Bittersweet Earth

Edited by Ellen Gray Massey

UNIVERSITY OF OKLAHOMA PRESS : NORMAN

By Ellen Gray Massey

(editor) *Bittersweet Country* (Garden City, N.Y., 1978)
(editor) *Bittersweet Earth* (Norman, 1985)

Library of Congress Cataloging in Publication Data
Main entry under title:

Bittersweet earth.

    Selections from a quarterly magazine called Bittersweet, published in Lebanon, Mo.
    Includes index.
    1. Ozark Mountains Region—Social life and customs—Addresses, essays, lectures. 2. Folklore—Ozark Mountains Region—Addresses, essays, lectur s. 3. Handicraft—Ozark Mountains Region—Addresses, essays, lectures. I. Massey, Ellen Gray.
F417.09B58   1985   976.7'1   84-20991
ISBN 0-8061-1927-6

The paper in this book meets the guidelines for permanence and durability of the Committee on Production Guidelines for Book Longevity of the Council on Library Resources, Inc.

The University of Oklahoma Press edition is the first publication of *Bittersweet Earth* in book form. Portions of this book first appeared in *Bittersweet* magazine, 1973–1980 inclusive.

To my daughter Ruth, who has never wearied of listening, suggesting, criticizing, and helping. She was always my sounding board and mainstay, from the beginning in 1973.

Contents

Preface

I never cease to be amazed at two things—the ability of high school students and the lack of understanding by most people of the time, effort, and talent needed to publish any written work. I have always been aware of these two things, but the ten years from 1973 to 1983 have emphasized them even more as I worked with the youthful staffs of *Bittersweet* magazine in an English credit class at Lebanon, Missouri, High School.

I have been teaching for twenty-eight years, most of them with high school students. To me they are no longer children, but young adults capable of doing what adults do if given the opportunity and guidance of older experience to help them. Treated with respect for their own individual worth, they will produce, as is evidenced by the continual high quality of the research, writing, photography, and drawings done by a constant turnover of students who worked on *Bittersweet* during the ten years of its publication.

"I suppose you get your pick of the most talented students in your school?" people asked me at the many talks we gave each year.

"No, I don't, not in the normal meaning of the word," I answered.

In the first place, the purpose of the class was educational. The quarterly magazine we published was just a device to teach the boys and girls many, many things in a real situation. Students were accepted on the basis of their interest, willingness and demonstrated dependability. The purpose of the magazine was to develop their talents, for every student is talented in some way. Some of them discovered they could take excellent photographs. Some related well to older people. Others discovered they liked to work with the business records or learned they loved local history.

Second, the typical gifted students were not usually attracted to the class. Wanting to take all the advanced courses, they thought they did not have room in their schedules, for working on the *Bittersweet* staff took a great deal of class time and time outside of class.

But once accepted as a member of the staff, each student knew that everyone depended on him to write his story, draw his picture, or show up for an interview. The rest of the staff members counted on him, and our readers expected a high-quality product for their money. Shirking the responsibility reverberated not only on the student's own head, but all the way through, a bit like the rhyme about the kingdom lost for want of a horseshoe nail. For want of more information the story was lost. For want of the story, the issue was lost. For want of the issue the subscribers were lost. For want of subscribers the whole project was lost—all because of one student's neglected responsibility.

Each of them understood this responsibility and responded. If one fell down, another would take it up. They did it for ten years, never missing publishing an issue on time. I now believe in miracles, because each issue was a miracle of student interest, willingness, dedication, patience, hard work, and, yes, talent.

However, the publication of forty magazines did not occur by magic. The main ingredient was work. The young people could do it, but it took time. Most people could not understand why it took almost a year to get a story published, or why we worked long hours all year to produce only four magazines. Accustomed to instant television and newspaper coverage, they thought that after a single interview the story should appear in the next issue. Professional journalists who have had years of experience and work full time with electronic editing typewriters and the facilities of a huge newspaper at their command do turn out stories quickly.

We, however, working with fourteen- to seventeen-year-old students with no journalism training, very little equipment, and only one or two hours a day, required a very long time. Many stories required several interviews. For instance, the story on cave crawling was written only after exploring about ten caves and talking with many people. The visit with Homer Massey was done in a period of three months, in four different interviews of about two hours each. The chapter on molasses took three years in research, making the molasses three different seasons to get it done just right and talking with many people who gave us help.

The students transcribed every interview word for word. An average interview is about two hours long. It took the students from ten to twenty hours to transcribe a half-hour conversation.

Next, they needed to type the transcriptions and organize all that material into an outline and then write the story. Inexperienced as they were, they needed help to learn every step of this process. Obviously, the first draft was not good enough, so after I gave them suggestions for improving it, they rewrote and rewrote (up to as many as twelve times, but usually five or six times was enough) until it was as good as they could get it. If I, or the student story editor, thought the story still needed work, another, more experienced, staff member would go over it. Of course it was typed several times, including the final draft that was printed in the magazine.

This listing does not even mention the time needed to work on the photographs or drawings. Sometimes we had to return to take photographs again, perhaps several times. Murphy's law certainly worked for us. If anything could go wrong, it usually did. We took pictures with empty cameras, accidentally exposed the film, used the wrong ASA number, lost the film, ruined it in the darkroom—these are just a few of the things that went wrong.

When we had developed a number of suitable negatives, we selected and printed the photographs we used.

When all the illustrations and copy were ready, the staff did the paste-ups, designing each page camera-ready for the printer. Writing captions for illustrations, coming up with titles and sub-titles sometimes took almost as long as designing the layouts.

When all the stories for a given issue were completed and they fit exactly in our sixty-eight-page magazine, we took it to the printer and then began all over again. Also, we had to publicize each issue, we had to address (by hand) all 3,500 labels, and on the happy days when the magazine came back, we formed an assembly line to package, affix labels, and sort it to mail out.

In this book, our second (the first, *Bittersweet Country*, Doubleday, 1978), all the chapters, photographs, and drawings have been previously published in our magazine. I have chosen these particular articles to fit the earth theme of the book and have organized and edited them, when necessary, for inclusion in the book form. These selected articles are the work of forty-five boys and girls from Lebanon High School in classes under my direction from 1973 to 1980. In addition to these students, many others assisted on interviews, edited, worked in the darkroom, or helped with layouts.

The students and I did not work alone. None of this would have been possible without the many people who invited us into their homes and lives and shared their knowledge, talents, and skills. Our research was mostly with older, life-long residents of the Ozarks, using the oral history approach.

Many of these people, born in the late 1800s and early 1900s, were descended from three or four generations of Ozarkians. The people who settled the Ozarks came from many places, but the great influx of settlers emigrated from the southern Appalachians. They brought with them their culture, which included their beliefs and legends. Obviously, much of the lore and culture of the Ozarks is similar to that of Tennessee, Kentucky, North Carolina, and other eastern states, as well as being typical of other pioneer regions.

Our goal was twofold: to record the life-style prevalent in the Ozarks in the early 1900s and to portray characteristics of the land that influenced that life-style. We recorded the stories, legends, and practices just as we heard them. Some may be unique to the Ozarks, others are widespread, but all combine to present a rich picture of a regional culture that many people from other parts of the nation find reminiscent of their own heritage. Since the Ozarks region was fairly isolated for a long time, these ideas and skills survived for a generation or two longer than in most other areas, making the Ozarks a rich source of an almost vanishing pioneer culture. The students and I tried to record as much as we could of that culture while the men and women who remembered it were still here to tell us about it.

Obviously, not all Ozarkians believed or practiced all the things we've written about. There is a diversity of people here, as there is anyplace. In many cases the cures and other lore we collected were from people who had heard of them from parents and grandparents, but who did not necessarily subscribe to the practice themselves.

In some cases our informants may have romanticized the situation when comparing a nostalgic, simpler time to the present. There were murders, grand theft, and other crimes as there are now. In our magazine we attempted to show all aspects of Ozark life, even drawing criticism from some readers for writing about such things as moonshining and outlaws. In this collection of articles, since we are concerned mainly with results of the interaction between the earth and the people, we do not include much about human morals.

Because we recorded the voices of the people on our interviews, we have used their exact words. We did not change their grammar or way of speaking. We sometimes deleted extraneous words, such as "you know," and irrelevant comments. For clarity we sometimes changed the order of the information, adding in the answer to a question we asked when that information should go in the context of the dialogue, but we did not add words or paraphrase the speech.

In summation, this book is a blending of youthful devotion, energy, knowledge, and talent with older devotion, energy, knowledge, and talent. We hope you enjoy it.

Lebanon, Missouri   ELLEN GRAY MASSEY

Acknowledgments

The publication of this book, which contains selected articles from the quarterly *Bittersweet,* was accomplished with the aid of many people. Without the support of the community, the school, our subscribers, the students and the assistant advisors, it would not have been possible.

The book exists only because of the many men and women in the Ozarks who shared with us their knowledge and resources. We were continually amazed at their willingness to talk and work with us as long as necessary for our research, to help us promote each issue in newspapers and on radio and television, to sell it for us at stores, and to serve on our advisory board and on the Bittersweet, Inc. Board of Directors. It is impossible to name all who have helped, but Dalton Wright, James E. Baldwin, and George Kastler have shared in guiding our corporation from its inception.

We could never even have begun without the willingness of Lebanon, Missouri, R-III School Board and the administrators, Vic Slaughter, Robert Payne, Gary Evans, Robert Duncan, Gordon Grant, and Richard Tiller, who let us conduct this unusual class that had the entire Ozarks as its classroom.

This book would not have been possible without the continued support of our magazine subscribers, who renewed each year and supported us in other ways by buying back issues of our magazines and our first book, as well as telling their friends about us.

The book obviously owes much to the high school students who did the work in publishing the stories first in the magazines and who have continued to be interested, even after graduation.

I would also like to acknowledge the professional help of fellow teachers at Lebanon High School and the following who worked with me for a time as assistants on the magazine: Ruth Ellen Massey, Vicki Cox, Delilah Amos Shotts, and Melinda Stewart.

Bittersweet Earth

Prologue

Climbing the rocky hill carpeted with pansy violets and soft moss, the young couple and their toddler son reached the comparatively flat ridge meadow. A few sweet williams were just beginning to show their lavender colon, which contrasted with the white blossoms of the dogwood trees scattered among the just-leafed-out timber all around the edges of the meadow. The mother was happy as she looked around. This was their land—their inheritance from five generations. As far as she could see in every direction—buildings, hills, hollows, fields, river, springs, woods, meadows, rocks—was the source of their livelihood, their toil, their pride, and their responsibilities.

The sense of ownership and belonging swelled as she surveyed the early spring beauty all around her. How new, how fresh and perfect everything was! Just to her right the spring pond her father had bull-dozed out twenty years earlier to catch the trickle from Drip Spring glistened and shimmered in the morning light. The black cattle, descendents from her grandfather's breeding program, were beginning to graze on the new grass of the meadow that she and her husband had revitalized and re-sown on this worn-out ridge field her great-grandparents had cleared a hundred years ago. Still standing in the hollow they had just crossed was the log springhouse where her great-great-grandmother had done her weekly family washing and from which she had carried uncounted buckets of water up the steep hill to the house.

Wherever the young wife turned she could see evidence of use, work, and loving care. Looking back across the hollow to their cluster of farm buildings on the next ridge, she saw the fading yellow of her grandmother's forsythia bush and her jonquils or "Easter flowers" as she had always called them. Her grandfather's tall concrete silo stood close to the big barn built in her great-grandparents' time. And closer, just to her left in the edge of the clearing, she could see the old, misshapen tree that, according to her grandfather, the Indians had bent many years ago to point down the hill toward the big spring in the hollow. In their time each generation had lived on the earth, taking

3

and giving back just as Americans have done since the Pilgrims landed at Plymouth Rock. Now it was this generation's turn.

Her elation was shadowed by a growing sense of responsibility. Already she and her husband were contending with problems caused by some predecessor who had taken too much. Too many trees had been cut, causing erosion and less ground water. The gravel bar on the river continued to grow each year, as the river became shallower. Last summer during the dry spell, for the first time ever known, the Drip Spring had stopped completely until fall rains began. What a tremendous obligation they had, to make a living on their three hundred acres of land and yet preserve it for other generations.

She knew their obligation had existed for every generation that had ever used this land, back to the first Indians. Some of these past "owners" had recognized the trust; others had seen the land only as a means to satisfy some immediate need or gratification. Of all, perhaps her grandfather best understood what was happening. His generation remembered the original white settlers, yet lived into the present age. She treasured the stories about the Indians and early settlers that he used to tell her when she would tag along with him on his daily rounds.

"The Osage Indians lived here before us," he would tell her. "They knew the earth and respected it probably more than we do. They believed they were the special people from the stars—that Grandfather the Sun had sent them to the Ozark land to care for it and bring order, for this was his favorite land, which he had formed of layered rock, timbered hills, running streams, and grassy prairies. So the Star People made sure things stayed in their order and man did not ruin it by waste. They were careful not to kill more buffalo than the tribe needed and they were careful to use every bit of the animal. They knew the forests had to be tall, the prairies must flourish, and streams flow undisturbed. Recognizing the place of each thing on earth, they knew the value of trees, for instance, not only for man's needs for fires, for tools, for food and shelter, but they also understood the place of trees in the total picture of animals, plants, rivers, and weather. They were careful to do nothing to change nature's ways."

Even their myths were lessons in ecology. One myth explains that rumblings heard beneath the depths of the floor of an old sinkhole were the drums of long-gone, wasteful Indians who ignored the trust of Grandfather the Sun. Because of their disrespect for the earth, which they called the Sacred One, they were imprisoned forever in its depths. While they were idling away their time in the cave, the earth had trembled and crashed stones over the opening.

Another myth explained why the earth suddenly had convulsions that resulted in the eruption of present-day Bennett Spring into the bed of a formerly quiet stream. The sudden out-pourings of the spring were tears from the eye of the Sacred One when he learned of his people's neglect of their trust.

The Osages believed that all things came from and returned to the earth. The pregnant woman ate of the fruits of the soil. Because of this food, the child was the product of the earth, and throughout his life he partook of the earth again and again. To them, death was nothing to fear—they only anticipated returning to the one who was responsible for their lives in the first place.

Her grandfather explained that when Christian settlers came to the land, many treated it with the same respect that the Indians showed; others despoiled it.

Many settlers, knowing they needed water year after year, protected the natural springs from erosion, animals, or foreign substances. Knowing they would need grass year after year, they were careful not to overgraze, even though tempted by immediate need. These people lived with the periodic rises of the creeks and rivers, knowing the rises were natural and necessary acts to purge the streams and let the fish come upstream. They lived with nature, comfortably in good seasons and poorly in dry years.

Strongly religious people, they knew that God had created the earth and called it good, and then He had created man and told him to guard the earth and keep it for generations to come. In death these people were laid in the earth with the words, "Dust to dust. Of earth thou art and to earth thou returnest."

Understanding now what her grandfather had said, she knew that on this land there were also many people who refused to listen to the meaning of the biblical words. They interpreted the words, "Man's dominion over the earth," to mean license to do whatever they wanted to do with the earth to make a living, get a profit, or enjoy themselves without regard to natural laws or future consequences. The buffalo ate grass that cattle needed, so they killed off the buffalo. Beaver pelts were valuable, so they trapped the beaver out of the river. Trees brought ready cash, so they cut the timber all down and plowed up the thin soil to plant corn. These practices followed by some of her predecessors, who looked at the land only for its economic value, seemed harmful enough. But more threatening still were the great changes to the land over which she and her husband had no control —changes caused by people far away who made decisions to build dams, spray the forests, dump wastes in the streams, or destroy the land for generations with lethal chemical dumpings.

The young family walked back down the hollow, following the direction of the Indian tree. The little son ran unsteadily to pick a wild columbine growing near his great-great-great-grandmother's spring house. "Drink, drink," he asked, pointing to the clear, quiet pool of water.

Sadly the mother shook her head. "It'll make you sick," she said. Just a few years ago, she remembered her grandfather giving her many drinks from the spring, when the water was still pure.

Her sadness deepened as she realized that people today are no more free from the grief or anger of the Sacred One than the few irresponsible Osages were. The earth is already injured. Perhaps some day again it will tremble and crash down stones, resulting in humanity's being forever lost in its depths with only an occasional far-off drum roll to remind the bittersweet earth man once had dominion.

"Pretty," the child said, holding out the delicate red flower to his parents.

1. THE EARTH

Making conversation at the Old Red Mill at Alley Spring, a native Missourian asked a visitor, "Are you from around here?"

"No, I'm from the east coast."

"I've lived in Birch Tree for forty years. Where in Missouri is East Coast?"

Birch Tree, High Prairie, Licking, Poplar Bluff, Pea Ridge, Mountain Grove, Lake Spring, Flat River, Wild Cat Hollow. Geographical names like these are common in the Ozarks, where there is such a variety of natural life and formations that a town called East Coast a thousand miles from any seacoast did not seem illogical to this Ozarkian. For decades her people had lived and worked in partnership with the earth. Obviously this nearness would be reflected in the names of their towns and villages.

Not only their names, but also their speech is filled with down-to-earth references. Living in a land "where the hills ain't so high, but the valleys sure are deep," it was natural to describe good and bad times, "If it isn't chickens, it's feathers," or to cheer up someone who'd have to have a stepladder to kick a duck in the "heinie" by saying, "Even a blind sow finds an acorn every now and then." Even their religious life carried a metaphor from nature. A man missing church too often would be classified a jimson-weed Christian. An eccentric person might be called one of the old blue hen's chicks, and a still-spry man who's slowing down might say, "I can plow as deep as ever, but I can't go as many rounds."

This partnership of people and land operated just as any partnership does. Ideally each partner works in perfect harmony with the other, but since neither the people nor the land was ideal, there were many conflicts. Sometimes the land, which was never very fertile even in the beginning, didn't produce according to the expectations and the efforts of the people. Sometimes the people demanded more from the land than it had to give.

Also, as in any partnership, each exerted an influence that perma-

nently changed the other. The land began by dictating to the people the ways they could make their living and spend their leisure time, so that the stamp of the land affected their morals, their speech, and their philosophy. Gradually the people began exerting their influence on the land until now, within the lifetimes of the older people, the situation has almost reversed; the people dictate what the land is to be. This power over the land is especially evident in two of the most appealing natural aspects of the Ozarks—its rivers and caves.

River Running Free

River running free is the way of nature. More than a phrase, it is an action, a happening, a thought with a meaning. River running free is a remembrance of the past, a fact of the present, and a hope for the future.

Through the four seasons the river flows, changing with the times of the year. Reflections of gold, red, and brown signal autumn. Crisp breezes bring a rain of leaves to litter the surface with discarded foliage. Gray skies and the frosty banks of early morning warn of the coming chill.

Clear and cold the water runs as winter envelops the river. The water appears shallow, the bottom within reach, but the illusion is six feet deep. Dark blue and silent is its course as ice forms on the edges. A sheet of ice seals the top, twenty yards wide and an eddy long. The scenery seems lifeless, but under the ice the river lives on.

The coming of spring renews all life and brings floods from early rains. Green buds and flower blossoms explode in color and fragrance, creating a myriad display of sight and smell. Insects and animals begin anew their fight for survival, and the strong are the only victors. Refreshed springs surge with crystal-bright water, and the run-off from a storm rolls down a gully. Churning brown water boils against trees and rocks, creating whirlpools of trash, leaves, and soil. As quickly as it has risen the flood recedes, continuing its path between green banks.

In summer a fiery sun burns the river, causing heat waves to shimmer across the surface and distort reality. The grassy edges turn brown and dry as the river dwindles to a stream. Soil and clay cook into rock, cracking and crumbling at a touch. In the driest weather the water vanishes underground yet follows the same path to resurface downstream. Less and less the river runs, until rains replenish the source. A season closes, another begins, while the river always flows.

River running free. Forever and always, without pause and without end. The way it has always been and the way it is now. The way the river should always be—running free.

The Geology of The River

A long, high mudbank leads you around slow, flowing curves. Then a final curve, and you shoot through rocky rapids, the banks changing to a sand bar, a gravel bar, and finally to a huge outcropping of rock. Wondrous how in just a few hundred yards such a change could take place. Surely, you think, the diversity present can only be the result of dramatic actions and influences. But to be so peaceful now, one can hardly imagine the violent destructive and constructive forces once present. It is almost a miracle. . . .

This miracle is actually a common sight along the Ozark rivers. In the heart of America one of the oldest geological formations in the United States, the Ozarks is a geographic region roughly two hundred miles square located in south-central Missouri, north Arkansas and a small part of western Illinois, and eastern Oklahoma and Kansas. It is defined by its topography, which is different from that of the surrounding regions. This difference was caused by the particular geologic history of the Ozarks. Because of the repeated uplifts and resulting deep erosion, the topography is one of hills, plateaus, and deep valleys.

The character of the rivers is the result of this land formation. To best understand just how and why the rivers are the way they are, it would be best to start at the beginning of the Ozarks.

About four hundred million years ago, Missouri, Arkansas and the surrounding area consisted of a metamorphic (mixed sedimentary and granite) and igneous (molten) layer of rock. Ancient streams running over the land carved the surface into a topography much the same as today's Ozarks, only with solid rock hills, mountains and valleys. This set the stage for the land's contours.

Later, the Ozarks, along with Kansas, Oklahoma, and Illinois, gradually dropped below sea level because of tectonic forces (those that caused land movement) and was flooded by streams running from Canada and the northern United States. These streams dumped loads of mud, clay, sand, and gravel, that became the building blocks of today's surface. Dead sea organisms such as brachiopods (bivalved

15

Bluffs, usually associated with eddies, are numerous. On the forty-five miles of the Niangua River there are about 120 bluffs, ranging as high as 230 feet. Their solid limestone faces, rising vertically, guide the river as it flows from bluff to bluff.

Approximate area of the Ozarks.

shelled animals) collected on the bottom to be covered by more silt. This region was, over several million years, alternately dry land and sea, and from the tremendous pressures of weight, the mud and clay became shale, sand became sandstone, and gravel fused into conglomerate. (These rocks now underlie the rivers and partly account for the clearness of the rivers). In some areas of the Ozarks the remains of dead sea organisms, composed mainly of calcium, are responsible for the limestone and dolostone. In other areas fossils are not present in the limestone, but, instead, limestone has simply precipitated out of the water.

Finally, after repeatedly rising and falling, about fifty million years ago the Ozark region rose to its present height, varying between a thousand and seventeen hundred feet above sea level. The rise is referred to by geologists as the Ozark uplift, and actually resembles a plateau more than a mountain. The land mass itself is called the Ozark peneplane.

This is where the rivers began.

The Ozark rivers started, literally, as a trickle. Rain runoff, seeking the path of least resistance, began cutting small channels downwards from the various high points in the area. Streams ran away from these "peaks" in all directions. Water eroded mud and clay as fast as it could move through them. Where limestone and dolostone were present, water moved underground, beginning the present spring and cavern system. In places where igneous rock existed, such as on the upper St. Francis River, the water could not cut through, so shallow, swift-running streams resulted in canyon-like shut-in formations walled in granite. These river paths were not influenced by the glacier movement of the ice age, for the ice did not reach as far south as the Ozarks, but the climate caused by the ice age—first drought, killing vegetation, then plentiful rain with heavy erosion—speeded the growth of the rivers. Given thousands of years, water gradually deepened and widened the channels to their present state.

At first the river cut deeply, its gradient sometimes several yards per mile. After reaching the rockbed, the river could cut only a little deeper and gradually leveled out, becoming slower and meandering. Often the river nearly doubled back on itself, with only a narrow strip of land between the two sections. This type of formation is called narrows or devil's backbones. During a flood the river would sometimes jump across the narrows, cutting a new path and abandoning the old. This is especially evident in the Gasconade River Basin and many other Ozark rivers. Entrenched meanders are common in the Ozarks. The

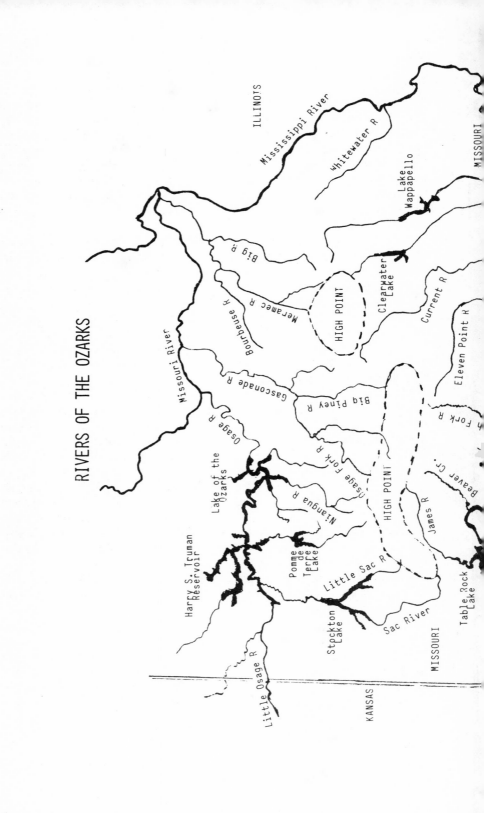

RIVERS OF THE OZARKS

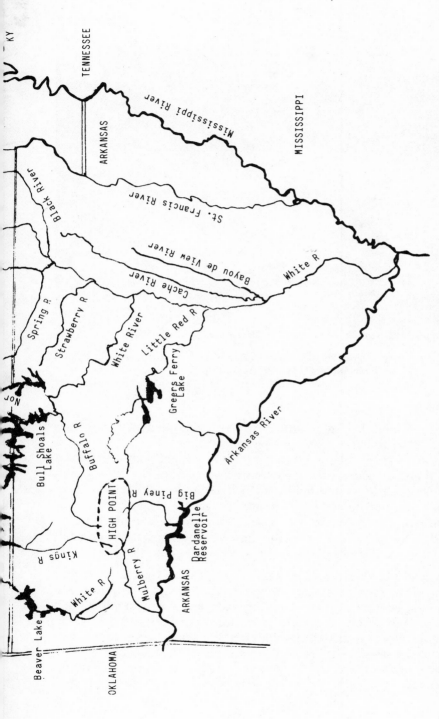

The rivers of the Ozarks, beginning from three major high points, run north to the Missouri River or south to the Arkansas River, eventually feeding into the Mississippi River.

Rising waters bulge higher in the middle. The Osage Fork River rises eight feet above normal to litter the low-water Davis Mill bridge with logs.

old path would fill with sediment and other eroded material from upstream, later to become a prime farming valley.

The rivers are still hard at work today. Seasonal floods continually clear land on both sides, except where rock formations check the river's path. Flooded bridges and fields, the collapse of a rocky wall with its base eaten away or movement of a sand or gravel bar several hundred yards downstream attest to the river's force and continued activity. Once born, the rivers will never die, but, barring any natural disaster, will go on to see the end of the world.

A typical Ozark river, the Osage Fork of the Gasconade, begins from one of the high points near Marshfield, Missouri, as several small streams join together in their quest for lower levels. Still small enough for one to step across, it trickles downward, gathering more water. Three miles from its distinguishable source a small spring feeds more water into the stream, still shallow enough to ford in a car. Five, ten, even twenty miles more, the Osage Fork doubles and redoubles in size as a multitude of seeps, wet-weather springs, and streams no bigger than a dribble slip silently into the river. Anywhere along this stretch, depending on the latest rainfall, a canoe or johnboat may be put in for a float. But if it is too heavily loaded, the bottom will drag in gravel on the riffles.

Winding through the countryside, feeling for the lowest spots to make its way, the river moves ever onward past farmhouses, barns, old mill sites, and low-water bridges that flood at every big rain. Trees, cattle, and long, green corn rows stand beside the banks in silence. At thirty miles from its start a shadow plays beneath the surface, a straight line between the river banks. The foundation of an old mill dam shimmers underwater, a reminder of days long gone.

Another half-dozen miles slip by, and a new steel bridge shows man's progress. A deep, dark eddy waits patiently for anything to sink, hiding from sight many lost treasures on its bottom. Fallen trees and log jams block the river's path, and water detours around, over, and under. Snags reach out with grasping fingers to capture any who come too near.

Another long eddy makes time stand still, but the hand of man is present here. Noticed first two hundred yards away, the water disappears over a ledge. Now only a hundred yards away and finally ten, the spillway of a small, weakening concrete mill dam creates a whirlpool as water thunders over, pushing the great wood and iron wheel. From twisting rapids in dense brush, the river straightens and shoots its water through the whistles of a low-water bridge. Next, more rapids and another quiet eddy.

Immense rock bluffs, first on one side and then the other, shade the sun from view. Turtles, snakes, fish, birds, and ten thousand insects move unharmed, undisturbed, through water, air, and on land.

Twenty miles or thirty more, the river unfolds a new view around each bend. Under bridges, past rusted machinery, around an island, or under high wires, it moves on and on, always different, yet in ways the same, moving toward its end.

Two miles more the river moves as tranquilly as before. At sixty-eight miles from its beginning, the Osage Fork quietly mingles with the Gasconade River.

The Groundwater System

Springs are the cool, clean essence of life to the Ozark rivers. Slippery stones glisten as clear water cascades down through rocks and fallen leaves on its way down a steep embankment to the water's edge. Another bone-chilling stream begins from a fissure in the ground, winding through gravel in its inevitable search for the river. And yet another spring feeds quietly into the river's bottom, its mouth at the base of a limestone wall. Springs make up the next facet of understanding the rivers.

The Ozark rivers described here are the streams that actually begin in the Ozarks, rather than those that flow in from outside areas. For example, even though the major portion of the Osage flows in mid-Missouri, it is not classified here as an Ozark river, since it has its source on the Kansas plains outside the Ozarks. The Pomme de Terre River, a tributary of the Osage, is considered an Ozark river, because it begins in the Ozarks. However, because much of the Osage flows through the Ozarks, the scenery and geography of the country along it are similar to that of the Ozark rivers. The difference is the water. The Pomme de Terre is much clearer. Where the rivers join there is a visible line between the murky and the clear water.

Ozark rivers are clear for two reasons—gravel and rock bottoms, and a unique seepage/drainage or spring system. The gravel and rock bottoms are the result of the rocks deposited eons earlier, and the springs the result of limestone deposits.

In the deciduous forests of the Ozarks the cover of fallen leaves causes seeping water to become slightly acid. As this acidic water moves downward, it readily dissolves the limestone and dolostone underlying much of the region. Over the years the slightly acidic water forms underground reservoirs, some small, others quite large. In fact, a spring in the Ozarks may often be thought of as a water-filled cave. The spring may exit the ground to create a stream on its own, enter the river along a bluff or hillside, or bubble up unseen below the river's surface.

All Ozark rivers are naturally clear, but the degree of clearness between two rivers may vary depending on the drainage basin of each, whether agricultural, developed town or city, forest, or grassland. Water from a heavily forested area will be inherently clearer than from an area with exposed soil. In addition, floodwaters will erode soil into the river, causing temporary murkiness, while at normal water levels the soil will remain untouched.

The clearness is especially evident when compared to the plains rivers flowing into the Ozarks out of the Kansas plains, such as the Osage River, which is somewhat muddy and slower moving. The difference lies in the fact that the plains rivers receive close to their total flow from surface runoff as opposed to subsurface runoff in the Ozark rivers. The land makeup in the plains is either clay and clay-soil, which allows only surface drainage, or deep soil, which causes water reaching the river to be muddy. The mud banks and bottoms add to muddy conditions. Because the plains rivers depend almost totally on surface water for their flow, the rivers nearly dry up during drought conditions.

Ozark rivers, on the other hand, receive nearly 85 percent of their total flow from the groundwater system. Hence the flow of the Ozark rivers is far more uniform, running the year around, although many small tributary streams go dry in the summer. During the rainy periods, the springs build up quite a supply of water, enabling their flow to last all summer. Vegetation in the shallow soil common to the Ozarks prevents the dirt from muddying the water (there isn't as much to make mud of), and both gravel and sand provide an easy path to travel as well as serving somewhat as a filter.

The Ozark rivers are also cooler than the surrounding rivers, since groundwater assumes a temperature about two degrees above the mean annual temperature for a region. For this reason, Ozark rivers maintain a temperature of about 57 or 58 degrees, ideally cool for swimming on a hot summer day.

The Ecological Story

Left on their own, the rivers would continue much as they always have—widening, deepening, cutting new channels, and leaving behind old valleys. The ecological system of life and death around the river lies in a delicate, but positive, balance until man enters the scene.

Several hundred years ago, before the white man pushed into this region, a small population of Indians lived along the springs and rivers in peaceful coexistence with nature. Later, white trappers and traders moved into the wilderness in search of fur for the St. Louis market. Neither had much effect on the river, but the trappers were responsible for opening the land to those who would change it.

Lead and iron mining and lumbering of virgin forests for products such as oak railroad ties and walnut lumber solved a need elsewhere, but often polluted and changed the character of the surrounding land. Available commerce brought people to the land that seemed so clean that nothing could defile it. Simple carelessness and economic development made polluting the land easier than keeping it clean. Rivers and creeks around large towns and cities now often bear the mark of many years of abuse, such as Wilson Creek south of Springfield.

In more recent years agriculture has had its effects on the river. During the period of the first settlement, farmers took advantage of the rich bottom lands created earlier. Some, but not drastic, damage was done to the river system, but without large machinery, it might take a lifetime for one man to clear forty acres. Today, spraying and bull-dozing timber has rapidly reduced the forest cover, with harmful results to the water system.

A nearby water table becomes muddy when the vegetation holding the soil has been cleared away. Without a cover crop to protect soil, heavy rains wash tons of the thin, precious topsoil downstream, mud-dying the river and making the land almost useless. Since without the forest cover to hold it back so it will enter the underground water system, more rainfall runs into the river as surface water. Chemical spray overruns and fertilizers by their very nature are poisonous to aquatic animals and other animals nearby.

Heavy overgrazing of river pasture by cattle has two effects — beaten-down cow paths become gullies for rainwater, and an overabundance of nitrogen from manure leaches into the water. Nitrogen, and some phos-phates, start the river plants in a race to outgrow themselves, choking the river with algae that finally leave backwashes and eddies with a stagnant, rotten scum over the surface. One isolated occurrence is relatively harmless, but constant practice is fatal.

Once thought to be the cleanest, purest water around, the Ozark springs now face contamination from sewage and dumps. Sinkholes have been used — almost as a ritual — as dumps for trash. Water draining into sinkholes becomes contaminated, in turn polluting the under-ground water, which becomes springs. Sewage from cities, septic tanks, or feedlots makes its way to the river as well, with the same disastrous effects. Because of the porous nature of limestone and the speed with which water moves underground the pollution is not all filtered out.

Man had the technology to move the land's contours to fit his wants and needs and to use the natural resources present. The effects of dredging for gravel and sand on the river are negligible unless carried to extremes. Gravel is constantly being moved downstream anyway, so if only a small amount of gravel is removed, it will be replaced by gravel and sand from upstream. Stripping a bank down to the soil, however, leaves the bank open to heavy erosion. A flood will drag as many tons of soil or more back into the river to match the gravel taken out.

Tapping the water table with wells for home and municipal sup-plies may have the same consequences. As long as the water taken out does not exceed the water replaced by rainfall, everything is fine. Using more than is replaced results in lowering water tables, drying up springs, and other problems as serious as land shifting because of vacant space underground. All this affects the flow of rivers.

Damming rivers is another example of man using natural resources.

A hundred years ago, old-timers said there wasn't enough gravel in the rivers. Today, gravel bars like this one on the Osage Fork River pile up, forcing the current to cut into the dirt bank. Then prime bottom land crumbles and falls into the water, silting up an already choked passage.

Seventy-five or a hundred years ago, men dammed rivers to back up and divert the river's course to power water-wheels in mills. When gasoline engines made waterpower obsolete, and better transportation made a trip into town easy, the mills and mill dams became deserted relics. No real change was made in the river, and it usually washed away the dams with time. Even those few small concrete dams still standing, like Orla Mill, present no real change or permanent danger to the river's environment.

The natural setting along the river—dark, ominous bluffs, gravel and sand bars, lily pads floating in quiet coves, snags and driftwood scattered about on the river, gnarled, intertwining tree roots on the banks, bubbling springs splashing into the river, and majestic sycamores reaching toward the sky—all make an Ozark river worth floating.

But people floating, or just being along the river, sometimes ruin the enjoyment for others. Discarded beer cans and bottles not only spoil the view but create a danger all their own. Many farmers complain of animals cutting hooves on broken bottles, or even eating trash accidentally, making veterinary care necessary. A partially-rusted can or broken bottle may pierce through shoes or slice open a hand, and doctors are few and far between on the river. An old rusted car, deserted and unclaimed, lies in a gully as an eyesore and a danger to anyone near it. Plastic, glass, and aluminum will outlast us all by several lifetimes, leaving an ugly spot on the river.

The pleasures of floating down a wild Ozark river, fishing in quiet coves and eddies, feeling the warmth of the sun, or enjoying the shade of a tree, shooting fast rapids and even dumping the canoe, swimming undisturbed except for the birds—all in this natural setting—is a precious inheritance to be carefully guarded.

The shallow draft of Osage River boats allowed them to land almost anywhere. Only a couple of boards were needed to load and board. Courtesy State Historical Society of Missouri.

Full Steam Ahead: Steamboating

The Ohio, the Mississippi, the Missouri, the Wabash, the Illinois, the Arkansas, and the Red. Cincinnati, Louisville, St. Louis, Cairo, Memphis, Natchez, and New Orleans. The names roll off the tongue like water rolling under the bow of a steamboat. And no wonder. Each is rich in the lore and legends of the steamboat.

Rivers were the nation's first highways, and lands along navigable waters were the first settled. Once an area was settled, trade soon followed. During the early 1800s, river trade used current or muscle-powered boats, flatboats and keelboats. The flatboat had a one-way trip. Early in the spring people upriver would build them, load them with produce from the rich river valley farms, and float them down to New Orleans, where the produce and wood the flatboat was made from were sold. The crews walked back home. Keelboats not only floated downstream, but also attempted the way upriver, hauled along the shore by main force. Men in the stern held the boat against the current. Using ropes fastened to trees along the shore, men on shore would pull the boat upstream until the rope ran out, fasten the rope to trees still farther upstream, and then repeat the process.

When steam-powered boats were introduced on the Mississippi in 1811 with the launching of the *New Orleans* in Pittsburgh, keelboats rapidly disappeared, a victim of the steam revolution. But flatboats continued on the river until the 1880s, when another steam revolution did them in, the steam engine of the railroad train.

The summer of 1817 marked the beginning of the steam age for St. Louis, with the arrival of the *Zebulon M. Pike*, its first steamboat. The number of steamboat arrivals rapidly increased until 1859, the heyday of steamboating, when thirty-one hundred boats arrived.

The big steamboats of the Mississippi River were a luxurious way for tourists to travel. The saloon of the *Eclipse* was three hundred feet long and eighteen feet wide and boasted imported carpets, magnificent draperies and French glass mirrors, paintings on the walls, and sparkling cut-glass chandeliers. The *J. M. White* was very luxurious, with im-

"Gasconade River Steamboating at Its Best. The shoals of the Gasconade presented a serious problem to the little boats. But the crafty skippers of those boats learned fast. They built their boats for extreme shallow draft, and then built barges that drew only a few inches of water when light. Up the Gasconade they would go, load up, and make the trip back over the shoals. Maneuvering beautifully, they would shape up, then float over with only an inch or two to spare. Years ago, while fishing on a dike, I saw a tow just like this picture coming down over the Wood-pecker shoals. It was perfection."—Dr. E. B. Trail. *Courtesy State Historical Society of Missouri.*

ported walnut furniture, hand-painted china, and an elaborate Brussels carpet three hundred feet long.

In addition to the regular crew, these boats carried barbers, cooks, bartenders and musicians. Many had ballrooms, elegant saloons, and bridal suites. Some of the boats were several stories high, with every inch of the exterior covered with an intricate lacework pattern in wood painted white. But these floating wedding cakes were more than a luxurious trip down or upstream. They were the lifeblood of trade in the United States. In 1840, New Orleans was the fourth largest city in the United States. In the next decade, it handled more export trade than New York City and more than 50 percent of the exports of the entire nation. In tonnage, merchandise shipped down the Mississippi River to New Orleans even exceeded that of the British Merchant Marine of the same decade.

Steamboating was extremely profitable, and soon after the first introduction of steamboats, daring pilots were taking them not only on the large rivers like the Mississippi, but also on almost all navigable rivers. In the Ozarks the boats had to be smaller and have a shallower draft than the Mississippi River craft, and they were not as luxurious; but for small towns along the Osage, the Gasconade, the White, the

Black, and the St. Francis, the steamboats played just as important a role as their more glamorous sister ships. They brought new immigrants in to settle the Ozarks, then hauled their produce out, forming almost the only link with the rest of the country. Even after railroads had replaced steamboats in other parts of the country soon after the Civil War, the rivers remained the sole highway in much of the Ozarks. The *Homer C. Wright* out of Tuscumbia, Missouri, on the Osage River ran until 1923, when railroads and highways finally reached the towns it served.

In the Ozarks steamboats regularly traveled up the Osage to Warsaw, which could dock seven boats at a time, up the Black to Poplar Bluff, the White to Forsyth, the Gasconade to Arlington, and all over the St. Francis. When the rivers ran full, free-lance pilots would attempt points farther up stream. Even the navigable parts of these rivers had to be continually cleared of shoals, rocks, trees, and submerged logs. Traffic depended on the season and the weather. Usually, unless it was an exceptionally mild winter, or wet or dry spring and fall, the steamboating season would run from March to September.

Steamboats on Ozark rivers were, on the average, eighty feet long and could make up to twenty-five miles a day upstream averaging five miles an hour and twice that downstream, depending on what kind of paddle wheels the boats had. The stern-wheeler (the paddle wheel at the rear) had more power and speed, but the side-wheeler (the paddle wheels on the side) could turn the boat easier, making it more flexible to navigate.

Wood, plentiful and easily obtained, was the major source of fuel in the Ozarks. Until the 1850s there was always a pile of wood scattered every few miles along the riverbank, supplied by farmers who sold it to the boats. When the farmer heard the steamboat's whistle, he would run to the woodpile in order to load it on. The number of stops the boat had to make for wood depended upon the size of boat and the amount of cargo. A heavily laden boat would not have as much room to carry wood, so would have to stop more frequently than a lesser-loaded boat.

The hulls of the Ozark steamboats had to be cut down to get over sandbars and submerged trees and to navigate the shallow rivers. They drew about a foot of water, while those on the Mississippi drew five or six feet. They also could not be as long as those on the Mississippi, because of the many bends and curves common to Ozark rivers. Don Boyd, a steamboating enthusiast, said that pilots claimed that at night the owls would twist their heads off trying to follow the lights of a steamboat winding its way up the Osage.

Boat hulls were made of elm because of its ability to weather. They were built on land and slid into the river when finished. It usually took about a month to complete a hull. The rest of the boat was built after the hull was in the river. It took an expert to build the hull, but after that, any good carpenter could finish the boat. It would take close to a year to build a boat and equip all the machinery on it. Boats would last forty-five to fifty years if they were not involved in too many accidents and timbers were replaced every few years.

Boats were named after various things. Some were named after the chairman or a director of the company that owned the boat. Others were named after family members, towns, or rivers. One of the last steamboats operating in the Ozarks, the *Homer C. Wright*, was named after Homer Wright, who said, "My dad was the pilot, but my granddad was president of the company. He thought I was a cute little grandson, so he named it after me."

Many of the steamboat landings and wharves in the Ozarks were simple and made of dirt. A landing could be made anywhere a gangplank of two or three boards could be laid down. Since everything was loaded by hand, steep banks were avoided. Each boat had scheduled stops to make, but would make unscheduled stops if a farmer along the river needed some produce hauled.

At first, most boats ran only during the days, but as the pilots gained more experience, they began making runs and stops at night. Kerosene lamps were the major source of light. These lamps were actually metal baskets stuffed with kerosene-soaked rags set afire. They were extended over the sides of the boat by long metal poles.

Steamboats carried everything from homemade whiskey to cloth. They brought into the Ozarks things the settlers did not produce themselves, such as bricks, shingles, cement blocks, lime, iron, mill machinery, drugs, saddles, and buggies. Often a farmer would trade something he raised or made for these manufactured goods. A trade might be some homemade whiskey for a machine, or a pig for wire or oil. Other items the farmers traded or exported were cotton, corn, hides, cattle, lumber, milled flour, sheep, and garden produce.

Steamboats frequently would push barges ahead of them. These barges would hold two or three train-car loads of merchandise, therefore a steamboat could move a great deal of material on one trip. One page from the log of the steamboat *J. R. Wells*, which ran on the Osage River in 1904, shows twenty-nine different items with a total weight of 37,231 pounds picked up in three stops. The summary for the same year shows 140 passengers and everything else from wheat and corn to sewer pipes moved by the steamboat.

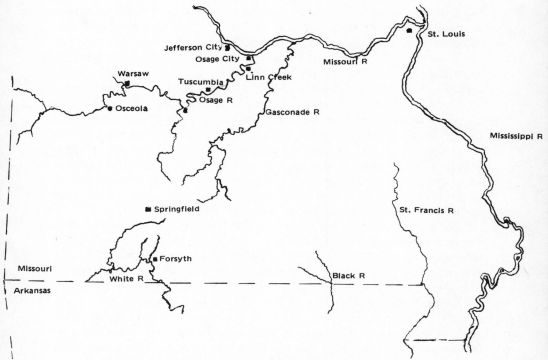

Southern Missouri Rivers with Steamboat Traffic

Homer Wright remembers that in addition to their regular runs, "Often they would run excursions. Maybe some Sunday, maybe some moonlight evening here, we'd just go up and down the river. They would put the Tuscumbia Concert Band on the steamboat and lots of soda pop and they would go for a boat ride."

On most of the smaller boats in the Ozarks the crew usually was ten men, the captain, the pilot, engineer, cook, foreman, and about five or six deckhands. Robert Zang, a present-day river boat pilot on the Mississippi, said, "I call the captains caretakers of the company's property. But they stood one watch and they would get out to make the landings and tell the boat to come in slow or this or that. They didn't do nothing much of the time."

The pilot ran the boat. He had to have the river memorized, all its turns, bends, sandbars, landmarks, and tricks. The responsibility for the safety of the boat, crew, and cargo depended on his knowledge of the river. A pilot had to be licensed for each different section of the river he worked on. He was the highest-paid crew member, earning as much as a thousand or fifteen hundred dollars a month on the Mississippi River. In the Ozarks they earned less.

The engineer's job was to stop and start the boat and to run the engine. Frequently he was studying to be a pilot. His was perhaps the easiest job aboard. The fireman fed the boilers to keep the fires going.

Deckhands, or roustabouts, loaded and unloaded the boat. They were the lowest-paid crew members and got a dollar a day and board on the *Homer C. Wright* in the early 1900s. "And a day was whenever they had work to do," Homer Wright explained. "It wasn't start at eight and quit at five. Might start sooner and load something at a landing here and may be an hour or so just coasting down the river and then be some more loading and unloading." Earlier deckhands, who were often blacks, received twenty-five cents a day.

On the Mississippi River before the Civil War, deckhands were slaves. Usually Irish employees had the much more dangerous job of stoking the furnace. That way, if a boiler exploded, the easily replaceable wage earners were the ones killed. The more valuable slaves were not in as much danger.

Steamboats were dangerous craft. On the Mississippi, Robert Zang said, "The old records show from St. Louis to Cairo was 180 miles. And there's a steamboat sunk for every mile of river." And on the Mississippi between 1831 and 1833 one out of every eight boats was destroyed, all by human error. The most common cause of accidents was racing, but accidental fires, collisions, and inferior boiler construction also took their toll.

On the smaller, shallower Ozark rivers most accidents were running aground or getting hung on a sandbar. "I don't know of any tale that I heard of any explosions here on the Osage," Homer Wright said. When boats did run aground, they would try to pull them off. But sometimes, Wright said, "They couldn't get off the grounding and had to wait till the river came up. They left a watchman aboard and went back to town."

Steamboating died out later on the smaller Ozark rivers than it did on the Mississippi, but many of the causes of its demise were the same. Insurance rates became so high many owners couldn't afford it. But the development of railroads and highways was the main reason that steamboating ceased in the Ozarks. Railroads could offer faster service and reach inland towns away from the river. Better highways were built, and where the railroads did not go, trucks did.

In 1923 the *Homer C. Wright*, the last steamer on the Osage, was sold to Union Electric in St. Louis, to be used as a ferry. Homer Wright explained, "They just ran out of business here on the Osage. When Union Electric finished with it, it was tied out in the river. They didn't sell it because no one would want a boat like that. She sunk one winter during an ice storm—that's the word we had."

Like the keelboat it replaced, the steamboat in turn became a victim of another revolution in transportation.

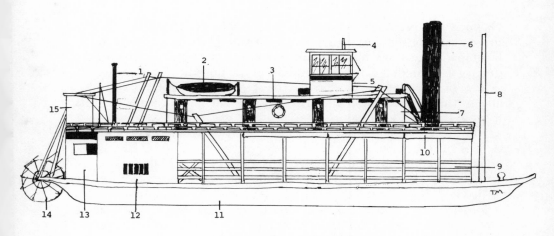

Parts of a Boat

1. Escape pipe (scape pipe) were pipes on the old time boats located above the boilers through which steam was wasted.
2. Yawl or rowboat.
3. Skylight found on fancier boat, was used for ventilation
4. Whistle.
5. Pilot house.
6. Smokestack.
7. Texas deck—the long narrow cabins occupied by the officers.
8. King post
9. Main deck—where cargo was kept.
10. Curtain—used as a shade and protection from bad weather.
11. Hull
12. Boilers
13. Kitchen
14. Paddle wheel
15. Outhouse

A Ferry Tale

Dawn is just breaking as a car pulls up to the river crossing. As the driver waits for the ferryman to come out and take him across the river, he impatiently toots his horn, introducing a foreign sound into the quiet, fog-shrouded valley. The sound of the horn brings the country-side to life—both in the valley, as the startled birds chirp frantically, and in the house, where the ferryman gets out of bed, knowing that it is the start of a long day.

This early morning scene was enacted many times at the ferry lo-cations on the Ozark streams from the early 1900s to as late as the early 1960s. Since most of the rivers in south central Missouri are not very wide and frequently flow over riffles shallow enough to be easily forded with horses and wagons or buggies, ferries were not often needed before the automobile era. The roads and trails led to the fording places, which were spaced every few miles. In normal weather the streams posed no travel difficulty for horses. However, the automobile did have problems crossing the fords. The narrow wheels got bogged down in the gravel or mud bottoms. If the ford had any depth to it, or the water rose any, the engines would flood out. The ford cross-ings became such a problem that often the nearest farmer was literally kept busy pulling people out with his team.

Obviously, as more and more people got cars, there was a demand for better crossings. Where bridge construction was too expensive, the solution was a current-powered ferryboat as near the original ford lo-cation as possible. So for many years, until the crossing was abandoned or a bridge built, ferries operated on many streams, including the Cur-rent, St. Francis, White, Gasconade, Eleven Point, and Niangua rivers.

However, certain conditions had to exist before the ferry would be successful, and not everyplace where there was once a ford had a ferry. First, the ferry had to be on a main-traveled road with enough traffic to make the operation financially successful. The approach and banks on either side had to be suitable for automobile traffic and landing points for the ferry. Above the flooding point on either bank there had to be something permanent, either a tree or post, on which to

With the widespread use of the automobile in the Ozarks, ferries instead of fords became the common method of crossing Ozark rivers. Moore's Ferry on the White River, about 1943, used the river current for power and cables to hold it in place. Courtesy Townsend Godsey, from Ozark Mountain Folk.

fasten the cable that held the ferry in the river. The river had to be at least three or four feet deep to float a loaded ferry, and the current had to be strong enough year-round to provide the power to push the ferry across the river.

Getting up at dawn was just one example of the confined life of the ferryman of past days. He had to be on duty twenty-four hours a day, seven days a week, year-round. He never had any time off unless he could hire somebody to run the ferry while he was away. Some ferrymen, during especially busy summer seasons, even put a cot out on the ferry. If a customer came along blowing his horn at two in the morning, the ferryman would get up, take him across, go back to bed and sleep until someone else blew his horn.

Often, running the ferry was a family operation. At many crossings, since traffic alone wasn't enough to provide a living for the ferry-man and his family, ferrying was combined with other businesses. Since everyone on both sides of the river for miles around had to cross the ferry to go anywhere, the crossing became a good location for a country store, a mill, or a blacksmith shop. As the community grew, the post office was usually located in the store at the ferry.

There was much more to ferrying than just taking the boat back and forth across the river. Many crossings were under the jurisdiction of the county court. In that case, each year the ferryman paid a ferry fee of about ten dollars to operate the ferry. He was sometimes responsible for building the ferry in the first place, and he was always responsible for keeping it in running condition and seeing that the approaches were maintained twenty-four hours a day. Then, the fare money that he received for the crossing was his.

It would be difficult to estimate the income of a ferryman. Euel Sutton said, "In the summertime, in the peak of tourist season, it was quite a bit, but in the wintertime, there wasn't many customers. And if the roads were bad, you didn't have any traffic. There was no way you could get a count to average it."

Euel Sutton remembered that when they first started the Powder Mill Ferry on the Current River, it cost ten or fifteen cents a vehicle to cross, "And if the customer didn't have the ten or fifteen cents, then some of the local farmers, if they were there with a loaded wagon, could bring potatoes, turnips, peaches, apples, whatever he wanted, and they'd trade them for the crossing. Kind of a barter system. Then as time went on and more cars got on the road, the fare went to twenty-five cents per car per trip of a daytime. Then of a night when you had to turn your lights on, it went to thirty-five cents.

"World War II came along, and then gas rationing took place, so the price stayed up all through the war. Then in '46, '47 traffic became a lot heavier, so they finally started raising the price, and then as the years went by, the car was seventy-five cents and a truck was a dollar because of the heavier load, and a dollar of a night."

Some ferries changed hands fairly often. The operators expected to earn more money than they were able to make. When they had trouble making ends meet, they sold out.

One ferry we found still operating was at Akers, in the Ozark National Scenic Riverways. The ferryman there has a much easier life than the old-time ferryman. To cross the ferry, the motorist rings a bell. Someone in the nearby store answers the call, or, on not-so-busy off-season days, one of the men working there in the store or at the canoe rental business on the bank takes the car across. Today's customers, not used to waiting, sometimes curse or bawl out the ferryman if he is slow to get there, as, undoubtedly, customers did in

times past. The ferryman must develop a thick skin, ignoring irate
passengers as he prepares to cross. Though the ferry is built with an
oarboard to use the current power, to make the Akers ferryman's job
still easier, he makes use of an electric motor to scoot the ferry across
the river and another motor to pump out the water from the hull.

The design of the current-powered ferries was not complicated.
They were constructed of wood available at the crossing site. Depending
on the traffic, they were made just long enough for either one or two
cars and usually just wide enough for one car. They were floored-
over, flat-bottomed floating hulls, designed so that they did not float
very deep in the water.

The framework of the hull was the gunnels. These were usually
four wooden planks eight to ten inches thick, about two to three
feet deep, and as long as the ferry—some about twenty-five feet long.
The gunnels were sawed at a slope on each end for approaching the
bank. Since the ferry did not turn around, both ends were identical.
Held in place with supports, they were boxed in all around to form
the hull, and the boxing boards were caulked to be watertight. Then
the two-by-six floor boards were laid.

Because it was impossible to completely waterproof the hull, three-
by-three trap doors were built into the floor to allow the ferryman to
get in and scoop out the water with a shovel. He didn't allow water
to accumulate to add more weight to the ferry and make it ride lower
in the water. The trap doors also allowed the ferryman to get inside the
hull to work on the bottom of the ferry, repairing leaks or punctures.

Fastened below the upstream gunnel was the oarboard. The oarboard, made usually from a two-by-six, was held in place by supports
several inches below the gunnel.

At each end of the ferry, there was what was called a wing or
apron. These were hinged to be raised or lowered, depending upon
which bank the ferry was approaching. In the stream they were usually
both up, though not all ferrymen raised them. When docked, the appropriate wing was lowered. Sometimes ferries had loading ramps or
boards built on the wings that actually lay on the bank to make it
easier for the car to drive on the ferry.

Along both sides of the ferry there was a precautionary railing
about three feet high. These barriers were usually just a few posts
holding boards, rope, or wire.

To secure the ferry to the bank, the simplest device was a rope
or cable thrown over a stob (post) in the ground or a handy tree.
Some ferries had winches, pulleys and cables with a hook on the end.
The winches, used to tighten the cables, were in the upstream corner

To keep the ferry from going downstream, a continuous cable runs from the ferry
through a triangular pulley on a main cable crossing the river.

of each end of the ferry. A cable went from each winch to a pulley
mid-point in the end and then off the ferry where the hook was fastened to a ring anchored on the bank.

Besides the actual ferry itself, there was machinery to keep it in
place. Stretching across the river and fastened to a stationary tree or
post on each bank was the main cable, which was usually about ¾-inch
in diameter. The ferry was fastened to this large cable with smaller
cables or lines. Riding along the main cable was a big triangular pulley,
suspended with the point hanging down. A long, continuous line ran
through this point, first to the pulleys anchored on each end of the
ferry. From each end pulley, the line was wrapped several times around
the windlass, located about mid-point of the upstream side of the
ferry. The windlass was a circular wooden tub-like device about a
foot in diameter with a handle to enable the ferryman to turn it.
Turning the windlass would shorten one line and lengthen the other,
thus pointing the ferry either upstream or downstream as needed to
control the ferry in the current.

After unhooking the chain that holds the ferry to the bank, Jim Purcell pries it into the water.

There are three basic operations in running a ferry. They are loading, crossing, and landing.

To load a car onto the ferry, the ferryman first makes sure the ferry is fastened securely to the bank and the wing is down, making a ramp to drive on. He then motions the car onto the ferry and has the driver pull clear to the front. The weight of the car on the front raises the rear to help the ferryman pry away from the bank.

To leave the bank, the ferryman must unfasten the line to the bank. If there is a winch, he must loosen it and unhook the cable from the ring on shore. After doing this, he has to pry the ferry away from the bank with a pole and jump on. He then raises the wing.

Normally, the quickest way between two points is a straight line, but if a ferryman tried to take an old-fashioned ferry across the river in a straight line, he would have trouble. He must take it across slantwise, like a sidewinder, for the current, going down river, not across, would take the ferry with it. Also, to use the power of the current and to control his speed, the ferryman pointed the boat either upstream to cast off or downstream to land. Hence the sideways movement. Today, most ferries are mechanically powered and they usually can travel in a straight line, since the motor has more power than the current.

The general principle of using the force of the current to cross the river is really quite simple. To cross the river, the ferryman turns the windlass, which in turn pulls the lines through the pulleys to point the ferry slightly upstream. Held by the big cable strung across the river so it can't go downstream with the current, the ferry is pushed across by the current. The force of the current, as it hits the oarboard and goes over it and under the ferry, causes forward movement. When more than halfway across the river, the ferryman turns the windlass to point the ferry toward the landing. Then, when the ferry is turned downstream to approach the landing, there is enough momentum left to glide gently into the bank. The lines and cable prevent overshooting the landing.

Once the ferry is out in the stream, the ferryman has the driver back his car to the rear of the ferry. The weight on the rear raises the front end slightly, making the approach to the landing easier.

Many times drivers would be afraid to back their cars for fear of backing off. The ferryman would then do it for them. There were incidents when the driver backed too far and the rear wheels went off the ferry. Though it was frightening, there was usually no harm done. Some men would push the car back onto the ferry when the boat reached the other bank.

If, for any reason, the ferry should stop in midstream, the ferryman got his ferry pole—a dried pole approximately fifteen feet long, three inches in diameter—and manually pushed the ferry the rest of the way across the river to the landing.

There were sometimes slight difficulties in controlling the speed of the ferry. The only way the ferryman could slow it down was to turn it more upstream so that less water hit the oarboard and the side of the boat. This position would allow the current to move straight through without exerting force against the oarboard. If the ferry was straighter (at right angles to the current), the force of more water against the side of the boat would cause a tauter cable, forcing the big triangular pulley to move on the big cable at greater speed. Sometimes, if the speed of the ferry wasn't controlled properly, the ferry would hit the bank too hard.

After coming into contact with the bank, the ferryman must lower

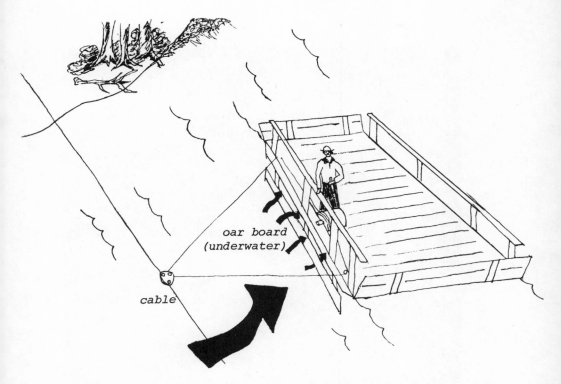

oar board
(underwater)

cable

Held in place by cables and pointed upstream, the ferry is pushed across the river by the force of the current going over and under the underwater oar board. The large arrow indicates river current direction.

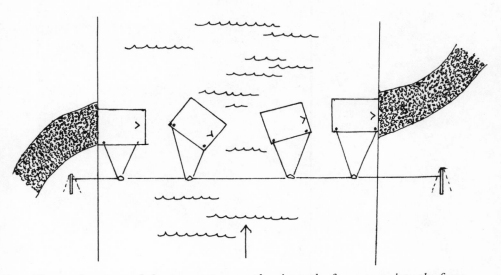

To use the power of the current to cross the river, the ferryman points the ferry upstream, using the windlass, pulleys, and continuous cable until over halfway across. Then he turns back downstream to land.

He guides the ferry across the river using the windlass.

How the car is positioned on the ferry can help in operating the ferry. (1) Pulling the car to the front of the ferry raises the back when leaving the bank. (2) In midstream the driver backs the car to the rear of the ferry, where (3) its weight raises the front for unloading.

the wing, jump off, and fasten the ferry securely to the bank. The car may then drive off the ramp and go on its way.

There were many hazards involved in the operation of a ferry, but the most costly to the ferryman were sinking, ice, and flooding, because these did the most damage to his ferry.

The ferry would not sink often, since the ferryman was always alert to avoid getting water in the hull. Even though builders used tar or pitch to seal the cracks, a ferry still leaked some. During a twenty-four-hour period, it might leak an inch or two over the whole ferry. Water also got into the hull from rainfall that leaked down through the floor. So using the trap doors in the floor to get into the hull, the ferryman had to bail water out every day in order to avoid water buildup.

Occasionally a ferry would sink during a flood, or sometimes a rock would punch a hole without anyone knowing it, so that during the night enough water might build up to sink the boat. If anything like that did happen, to recover the ferry the ferryman had to use pumps that would pump the water out of the hull faster than it was running in.

Ice was another danger. The problem wasn't the ice in the river, but the added weight of ice frozen on the ferry, for if enough ice accumulated the extra weight might sink it. When ice accumulated on top, the only solution was to chop it off with a pole or break it off any way possible. Very rarely would the river freeze entirely over. The current was usually strong at the ferry crossing, and most of the rivers were fed by spring water that normally kept the river temperatures above freezing.

Euel Sutton said of the Current River, "I could remember ice coming down only two or three times in my lifetime. Big chunks of ice would float down the river, huge chunks, and in old times, way back in the 1800s, she'd freeze over. People drove across in wagons. Now I've seen that.

"The Current River is fed by springs all the way from Montauk to below Big Spring—and the spring water stays a minimum temperature of 58° year-round. Therefore, the river has a fluctuation of warm water and is rather hard to freeze over."

Flooding was probably the most common natural hazard, since Ozark rivers rise quickly during heavy rains, sometimes six inches an hour. Because of this, the ferryman had to constantly watch the water level.

When the river reached a certain stage above normal—two to five feet, depending on the particular river—the ferry had to be shut down. As the water was rising, to keep the ferry out of the current the ferryman had to keep pulling the ferry up in the road, and as the water receded he had to gradually lower the ferry back into the river. Failure to keep the ferry pulled up might result in its being washed downstream, and failure to lower the ferry back into the falling river might result in its being stranded until the next high water.

Other flood damage resulted from trees and logs being swept downstream. Should one of these hit the ferry, the force might be enough to sink it, or snap the main cable or lines and wash the ferry downstream. During flood times the ferryman stayed up all night to keep watch on conditions. If possible, he might pull the ferry to a cove away from the current until the river subsided.

Flooding danger could happen any time of the year, but it was most frequent in the spring. Depending on the size of the rivers, usually the water would crest and fall within a twenty-four-hour period after heavy rain. When the water receded, the ferryman had to repair the washed-out landing, fix the approaches by hauling in clay and other materials, and remove any debris left in the way, as well as inspect the ferry and make any necessary repairs, such as replace broken railings, repair any new leaks, and, of course, scoop out water.

Even without flooding, water levels fluctuated, and some ferry locations had special high-water hookups for the ferry. Ferries with permanent concrete landing ramps on the bank made provision for higher and lower water levels.

In the opposite extreme, sometimes in summer or early fall there would not be enough water. This condition, though not as potentially dangerous as a flood, was of major concern because it caused the ferryman greater work. During a drought, rivers occasionally got so low that the ferryman had to scoop out the gravel from the landing approach to enable the ferry to get close enough to shore to unload the cars. And if the river became sluggish enough that the current wouldn't take the ferry across, the ferryman would have to pole the ferry to and fro across the river.

It is difficult for modern motorists to envision all the work and trouble it used to be just to cross a river they could easily throw a rock over. Accustomed to speeding on high bridges over streams they hardly notice, most of them would be frustrated and impatient to have to stop, wait in turn, and then, one or two cars at a time, float at a snail's pace across a hundred-foot river. But, on the other hand, some motorists drive miles out of the way just to experience riding a ferry. They consider it an adventure into the past to drive onto the rattling, unstable ferryboat and glide silently to the other bank.

There are very few current-powered ferries left, except for places such as Akers, in Ozark Scenic Riverways, where for old times' sake a ferry still crosses the Current River. Either because there wasn't enough traffic to make them economically feasible on out-of-the-way crossings or because bridges were built to replace them on heavily traveled roads, one by one the ferries have disappeared.

Powder Mill Ferry

Interview with Euel Sutton, Eminence, Missouri, September, 1978

From the early 1920s, when it was built, until a highway bridge replaced it in the late 1960s or early 1970s, the Powder Mill Ferry played a prominent part in Euel Sutton's life. "It lasted from the horse and buggy days until the jet age," he said, remembering his experiences growing up near the ferry.

During the height of the Vietnam War, the mission of the boys from Chanute Field, Kansas, and Colorado Springs was to fly their jets and "bomb" Powder Mill Ferry, and the Cooley Ferry and possibly the Akers Ferry—simulation bombing. These young trainee pilots would have to fly a jet from Colorado Springs, fly through this range of mountains to this river and find this little bitty boat. It was quite a navigational chore. Those boys were good. Once they found the ferry, they would "dive bomb" it from a certain height and turn their cameras on. Some of them got real good at it. They could come right down on it.

Right at the start it would scare the hell out of everybody. They didn't warn anybody. They just started bombing. We didn't know what was going on until someone said, "Those boys are practicing to go to Vietnam."

Sometimes they would come in at about 600 miles per hour, and we didn't hear them until they had "hit" the ferry and started back straight up. We could be standing at the ferry, and we couldn't hear them if we weren't looking in the direction they were coming. Then all of a sudden they'd be there. Those things were so fast it demonstrated how a jet would sneak up on you and bomb you before you knew what was going on. And you would be surprised at how big they were once they got down there on you.

When the pilot would bomb his ferry, he'd turn that jet to go straight up at a terrific speed, fall over on his back, do a sweep back under himself and bomb it again. Then he would turn west, wiggle his wings as if to say goodbye and go back.

Sometimes they would miss the ferry like four or five miles below

FERRY LANDING CURRENT RIVER HY. 106 MO.

*The ferryman at Powder Mill in 1940 has almost completed another crossing.
Courtesy Edna Staples.*

it. Then they would go back up, get their altitude, and come along and swoop that ferry just like a hawk coming in. Some of those boys would come so close to that ferry that we would just back off. They would shake that ferry all to pieces.

Some days five planes would "bomb" it. And then they sent over the large planes, big bombardiers, that would fly up high and "blow the ferry up." That went on for three years.

I talked to one of the boys from out at Chanute Field whose mission was to knock out Alley Springs and Powder Mill Ferry. He came down on vacation later, walked in the store at Alley and said, "I just wiped this thing off the face of the earth about three weeks ago. The Powder Mill Ferry's not there anymore, either. I wiped it off, too."

Even though the Air Force boys didn't really bomb it off, the ferry doesn't exist anymore. There is a bridge there now. Powder Mill is halfway between Ellington and Eminence. They had a tourists' resort there, at Powder Mill, a few cabins and a store there with fishing equipment in it. On the west side of the river there was a post office named Owl's Bend that lasted until sometime up in the sixties before it went out. On the other side of the river, it was called Powder Mill. Now there's a high bluff, four or five hundred feet high on the other side. It was said that back in the Civil War days that there was a saltpeter mine in the area where they made their gunpowder. They had the lead, and drop-shot—or as some call it, tearshot—off the bluff. That's why it was called Powder Mill Bluff. When they built the ferry, they called it Powder Mill Ferry instead of Owl's Bend Ferry.

The Powder Mill Ferry was started sometime in the twenties. The first time I saw the ferry, I was about five or six years old. I really think it was built in about 1928 or '30 when the Model A's were getting started. Now the original 106 Highway between Ellington and Eminence that crosses the river now was nothing but a country road used by horses and wagons and people afoot. A fellow named Tom Nash built the ferry out of wood. It was approximately twelve, maybe fifteen feet wide and two car lengths or better, say twenty–twenty-five feet long. It was made out of heavy plank timber, sawed of rough pine, not dressed out, just sawmill sawed.

In the sixties they had as high as 150 cars cross there in twenty-four hours. Sometimes people'd have to wait as high as twenty or thirty minutes. Some people got a little hostile about it, but some of them enjoyed the river so much that they'd sit on the banks of the river while they waited their turn.

This is a tourist town and it was utterly ridiculous to leave that ferry there that long. But the Highway Department was slow, and it took them a long time to build that bridge. Today it's a barrage of cars that cross.

There were several wrecks involved with this ferry, especially as they got faster cars. It started out with the first hydraulic brake systems. Those things had a habit of leaking out fluid to the point where you wouldn't know that you didn't have a brake until you stepped on it and it was gone. On the west side of the river at Powder Mill, they had a long hill coming down to it. Just before you'd get to the ferry there was a sharp turn that dipped down to it. The east side was a long flat field so there wasn't too much problem there, but there have been several vehicles come down the west road and when they started to hit their brakes, they didn't have none, so here they come right on toward the ferry. The local people who knew the ferry would go by the side of the ferry into the water which was maybe waist deep all the way across the river. They'd run down in there and just drown out. Then they'd get pulled back out of the water with some mules or horses, maybe a rig, and they'd dry out their motor and go on. But if people didn't know the situation, they'd get excited, and some of them would cut into the bluff there. There have been a few people killed there, not too often, but there have been several of them with their heads banged up.

The funniest one of the wrecks involved a dairy truck that crossed the ferry every day with dairy products. He would go around to local farmers, pick up their milk in milk cans—regular creamery cans—haul them all the way to Willow Springs and come back with the empties. Well, he had an old bed on an old Ford truck and he had a top on this. We could hear the milk cans rattle continuously. We could hear him coming for half a mile. Well, this one particular day, he was coming rather fast, and we could hear him trying to hit gears on that old Ford truck, for he had discovered he didn't have any brakes. He had crossed the ferry enough he went to blowing his horn to get everybody out of the way because he was free-wheeling. When he came around the curve toward the ferry, it was all clear. The ferryman was standing there watching him. By this time the driver had reached a speed of probably forty or fifty miles per hour. He drove right out on the ferry and momentum of the truck carried him clear and on out into the water. His truck almost floated.

Of course they tell some good tales on this fellow, what all he said when he went out and hit the water. He really didn't say anything, but they said he was a-hollering and praying at the same time, but he didn't. The funny part was all those tin milk cans rattling around in that old tin bed. He knew the river was about four feet deep, so rather than to hit the water at the bank or swerve his truck, he went right out on the ferry and right off.

Now when something like that happens you have 106 Highway shut down from Ellington to Eminence. Before you can move the ferry you have to call Ellington on the east side, get a wrecker to drive the thirteen miles, hook a chain on to his truck, take a boat and go out and hook the other end on the truck and pull him across. So anybody that showed up wanting to cross the ferry in that length of time had to sit and wait until this happened, or they had to drive around through Van Buren to Eminence, about a forty-mile drive. Now they had signs in Eminence and they had a sign in Ellington, right on the highway, that would say the ferry's closed.

One of the other times—I was about fifteen years old—a fellow came down through there with a pickup full of watermelons. He didn't know the ferry was there, even though there was a sign that said ferry, but he had missed it. He came flying around there and got scared and ran off the end of the ferry with his watermelons. So here's all his melons floating and bobbing up and down in the river. He tells us boys, "Catch those melons and bring them back, and I'll give you a nickel apiece for them." So four or five of us got in a boat and started going down the river over the shoals and out of sight. We put a lot of those melons over on the bank but gathered the rest and took them back to him.

Then we collected five cents apiece for the ones we'd got to him. We still had fifteen or twenty that we'd stole off him while we were getting them, and we tried to peddle them.

The only time the ferry ever sunk was when it would hit the bank and punch a hole. No one would know it, but the next morning it would be sunk. That didn't happen too many times. They pretty well maintained it.

Sometime in fifty-eight or nine, sometime along in there, the old wooden boat was replaced by an iron metal barge that was motor-powered. They put on a car motor and rigged it up to the windlass, and fixed it to where it would push the barge across the river and back. That one could haul four cars at one time. The old wooden one could only take two cars and the first one could only take one car.

The first time I saw the ferry when I was real young, we crossed the river in wagons and teams, for we didn't have an automobile. And in the space between the twenties to the sixties they were bombing with jets. They had walked on the moon by that time.

The Spans of Time

The expression, "I'll see you if the creek don't rise," holds much meaning for inhabitants of the Ozarks who must cross creeks and rivers for almost any travel. In many gatherings of people reminiscing about old times, someone will tell a tale of a troublesome crossing.

"About fifty years ago old Mr. and Mrs. Albert Claxton were driving home," Lavern Cravens said. "It was raining pretty bad when they got to the Elk Creek ford in Wright County. Now that ford's tricky. You got to know just exactly where to cross or you'll get stuck. Albert saw the creek was coming down—you know, you look up the creek and see the rolls of water coming—but he thought he could make it before the water got to the ford. He'd crossed it hundreds of times. Well, he got stuck right in the middle. He was old and his wife was an invalid, so all he could do was go get help. He waded out and came to our house. I wasn't very big, but I remember. We got ropes and the tractor and rushed back there. While we were getting there, a big log come down the creek with the rolls of water. Mrs. Claxton opened both the car windows and somehow guided that log through the car. If she hadn't, it'd have hit the car and probably turned it over. When we got there, she was sitting in water up to her neck. They took ropes to keep from being washed down the creek and went in to get her out, but we couldn't get the car out till next day when the water run down. The car was clear ruined.

"Then another time three car loads of us, kids and all, were coming to a family dinner when we got to the low-water bridge on the Osage Fork River—there at Pease Mill where the county road crosses. It had been raining all night and the river was up—plumb across the bridge. All you could see of the bridge was the two rows of swells where the water went over the little raised edges. My brother-in-law drove across first by himself and came back to say it was safe. We headed into that water, one car right behind the other following him. We started close to the upstream edge of the bridge. Water ran through the floor of the car and we could feel the car being pushed toward the other edge of the bridge. It was really scary to be driving straight ahead, yet going

51

sideways right toward the edge of the bridge and twelve feet of raging water. My car was big and heavy, but the one behind me was light. I watched in the mirror and thought sure the current would push him over the edge before he could get across. If he'd gone over, there would have been nothing to do. They'd all have drowned. But we made it. In just the time it took Lester to cross and come back, the water had risen enough to make it dangerous. It was foolish of us to do it, but it saved about a thirty-mile drive to go around."

Incidents like these often occurred in the hilly and forested Ozark land drained by many hollows, creeks, and rivers. From the days of earliest settlement when the first settlers inhabited the rich creek and river bottoms, crossing rivers was frequently necessary, even in high waters. Roads were generally rocky soil, gravel, and hardpan, uncomfortable to travel on but passable under most conditions. However, river and creek crossings were not predictable and not always passable because of frequent and sudden rises during rainy periods. Getting across the river demanded a secure method of crossing for man, horse, or machine.

The various methods of crossing employed were dependent on the terrain of the site. Rock bluffs precluded any bridges except for large, steel-frame or suspended cable. Mud banks and gravel and sand bars necessitated clearing for a solid base. Banks could wash away, and loose gravel or sand bars might shift with the next flood. Since the waterways are lined predominantly by gravel, sand, or solid rock, acquisition of these building materials was simple. Abundant hardwood forests supplied other materials, and oak lumber played a major role in many constructions.

Natural Fords

The first joining of river banks to occur obviously was by means of natural ford crossings. A ford is merely a shallow spot on a river or creek, preferably narrow, with low, solid banks for easy entrance and exit and a hard-packed gravel or rock bottom. In case of several possible choices, the road generally went to the best ford. An extra distance overland was easily justified by an easy crossing.

Fords often had one place that was firm enough to drive across. Persons familiar with the ford usually had no difficulty, but strangers were not always so fortunate. Even with normal water flow, they might get stuck by heading in wrong, especially on longer fords, which usually did not go straight across but curved to use the firmest footing or angled downstream to avoid fighting the current.

No matter how good the crossing might be at any one time, fords were unreliable and unpredictable. The slightest rise in water terminated the usefulness immediately. Heavy flooding could wash out a once-secure footing, leaving gulleys and an uneven bottom, or deposit heavy layers of gravel. Since the footing was never surely safe, a simple crossing with heavy vehicles could become several hours of sweating labor as wheels bogged down in the newly washed-in sand and gravel. Winter months added a special danger because neither men, horses, nor car engines could last long struggling through cold water.

Whenever wagons or cars became stuck, customary courtesy and neighborliness required the nearest farmer to pull them out. During especially bad weather, the farmer might leave his team or tractor handy for aiding unlucky travelers. The farmer usually didn't expect neighbors to pay anything and would probably refuse to take money if offered, but he would sometimes appreciate some compensation from a stranger. A dollar was the usual amount.

People accustomed to crossing fords had various methods of crossing in high water. A common precaution was to loosen the fan to keep it from throwing water on the engine and drowning it out. A car's engine will run in fairly deep water if water doesn't get into the oil. One particularly deep but narrow ford that Lavern and some high school boys had to cross to get to school activities required preparation when the creek was up. Rather than miss out on the fun at school, the boys would bring ropes and extra cans of oil. On reaching the ford, they fastened the ropes to the front of the car. Two boys rode on the hood holding the ropes. After loosening the fan belt, the driver moved into the water. If the car got stuck or flooded out midstream, the two boys jumped to the other side and pulled the car on through. They checked the oil to see if it had water in it. If so, they drained the oil, put in the new cans of oil they had with them, tightened the fan belt, and went on their way.

For a permanent crossing often used, natural fords were a poor choice.

Paved Fords

The first improvement for natural fords was insurance of a solid bed for traction. A slab of concrete in place of an often-shifting gravel bed provided a secure surface for people, horses, wagons, and automobiles.

The decision to put in a paved ford usually fell upon the residents living near the crossing. Those who would benefit from a paved ford donated time, money, materials, and labor toward the construction.

This concrete slab on the Niangua River at Moon Valley only assures motorists that they won't get stuck in the gravel. As long as the water isn't too deep or the current too strong, it is safe to cross.

During the summer months, when the river or creek reached its lowest point, work began. Workers first dragged the pathway of the ford free of loose sand, gravel, and mud with horse teams and double shovels, or with a tractor and scoop, depending on which was available. Next, they built wooden forms across the width of the river, between one and three feet deep. Large rocks filled the bulk of the form, while cement, sand, and gravel, mixed by hand or tractor-driven mixers, filled the remainder. If the water was running more than a few inches, they mixed the concrete thicker to set under water. After several days of actual work and a week for the concrete to harden, the paved ford was ready for use. If the concrete set and settled correctly, then no further work was required, barring mishaps.

The solid platform gave ideal footing compared to the natural river bottom, but the advantages ended here. No allowance was made for water flow, so water moved underneath the slab in cracks or over the top. Except for the driest weather water ran over paved fords, causing a layer of green slime to grow on the ford and make a slippery surface. On occasion, extremely heavy flooding would wash out around the ends, cutting across the approach or washing it out altogether. Water underneath the slab could result in a shifting and breaking up of the concrete, which meant a complete rebuilding of the ford. This often happened in winter as a result of freezing and thawing. Because the ford was nearly level with the river bottom, high water over the paved ford was the same as high water over the natural ford—impassable. However, as soon as the water receded, the paved ford was ready for use again.

Concrete Low-Water Bridges

One difference between a low-water bridge that is at bank level and a paved ford is that the bridge allows water to flow primarily underneath, while a paved ford has water flowing over the top. There are two different types of low-water bridges prevalent, with many variations in height, width, and length. One type consists of metal whistles (culverts) through a sort of dam, the other of concrete slabs and pillars. Funding for concrete low-water bridges also varied depending on site selection. For a little-used crossing, local residents would often be responsible for all expenses. For a heavily-traveled crossing, part or all the expenses might be paid by the county court, through the road dis-

The approach of this low-water concrete fill on Brush Creek in southern Laclede County extends well past the present creek channel, in order to prevent washouts of the road.

The whistles (metal culverts) of this low-water bridge on the Osage Fork at Orla fail to carry all the flow during rising waters.

trict tax fund. This fund was part of the county property tax levied upon residents of the county and was used expressly for county roads and bridges. Both these types of bridges have been built occasionally in recent times. Over secondary state roads and county roads the concrete slab low-water bridge is utilized when practical.

The construction of a solid, dam-like bridge with whistles began similarly to that of a paved ford. The site was cleared of loose gravel and sand before setting the wooden forms. The height above the water varied from two to six feet, depending on the size of the waterway. The length was sometimes twice the actual distance across the river, with an extra length serving as an approach on each side. Since the bridge was usually level with the roadbed, no special effort was required to slope the approach. The width was approximately twelve feet, for only one lane of traffic.

The whistles were set into place to accommodate normal water flow, with large rocks and gravel fitting in the bulk of the form. Concrete was poured into the form and allowed to cure. After a week or two for settling and drying, the bridge was ready for use. Because of the nearly water-level height and the limitations of the whistles for handling large amounts of water, rises of only a few feet would cover the bridge, making it useless.

This type of bridge was relatively inexpensive, but it had several other limitations besides flooding. Its length and width were restricted by the fact that the bridge's strength faded in long spans because of poor supports. Obviously, longer crossings required a more complex bridge.

The second type of low-water bridge used concrete slabs and pillars supported by enclosed steel beams. The use of steel beams was mandatory, because without them the slabs would break apart of their own weight. This type of bridge allowed almost unrestricted flow of water underneath during normal river conditions and was generally more resistant to flood damage than the solid construction.

The first construction job was to dig the pillar sites down to bedrock and then build the wooden forms to contain the pillars. Steel mesh and reinforcement bars were used in the pillars for strength. Concrete was mixed and poured into the forms. Bolts projected from the top of the supports. The steel beams were manhandled into place on the supports and secured by the bolts. The beams were often scrap from junkyards or rails from a railroad. At best, finding the steel beams for a privately-built bridge was a hit-or-miss situation, depending on the chance availability of scrap beams.

The next job was to build strong wooden frames for the poured concrete roadbed. Steel mesh and rebar stretched across the frame provided inner support for the concrete. The steel beams were enclosed in the wooden frame. In addition, each edge of the bridge had a raised concrete bumper to prevent vehicles from running off the bridge. Slots in the edge allowed water to drain off the top.

On each end usually a concrete abutment winged out into the bank on the upstream side, preventing water from eroding the approach to the bridge.

The many concrete low-water bridges, like this one on the Osage Fork south of Morgan, offer safe crossing as long as the river stays within its banks.

This bridge required more labor and care during construction than the bridge described above. However, the strength was greater and the danger of washing out was less, since the bridge offered less resistance to water flow. Still, the bridge had its drawbacks. Since it was only bank high, flooding was possible. Although water went over the bridge usually only a few times a year and for only a few hours at a time, high waters did prevent year-round use. After each flood someone had to clear the bridge of accumulated driftwood. And there was always the possibility of a heavily loaded vehicle breaking a slab in two, sending everything tumbling into the river.

Probably one of the greatest difficulties with this type of bridge was keeping the approaches to the bridges passable. High waters jamming logs against the bridge have often diverted the water to the less resistant banks. When the waters receded there would often be an impassable gap washed out between the road and the bridge.

The fords and low-water bridges made travel easier and out-of-the-way places more accessible before steel and concrete high-water bridges spanned almost every creek and river so effectively that the traveler hardly realizes the hollow he is crossing was once a major obstacle. Yet today there are still many fords and low-water bridges being used because they save many miles and much time. The creeks continue to rise and temporarily prevent people from traveling. Even today school busses cannot pick up all the children on the route when creeks are up. Yearly, on highways and main roads better bridges are being built and old ones bypassed or torn down, but on the back roads the old bridges are still greatly needed. These spans have withstood the test of time.

Swinging Foot Bridge

Years ago, when the land was surveyed for settling, school districts were not divided geographically but into squares, with each containing six to nine square miles. As early as 1789, Congress passed an ordinance to subdivide the millions of acres of land west of the Appalachians into square townships and sections on north-south, east-west lines. School districts were formed on these lines regardless of geographic conditions. Placing the schoolhouse in the middle of the square assured that no child had to walk more than two miles to reach school. For most school districts this plan worked, but to the children of the Stony Point school district the plan presented a unique problem, because the Osage Fork River divided the district into two almost equal parts. How to get the children across the river to attend the school became a real community problem, for the only crossings for miles were fords.

After considerable planning, the members of the school board resolved the problem by constructing a swinging foot bridge at a halfway place where there was already a natural ford and well-used travel way. In 1912 the patrons of the district built a bridge of wooden slabs. Since it reached only from one side of the river to the opposite bank, this bridge had one big disadvantage. On the east side of the river the bridge came out at the base of a twenty-foot limestone bluff. The students had to climb the near-vertical rocks or walk down the river until they could find a place where it was easier to climb in order to reach the path through the timber that led to the school, for the road went in another direction.

To solve this problem, when the big overflow in 1914 took out the first bridge, the patrons again provided the labor (at twenty-five cents an hour) to build a better bridge—a swinging bridge. This bridge came out at the top of the bluff instead of at the bottom and was well above floodwaters. About one-third of the new bridge was suspended over dry land. Large oak and cedar trees on each side provided vertical support for four steel cables that spanned about a hundred feet between the rock bluff and the opposite bank. For added strength, cables were tied to huge logs buried in the ground.

The last child crossed this bridge to school in 1960. Although now in disrepair, the supports and cables are still strong. It was built to last.

Fastened securely between the hand-twisted wire cables, welded wire formed two sides about three feet high and a bottom about four feet wide. Stapled crosswise to the wire in the bottom were two-by-fours placed four feet apart. On these, one-by-sixes were nailed four inches apart to provide a walkway across the bridge.

On the west side of the bridge, steps were constructed to reach up to the walkway, which was about ten feet from the ground. The steps, protected by hand rails and made of sturdy oak two-by-sixes were placed close together so the smaller children could ascend them easily and safely.

The bridge proved to be very rugged and required surprisingly little maintenance. Portions of the wooden walkway had to be replaced occasionally, but the steps needed repairing less often because the large trees offered protection from the elements and because the native oak is very durable. This durability is really remarkable when you consider the abuse the bridge has taken from the children and the years.

Although each season presented its own problems, winter was the

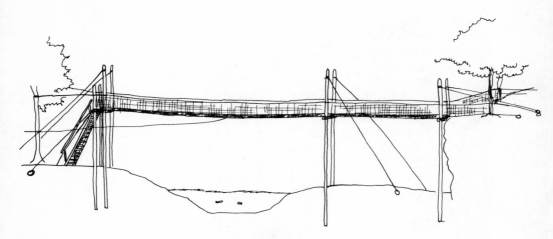

Structural drawing of the footbridge.

worst for crossing the bridge. Because of the spaces left in the flooring
of the bridge, snow could not form in the winter. However, ice certainly could, and when it did, the bridge would become very slick and
hard to cross. The older boys would help the first- and second-graders
by placing the smaller children's feet on top of their own and walking
them across the bridge.

Flash floods caused by heavy rains were a year-round danger. The
water would never get up to the bridge, but would fill the slough,
flood the bottom field over which the children walked to get to the
bridge, and sometimes would rise well up the steps on the west bank.
The older boys sometimes would swim horses across the low slough
nearest the bridge in order to pick up the children as they came home
across the bridge. Sometimes the river would rise so far that it was too
dangerous for the horses to swim. If this condition developed when the
children were at school, they stayed all night with neighbors on the
school side of the river. If it happened during the night, those children
had a holiday next day.

Because the bridge was one of the few swinging bridges in the region, it proved to be quite an attraction. Relatives and friends who
came to visit school patrons wanted to see and walk across the bridge.
Most of the children who grew up around the bridge did not find it
particularly interesting. The majority were not afraid of the bridge and
crossed it daily as easily as if they were walking through a field. On
the other hand, there were some weak-hearted students years ago who

would not cross the bridge. They used a flat-bottomed johnboat, which was the only means of crossing the river before the bridge was built.

Many times the eighth-grade boys would catch smaller children out on the bridge and frighten them by making the bridge sway. This prank would really terrorize the youngest children, because the bridge, a good twenty feet from the surface of the water, probably looked a great deal higher to those youngsters. Actually, it was almost impossible to fall from the bridge, because the welded wire bottom and sides would catch anyone who slipped off the walkway.

I have visited the swinging bridge four times, and I am still amazed at the durability of the structure, which hasn't been used or repaired since crossed by the last child in 1961. It leans to the left now, and all the boards on the walkway are gone, but the rusty cables and wire are surprisingly strong. The oak trees anchoring the cables are vigorous. With care, even the steps can still be walked on.

There is no sign now of the former ford in the river for horse-drawn vehicles. The once frequently traveled road is now only the farmer's access to his field, but the foot bridge, almost hidden by trees, is still suspended over the small springfed river, a reminder to the few fishermen who pass under it of the care and interest the people of the Ozarks have always had in their children's education.

Corkery: Once a River Village

All that remains of Corkery are aging bridge piers, crumbling foundations, the walls of a store with a caved-in roof, and, of course, a graveyard. There isn't even enough left of this one-time river village to be called a ghost town. Whether approaching by the narrow, rutted road or from the river, it takes an alert observer to notice even these remnants. Only the three still impressive-looking bridge piers, one on each bank of the river and a third close against the high bluff, make the visitor aware that there once was a settlement on the now deserted and overgrown banks of the Niangua River.

Over fifty years ago, however, there was much activity and business here, based mostly on the river location. The original mill built near the natural ford attracted business and people. Thousands and thousands of railroad-tie rafts were assembled here and floated down to market during Corkery's heyday. Then, when the hoped-for bridge was not completed beyond the piers, the settlement dwindled away to nothing. But today, ironically, every pleasant weekend hundreds of canoeists make the traffic on the river heavy once again, though very few of the nature lovers and pleasure seekers who float by even consider that there must be a story behind the silent bridge piers.

In the late 1800s and early 1900s Corkery became the main crossroads for the whole area because of the natural ford, which people crossed by foot, horseback, and wagon. The river traffic provided a feasible location for stores and made mail service a necessity. The traffic also helped develop tie rafting into one of Corkery's major businesses. Forrest Bradshaw, who had lived in the same house about half a mile from the east bank all of his life, said, "There was two or three places between Bennett Spring and here where they stacked railroad ties. They used to float them down the river to market by the millions! I've seen rafts that'd be a mile long."

The ford wasn't the only crossing. At one time there was a do-it-yourself ferry tied to the bank. People towed themselves and their belongings across on a raft-like ferry held in place by cables. Later a low-

Near these long bridge pillars on the Niangua River there once was a thriving river village called Corkery. When the bridge was never built, the community eventually died out completely.

water bridge provided adequate crossing for cars. As a logical response to Corkery's traffic, in 1920 workers began constructing the bridge piers out of cement and native rock, as the first step in making a permanent crossing.

David Bradshaw, Forrest's cousin, said, "My dad furnished a lot of the rock for the piers. He picked them up around our place. My dad got seventy-five cents a wagon load."

The cement bags that Forrest helped carry to the construction site were stored in a shed that was reputed to be the longest in the county. The completed bridge would have been the only all-weather crossing over the Niangua for miles, and would have secured Corkery's future. But the bridge was never finished. The steel for the bridge frame had been ordered and the lumber purchased, but the Dallas County Court ordered the work discontinued for lack of funds. The work was never resumed.

Later, a bridge across the Niangua was constructed near Bennett Spring, and it attracted the traffic that was once Corkery's mainstay. After the ford and the low-water bridge both washed out, there was no way to cross the river at Corkery. The main road was moved from the bank of the river to the top of the bluff, and with no river crossing and no traffic, Corkery was no longer the main crossroads for the surrounding area.

"Corkery was a thriving business a long time," David remembered, "but we were pretty well isolated once the river crossing washed out. The Model T's did fairly well, but after the new lower cars came, we didn't get across if we lived on the other side of the river."

Gradually the town dwindled. The piers that first promised a better river crossing soon became a symbol of Corkery's demise.

Before its decline, Corkery served the outlying area for about a five-mile radius. Most people lived on nearby farms and traveled by foot, horse, or wagon to Corkery to have horses shod, catch up on gossip, mail a letter, go to school, trade at the general store, or pick up flour or cornmeal at the mill.

The first mill, which was powered by river water forced over a dam, was used to saw lumber and grind cornmeal and flour. It was started by David's great-grandfather. "The old mill was known as Poynter's Mill," said Maude Bradshaw, David's mother. "Poynters came from Kentucky and settled down here around Lebanon. Mr. William Poynter wanted to put a mill in, and that's what took them down to the river. He put in that old mill in 1863. The old mill washed out in 1902 in a big rise in the river. Everything was lost. They did find the burrs that ground the corn."

Forrest's wife, Ethel, said, "There's an old mill wheel that stayed in the river for years until the folks down here at the campground pulled it out and laid it down in the front yard. Everybody looked for that mill wheel when they came over that old dam."

After the flood, Fred Johnson rebuilt Corkery with a large general store, blacksmith shop, grist mill, and sawmill, both powered this time by a big gasoline engine.

Beginning in 1884 the mill served another function. Ed Corkery had bought Poynter's Mill some years earlier and established a post office there, hence the name of the village. He delivered the mail twice a week on horseback. After two more postmasters, the post office was moved to the general store.

Gertie Bradshaw, Forrest's mother, became postmistress in 1919 when the office was moved from the store across the river to the Bradshaw home. Gertie retired in 1944 when she broke her hip and was unable to manage the post office. The mail then became part of a Lebanon route.

"The post office was moved over here to our home," Ethel said, "because the man who owned the general store was never there. The first class mail was all in a lock box, and those mail carriers never let that first class mailbag out of their possession until they got into the post office."

"Now, believe it or not," Forrest added, "the pay Mom got for years was whatever stamps she cancelled. If the letter was mailed here, she got paid, and if it wasn't, she didn't."

"When they first got the mail route," said David, "The mail only came two days a week, but forty years ago or even more than that, the mail usually came every day. Sometimes the team couldn't make the round trip in a day. They would be too worn out to come back. Mail carriers had to have poles to pry them out of the mud, because the roads were just terrible. They would cut poles and leave them out along the road, and it was so far from this pole to the other. If the mail carriers couldn't cross the river when the water was up, they would go across by boat, carrying the mail across their backs up to Forrest's. Can you imagine that now? Mail carriers didn't have it easy back in them times."

The general store, as in any small community, was probably the most popular place in Corkery. The store was located between the retaining wall and the river, with the rough gravel road running between the store and the river. The store building had a basement and was three stories high at the back. "I was just a little wart," Forrest grinned, "but the best I remember, that was the fullest store I ever walked into. You could get anything from a sewing needle to a threshing machine—just whatever you wanted."

Maude added, "They tried to keep a little of everything. We didn't come to Lebanon very often. We come about twice a year in a covered wagon to get a good supply."

Corkery was self-sufficient enough to boast a springhouse that provided running water. "Down in that little field," Forrest said, "between the store building and river was a springhouse. It was automatic—it ran on its own after it got started. On the hill there was a tank. Now a ram forced the water up into that tank and gravity fed it back to the house. Whenever the water level got so low, it started pumping."

No community is complete without a final resting place for its citizens. Corkery's cemetery was an eighth of a mile upstream from the general store and springhouse. Many gravestones lean at odd angles, some have already fallen over, and the wire fence enclosing the small graveyard is in disrepair. Although unkept and crowded, the graveyard is a peaceful, quiet place, where the river's murmurs and gurgles create a lullaby that adds to its restful aura. The designs of the professionally-engraved headstones are still clearly visible, but the depressions of the hand-carved ones are barely discernible with fingertips.

"Many years ago I could read those stones," Maude said. "They were taken out of a cave and they say the cave rocks were soft when they made the markers."

The legible headstones indicate the graves of many infants and youth. "Typhoid was awfully bad way back then," she continued. "My mother-in-law's first husband died with typhoid and then in a short time the little girl, four years old and the youngest, died. The next June her two boys died with typhoid—one died one day and the other one the next. There were four that went out of a family of seven in less than a year. She didn't talk very much about when they was gone—they was just gone."

Although sickness and death were sad and sometimes cruel, there were happy times, too, and recreation in Corkery was never hard to find. "There at the general store almost every Sunday," David reminisced, "there'd be thirty-five, forty kids coming there from around the hills. If there was nothing pushing to do, we had to climb that bluff. We've been up it a thousand times. We'd go on hikes, explore caves, play cards, ball, all kinds of games, and of course in the winter, sleigh ride. In the summer we'd live in the river and swim all day." Maude added, "I don't know what kept the children from drowning. All the kids up and down the river did that, but nobody got drowned."

The hospitality and neighborliness common in small, close communities showed itself when Forrest said, "There was always somebody else's kids here. Mom never knew just exactly how many kids she had. Everyone had a place at the table, and we would just count noses to see who was gone. When Mom fixed a noon meal, she'd never know how many she was fixing for. The mail carriers would all plan on meeting here for dinner. Anybody that knew Dad knew that if they ever landed here around mealtime, they would never leave until Dad had them fed."

Forrest also noted the differences in entertainment and discipline. "You kids have a lot more in entertainment. When I was a kid, we had to make our own entertainment. Sometimes we'd get into trouble, like for stealing watermelons. Say for instance I was up at one of the neighbors and I done something I shouldn't have. If the fellow thought I deserved a thrashing, he didn't wait till I got home. He gave it to me there."

Life in Corkery was certainly not boring. Stories about everything imaginable still abound and help to complete the picture of work and play in a small river village.

"I know a bunch of stories," Forrest said, "but I don't know whether I should tell them or not! I remember I was over there at the general store one time. A big old fellow chewed tobacco all the time. When that old fellow was around, a whole bunch of young fellows'd bug him for a chew of tobacco. They wouldn't stop until they'd get every bit he had. One day he was over at the store chewing. At that time tobacco came in long sheets—plug tobacco—and it was cut off in nickel's, dime's or quarter's worth with an old tobacco knife. He got a dime's worth of tobacco, which was two or three times what it would be now. There was four or five of us around there, and he said, 'Come on, boys, have a chew.' He had just bought it, but nobody would take it. 'Well,' he said, 'evidently something's wrong with it.' He just threw it over the back of the store building out through that field and into the river. He said, 'Now boys, don't ever ask me for another chew of tobacco!' As far as I knew, he stayed with it. I can't tell that part about why they didn't want any." He paused, and with a smile added, "Something happened to that tobacco.

"Me and my oldest brother was down there by the old mill in the summertime. There was a couple of old guys by the river—I thought then they was old, but I imagine they was up around their fifties. They pulled their underwear off, so they'd have dry clothes to put on after they got done working around the water with the ties. They had them hung up there on a bush. Then they got out there in the river. I and my brother both got into the one seat of the underwear. Both of us in one pair, but we didn't get going in the same direction. We tore our way out of them!

"Soon as we got out of that underwear we left. We didn't leave too soon 'cause one of the men was coming. He got pretty close to us, and we knew what that would be. He caught him a good hickory and he give us a sound thrashing right there. He knew us, but we didn't dare tell Dad. Anyhow, later Dad found out. He said, 'It's all over with now, but I ought to give you a good thrashing!' I thought he was a-going to anyhow, but he didn't. If he'd a-gotten hold of us that day, he'd a-done it. We'd a-gotten two thrashings, because when we'd a-come in the house with switch marks all over us, Dad would've wanted to know how come. We'd a-had to told him and he'd a-give us another one. Ah, when I was a kid, I'd a-done anything!

"Never hunted a turkey in my life, but I killed one—near nigh choked him to death. I was eight, nine years old. Dad had this field up here in corn. It was cut up, shocks still standing. There was turkeys up there and they got to feeding on that corn. I wanted Dad to let me take a shotgun up there and the next spring kill them. Mother had tame turkeys here and the wild turkeys would come up and fight the old gobbler through the fence. 'Course the old gobbler was just boogered up.

"I'd watched them and there was one path that came up the hill over there. There was a little gulley across the path with a big log across it. Them turkeys would fly across from the other hill to just below that log, walk up that path, hop over the log and walk on up over that hill.

"I laid down behind that log and covered myself up with leaves with my hands up. The log was high enough up I could squint in under it. I just got laid down there and I heard wings a-flopping. I peeked under my log and a hen looked down off the hill, walked up and walked on the log just over me, hopped off and on up the hill. Then one gobbler lit down there, walked up and hopped on the log. When he walked up there, I grabbed. I accidentally caught him by the leg. There I was, down, and that old turkey—he seemed to me like he weighed thirty pounds—was literally beating me to death! I guess he would have finally got away, but wrestling around there his head come in contact, and I got him by the head and just absolutely choked him to death. That's the only wild turkey I ever killed in my life. One of those big turkeys can really claw you up!"

Maude said, "I remember a story that happened at the post office during the Civil War. There was a boy that was carried away, and years and years later a young man come back and told that he was the boy carried away, but he was forty years old and he didn't remember much what happened. You see, some of the boys was dragging up the wood in the snow and they saw three men riding up in the field. When his family went to call this child up for dinner, he wasn't to be found. They tracked around in the snow and they saw where he got on a horse with these men. When he came back they couldn't hardly believe it was the same boy. He didn't look like the other children and he didn't act like them.

"On the same place several years ago, there was a woman and a little boy that had to cross the river. I don't know why the woman was foolish enough, but the river was up, and they got drowned. They had an old mule and an old buggy that a man had thrown away. The old mule got out a ways and then turned around and came back. Well, they found the woman after a day or two, but they didn't find the four-year-old boy till several weeks later."

"There must have been Indians down around our place," David said, "because there were lots of Indian arrowheads. There was a tribe supposedly camped up on the hill there between our place and For-

These stairs led to a busy general store in Corkery's heyday.

rest's. Legend has it they buried their gold under huge flat rocks out
in the field. I don't know what they was doing with gold; but anyway,
that was the story. They buried the gold there, stayed that night and
moved on. I had a fellow doing some dozing there several years ago.
I told him about that, and I said, 'I got to go to town, but I'll be
back in time to help you look for that gold.' He said, 'If I find it, I'll
give you half of it!' But he had the rocks all pushed out by the time I
got back. He bought a new Cadillac and a new dozer after that. Nobody never knew if he found the gold. I doubt it very much, but it
makes you wonder. I didn't really believe it.

"Several people operated a general store over the many years. One
store had a basement under a basement and some owner brewed his
moonshine off in there. The smoke went up through the store building
through a flue that went clear down into this second basement. He'd
always have a little fire in the store stove so smoke would go up the
flue to camouflage what he was really doing. It was a pretty good
business.

"To get down to the still you had to move a counter. There was
a trap door under the counter in the store. Officials raided him several times. They knew he was making whiskey, but they never found it.

It changed hands a time or two until a family moved in named

Gann. He found the still. He said he was sitting there one day and noticed that trap door under the counter. So he raised it up and saw the stairs leading down. The Gann kids told us, so we all went down in to look it over. We were little kids and it was hard for us to climb the high steps. It was real exciting finding a still."

Corkery as the Bradshaws knew it is dead. Nevertheless, its spirit still lurks among the skeletons of this hidden town—the bridge piers, the graveyard and the foundations—and in the bittersweet reminiscences of the people who lived there.

Corkery was once an excellent location for a multi-purpose river village. Later its once-excellent location became the very reason for its decline—no way to cross the river. But now Corkery's location is ideal for the growth of a new enterprise—the canoe rental and campground businesses. Because of this new era, Corkery probably sees more traffic now in one canoeing season than it ever did seventy years ago in a year of ferries and railroad ties.

Floating Downstream with Boat and Paddle

Some people are content to view the Ozarks scenery from the comfort and convenience of an automobile, which is a reasonable method of observation. The advantages are quick and easy access, the possibilities of covering a hundred or more miles a day, and leaving whenever you find it necessary. The disadvantages are being locked up inside a vehicle and not getting out into fresh air except for short walks.

Other people like to throw themselves out into nature and experience the sights, sounds, smell, feel, and even taste of the outdoors. For these people, a hike in the woods is great. Even better is a float down an Ozark river.

Truly, a float down the Ozark rivers is one of the best ways to get into the Ozarks. Rest and solitude alternate with speed and excitement for every mile of water. Animals and plants flourish in and around the river. A chance to get-away-from-it-all, and at the same time a chance to get-into-it-all is what the float trip is all about.

The qualities that make the Ozark rivers special are evident when you compare streams with rivers that flow outside the region. Parts of seventy-five or more rivers and streams are floatable, and some of them remain almost as they were a hundred years ago. For persons interested in running the river in a canoe, kayak, or johnboat, the chance is readily available.

The rivers' winding channels run through gravel, sand, and rock, and are fed by cold, clean springs that make the rivers surprisingly clear. There is a minimum of soil runoff, except where vegetation has been destroyed. Compared to muddy rivers in the plains, the Ozark rivers are much more enticing. Also, because of the springs, the Ozark rivers seldom go dry, whereas plains rivers may turn into muddy trickles during summer.

The Ozark rivers have nearly everything to offer in abundance. Quiet stretches of water called *eddies* ranging from four to ten feet deep, fifty to two hundred feet wide, and from a quarter of a mile to two miles long or more offer silence and solitude—the fisherman's dream.

After a lazy float through Amos Eddy, the boys pick up speed in the swifter riffle.

The eddies are separated by *riffles*—shallow, fast water rushing over rocks. The term *rapid* is a misnomer for Ozark fast water, since a rapid is more often thought of as churning, boiling white water breaking against rocks and boulders. A riffle is a tamer version of a rapid. You can wade through some Ozark riffles, but rapids would sweep you off your feet. Even so, the riffles offer excitement, because the water not only moves swiftly, but in right-angle turns, s-curves, double s-curves, and 180° turns. And more than likely a tree limb or rock is hidden around that curve right in your path. But don't let this frighten you away. Most Ozark waterways are safe enough for even the inexperienced boater who respects the power of the river. With a little common sense you won't get dumped out into the water. Even if you do go swimming unexpectedly, the worst damage will be to your pride.

All of the rivers offer good fishing opportunities, and it is difficult to say which is best. Any resident of any river will tell you his or her river has the biggest fish around. But don't count on their showing you the best fishing hole!

For really inexperienced visitors, or those who don't have canoes or don't want to bother with getting them and who like being with a group of people, organized float trips are available. On the Niangua

River by Bennett Spring, the Current River, the James River, Buffalo, Eleven Point, and other rivers, groups of boaters leave nearly every day during the summer months. There are crowds of people on these rivers, so if you want to be alone, find another river.

The only really dangerous rivers in the Ozarks are the St. Francis River and its tributaries, the Little St. Francis and Big Creek. Solid granite formations called shut-ins have been formed where water cut narrow channels through rock. In swift water, shut-ins, with boulders scattered throughout, are hazardous to move through in a boat. All Ozark rivers are dangerous in flood, and even if you are an expert you should stay off them during high water. Of course, anytime you are on water you should exercise some caution.

Outfitting for the Float Trip

When you decide which river to float, figure how many days you have for floating. To plot your river route, put-in, camping and take-out points, consult a county map, which is available at the courthouse of each county. The map shows great detail, with every bridge and river crossing marked. To plan your mileage, figure six miles in six hours for a slow fishing trip. Eight miles in six hours for viewing the scenery. And if you're in a hurry and want to paddle your head off, ten miles in six hours.

Outfitting, or getting supplies and equipment together, depends on whether it is a day float, overnight float, or longer. The longer the trip, the more supplies and equipment necessary.

If you are going on an organized float trip and paying an out-fitter to have everything ready, then you need not worry with out-fitting. On the other hand, if you embark on your own, you had better be sure you're well supplied.

Equipment for a day float will only be the boat, paddles, seat cushions, life jackets, drinking water and, lunch. Overnight trips add sleeping gear, cooking equipment, and a change of clothes. More than one night requires more clothes and additional food.

One thing to remember is to pack light—take the bare minimum of equipment. If in doubt, leave it out. The purpose of a float trip is to enjoy yourself, which is nearly impossible if you are burdened by a stack of gear you'll never use or need.

If you don't own a canoe or boat, and cannot borrow one, the next best alternative is to rent one. Near the more popular rivers, canoe rentals abound, where you can rent a canoe for as long as you need. Paddles, seat cushions, and life jackets are available with the canoes.

Don't overload the boat or you will drag bottom through shallow spots and exhaust yourself paddling in the eddies.

Often other camping gear is for rent, but suppliers vary. Check the rentals to be sure what they have for use.

In addition to supplies and equipment needed there are certain other preparations you should make before you leave, to save time and trouble during your float trip. Headaches can be prevented by a few preliminary precautions.

Know the river. Every river is different. While one may be perfect for quiet bass fishing, another may be completely white water. You can't know everything about a river beforehand, but you can have a general idea of the river's nature by asking local residents and reading literature about it. If possible, take along someone who is familiar with the river. Even this is no guarantee, since the river changes with every flood. Still, get some idea of what the river is like before floating it. (An excellent guide to Missouri rivers is *Missouri Ozark Waterways*, Missouri Conservation Commission, Jefferson City, Missouri, 65101.)

Check the river. Depending on the season, a river may be at the perfect level for boating, flooding its banks, or too shallow to float. During spring, rains usually fill the river to an adequate level. Summer will probably bring a drier season, but most rivers usually stay about half full because of the water supply from natural springs. Fall usually brings the rain again, which refills the rivers. Sometimes winter is also dry. However, Ozark weather is known to be finicky. Droughts can occur in spring, or a deluge can fall in summer. It is disheartening at best to drag a canoe over gravel on a low river farther than you ever paddle, and it is much too dangerous to run a river in flood. For the most enjoyment, float when river conditions are best.

Check the weather. Even though the river is at the perfect level

*Check the weather
situation before
leaving on a float trip.
If heavy rain falls
during the night,
move to higher
ground. Don't be
caught on a low spot
if the river rises.*

for floating, heavy rains along the river may raise the water four to eight feet in hours. A sudden downpour may flood the low-water bridges, gravel bars and low banks, and wash away anything not tied down. Flashfloods can occur on the smaller tributaries, but are not as likely on the wider rivers. The rise of water will be more gradual on wider rivers, but the danger still exists. A wall of water several feet high poses a dangerous and frightening prospect. Besides, it is very disturbing to wake up underwater on a gravel bar with all your gear bobbing around you. The floater and camper should always observe the weather and river conditions.

Check out all your gear. Look over the boats completely for cracks, leaks, broken rivets, or other damage and repair them before you start. For added ease in sliding over rocks, apply car wax all over the bottom of metal boats, but do not wipe it off. Make sure the paddles do not have cracks or splinters in the handles. Check tarps, river bags, and plastic gear sacks for holes. Double check everything just to be sure. Ten miles downstream is no time to find out half your gear is missing and the other half is faulty. Be sure all equipment is together and sound.

Notify friends. With care, probably nothing will happen to you on the river, but it is reassuring to know someone is expecting your return. The Ozark rivers are not generally dangerous, and someone's farm or house is usually close by in case of emergency. There are, however, some stretches of river so lonely nothing but animals passes by for days. So be sure someone knows where you are going and when you plan to return.

Get permission from the landowner. Whenever crossing private land for access to the river or when camping on someone's land, *ask* first. More than likely you'll get yes for an answer. The laws defining the line between public and private lands on the river are disputed, and no matter what you think your rights are, it's very difficult to argue with an angry landowner on his ground. Respect private property, and you can leave with a friendly "Come back anytime" from the farmer.

Getting on the River

With everything stacked into the back of the car or pickup, you're ready to load the boats onto your vehicle. With a pickup or truck, you can either tie the boat over the cab and bed or let it stick out the tailgate. If you rest it on the cab lay an old rug or mat down to protect the finish of the car. If you stick it out the tailgate, tie a red flag on the end. Tie the boat to the bumper and front of the truck bed, or it may go bouncing down the road in the wrong direction.

If you use a car, place a mat on the top and balance the boat carefully. Tie to the front and back bumpers. Also, wrap a cloth or foam rubber around the rope where it touches the car, to prevent rubbing off paint. Make sure your vision is not obstructed by the boat or the tie ropes. Removable luggage carriers that fit on the tops of cars are excellent for transporting boats. They can be extended so that two boats ride as easily as one. Just be sure there is no danger of the boats falling off.

Of primary concern is the way back home. After you know where you are getting out, you need to arrange for a ride to pick everything up. Here are two possibilities of getting home. Shuffling cars is first. You'll need two vehicles, at least two people, and some extra time to spend while putting in and taking out. First unload the gear and boats from the two vehicles at the starting point. Next, drive both cars to the take-out point and leave the first one there. Drive the second car back and leave it at the starting point. When you finish the float, the first car is there waiting. If you travel light and can carry your boats and gear in one car, load up and return to the starting point to pick up the second car. Sometimes it takes both vehicles, in which case both will return to the take-out point to get the rest of the gear.

The second way to get home is to have someone take you to the river and meet you at the end point at a specified time. This is much simpler, but you must depend on someone other than yourself and your time is pre-determined. You can't take an extra day or even an extra hour on the river with someone waiting for you.

With all your gear together in waterproof bags, canoes on the riverbank, and feet itching to get on downstream, you're ready to load the boats. But load up correctly, or the first bump in a top-heavy canoe may dump you into the river. When loading, place the heaviest items in the bottom center of the canoe, slightly back from the middle. It is better to have more weight toward the back than toward the front for stability. Keep the weight low and toward the back. Use a waterproof tarp, if desired, on the bottom of the canoe, extending over all the gear. Gear piled higher than the gunwale can be jerked out by tree limbs. Fishing rods, especially, have a peculiar habit of snapping off in trees. Place small valuables in waterproof sandwich bags so they will float if you upset. For larger or expensive items you will be using constantly (such as cameras or fishing rods) tie a string or rope onto them, then tie the other end to a tire innertube. Then, even if they sink, the innertube will float and you will be able to retrieve them.

After loading, the boat should float about six to eight inches above the water for safety and greater ease in handling. You are then able to enjoy yourself and not be a freight barge.

Keep the gear you will use during the day on top, the camping equipment on the bottom of the canoe. Keep the extra paddles close at hand, so you will have little trouble grabbing one if you break or lose one in the middle of a riffle.

Basic Paddle Strokes

There are three ways to get around on the river—drifting with the current, poling, or paddling. Outboard motors have been omitted from this article on purpose. We do not condemn their use on the rivers, for many trappers and trot-line fishermen use them to run the eddies. But a boat motor defeats the purpose of a *float* trip. The noise, fumes, and troubles of the motor disturb the silence and stillness of the river. Electric motors remove these factors, but even they can be used only in the deep eddies. The propellers must be raised up through riffles, and even a snag in the eddies might snap a prop off the shaft. Motors are fine for some purposes, but on the float trip they are useless.

Drifting with the current is what you do on a float while fishing or lying in the sun asleep on a mile-long eddy. Here the current does the work for you. Drifting takes a long time to get anywhere in the big eddies, but you're not in any hurry. An occasional paddle thrust is all it takes to keep you on course.

It is doubtful you will need or want to do any actual poling with a pole. What you will do is use your paddle as a pole—and as a brace, rudder, drag, steering wheel, anything to keep the boat upright and going in the right direction.

To save wear on your back, pick a long paddle. For the bowman, the paddle should be chin level or a little below when stood on the ground. For the sternman, eye level or below. Grasp the paddle by putting one hand on top and the other hand just above the blade. This grip gives the most leverage.

The way you paddle depends on your position in the canoe, front or back. The bowman (front) uses a straight-back stroke or a sweeping stroke in normal paddling, switching sides back and forth as either arm gets tired, or to correct the bow's position in the water. A third stroke is pulling water toward the canoe, which will swing the front end in the opposite direction of the pull.

The sternman has the most power and control of the canoe, owing to his ability to swing the back (and front) in either direction easily. This is not to say the bowman has no control, but that the sternman can overpower him.

The sternman has three strokes. The straight-back method is perhaps the worst way for the sternman to paddle. With every stroke on the left side, the bow swings to the right. Switch sides and the bow runs to the left. Either you must switch sides every two or three strokes, or the bowman must paddle twice as hard to keep straight. Keep paddling on one side, and you'll paddle in circles all day.

The J-stroke is better than the straight-back stroke for the sternman. The backwards pull sends the canoe forward, and the hook of the J keeps the bow straight. Although this stroke keeps the canoe in a straight line, the hook has the effect of slowing down the canoe from the drag on the paddle, which acts almost as a brake. This means the sternman has to paddle harder to make any distance.

The pitch, or guide stroke, is the best of the three. This stroke is actually a modified J-stroke. In the pitch stroke, the sternman pulls the paddle back and then moves it outward and back, feathering the blade out of the water as he does so. The feathering keeps the canoe on course and keeps drag to a minimum. It takes practice to use this stroke effectively, but mastery will allow the canoeist to travel many miles with minimum effort.

Most people floating rivers today use canoes, and a few daring individuals use kayaks. But before the interest in these boats, fishermen used the wooden johnboat on the river. Many today still prefer the wooden or aluminum johnboats to canoes for fishing.

The major difference in johnboats and canoes is the shape. With its flat bottom and squared-edges, the johnboat resembles a rectangular box. The johnboat has a much greater stability in the water because of its wide bottom, and it rides higher, so it can float in shallow

Johnboats are preferred by older Ozarkian fishermen for circling eddies and for their stability when a fisherman stands in them.

water without dragging bottom on gravel. However, the johnboat cannot cut through water as quickly as V-shaped craft, and is not capable of quick maneuvering in riffles. The johnboat was designed for long eddies, quiet floating and fishing in a limited area.

A johnboat can carry more cargo because of its space, but loading remains the same as with a canoe. Keep the weight low and to the back. Don't overload, and don't stack gear over your head.

One way for the back man to paddle consists of pulling the blade to the back edge of the johnboat and then ruddering the paddle behind the boat. This is not the only way to paddle a johnboat, but it is a common method.

These basic paddle strokes of canoes and johnboats can be easily understood and learned individually when used in the quiet water of lakes or river eddies. But a river's current as it rushes around log jams, over riffles and through bends makes river boating much different. Instead of there being only two people in control, there is a third element with a mind and power of its own—the current. In order to take advantage of the current when it is going where the boat needs to go to counteract it when leading into dangerous places, the paddlers must act as a team. The bowman must watch for obstructions in the river, pick out the best course to take and give instructions to the sternman. The sternman then moves the canoe with the bowman's help. In essence the bowman must help make the decisions and the sternman must have the skill and power to guide the canoe.

Still, there are three items of caution to consider. When floating down one of the Ozark rivers, you place yourself at the mercy of the river the same way you are at the mercy of the other drivers on interstate highways. In both cases there are unpredictable variables. When you come through safe and sound at the end of the trip, it is not because you have tamed or conquered the river. You have become part of the river and made it because the river itself came through.

Second, the instructions here are misleading because you may think each action is governed by careful thought and communication. In some instances they are, such as when you choose to go left (or right) after studying a short riffle from the bank. But after you have entered a fast riffle and round a corner to view a log jam laced with barbed-wire throughout, there is little time for thought, much less communication, before action. Instead, this situation would produce reaction to a crisis. One hopes that the bowman and sternman will react enough alike to beach on the left, where there is a bit of gravel, and not each paddle in opposite ways. Perhaps the bowman will have time to yell "Left!" and the sternman will understand he means to go to the left bank but not to paddle on the left side. But more than likely each reacts automatically and, with any luck, as a team.

This brings up the third point. Canoeing Ozark streams is not a dignified orderly paddle-by-the-rule-book activity. Quite the opposite. It is a humbling, extremely haphazard, and devil-may-care sport. Remember the river is in charge. If a tree or boulder lies directly in your path, don't try to execute a perfect reverse stroke or curlicue. Stick out your paddle and push away from it. If you get caught on a rock, shift your weight to one side and use your paddle as a pole to get free. For reasons like these, paddling Ozark rivers has sometimes been called "stroke-one, dodge-two," and the name fits. This method isn't professional, but it will keep you (almost) dry. When approaching riffles, head the canoe into the longest "V" in the current and keep the canoe moving straight with the current, unless a rock or limb lies in your path. In this case, the bowman pulls water in on one side to pull the front over, and the sternman paddles on the opposite side. After passing the obstruction, the bowman pulls the bow back into the current. This is, of course, not a set rule, for different strokes can achieve the same effect. The sternman could just as easily have swung the bow around by ruddering and brought the canoe back into line by paddling harder on the side.

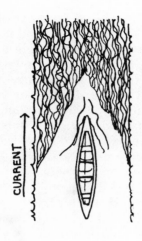

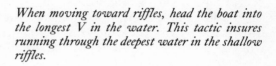

When moving toward riffles, head the boat into the longest V in the water. This tactic insures running through the deepest water in the shallow riffles.

If pinned against an obstruction by the current, lean toward the rock or log, working around it.

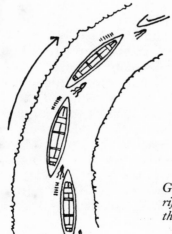

Going around a bend while floating through riffles. Keep both front and back of the boat in the current.

If the riffles curve, hit the first V, then move the canoe straight to the middle of the river, where the current is strongest. Next swing the stern into the current, being sure to keep the bow in the current also. If the bow moves out of the current and the stern is caught in the current, the back end will swing around. Unless you enjoy running the river backwards, continue in the swing until you move full circle. Stay in the current except to dodge rocks and move onward out of the riffles. This type of maneuvering calls for timing and teamwork, so it would be best to practice in an empty canoe for an afternoon before venturing out with a fully loaded one for an extended float.

If you cannot avoid hitting an obstruction in the river, try to hit it with the bow of the canoe rather than the side. A head-on collision will jar your teeth, but a side-swipe may dump you overboard.

If you get pinned against a log or rock, lean toward the obstruction, not away from it. If you lean away, the gunwale will likely drop below the water and the current will flood the canoe. Instead, keep your weight next to the log or rock, and work your way around it keeping the bow pointed downstream.

If you are snagged on a rock or underwater tree limbs, push off with paddle, limbs, hands, feet—anything available. Just don't tip over with your efforts.

If your canoe fills with water and sinks under the water level but still floats upright, you're swamped. The canoe will remain afloat, unless a shift in weight or so much as a soft nudge flips it over and your gear falls out. Stay seated and get the canoe to the bank by paddling gently, throw out your soggy gear, and empty the canoe.

On the other hand, if you turn completely over and dump everything out, push the canoe to the bank and gather up any floating items. If the weather is warm, then you get to go diving for everything. Usually this is no problem, since Ozark rivers have gravel bottoms, except for a minor layer of silt, and are generally not deeper than five to eight feet. There are exceptions, however. Around bluffs and rock outcroppings the water can be twenty feet deep or more, with swift undercurrents that may pin you under a rock ledge or strike your head against rocks. In winter, the river is cold, and with the added exposure to wind, your endurance is limited. At sixty degrees water temperature, you can stand an hour or more submersion; from fifty to sixty degrees, fifteen to forty minutes; from forty to fifty degrees, five to twenty minutes; below forty degrees, less than ten minutes. If you do get wet in cold weather, get to the bank and start a fire with the waterproof matches kept in your pocket. If it is extremely cold, then strip and get into a sleeping bag. Use common sense and

Occasionally the rivers are blocked with concrete dams left from old grist mills or by log jams, necessitating a short portage.

remember that even a $500.00 camera is not worth your life.

To avoid a risky spot where you might ditch, pull over to the bank to make a visual inspection of the river before you go on. If the river is choked with trees, you might try to get out and push the canoe by hand. If the river is too bad even to walk through, then unload your gear, carry your canoe and gear around the spot, reload, and get back in. Portaging will also be necessary at the small concrete mill dams still standing on some rivers.

Deadfalls and logs abound below the water, and limbs above. It is the bowman's job to locate snags, rocks, and shallow places and inform the sternman of the new direction to by-pass it while keeping his paddle ready to avoid it.

Occasionally (and embarrassingly) you may barrel into a tangle of tree limbs. This possibility is the main reason for keeping your gear below the gunwale. The impact will snap fishing rods and scatter lighter articles all over the river. If you get entangled, the only answer is to push out. But keep your weight steady, for a sudden shove could drop you or the canoe underwater.

If you grind to a halt on a gravel or sand bar, push off with a

The bowman and sternman need to keep watching ahead to locate and avoid rocks and limbs. If you are snagged on a rock, keep your weight steady and push off.

paddle. If you're stuck for sure, don't break the paddle with your efforts. Just hop out and get your feet wet. In most cases only the heaviest person needs to get out.

You don't have to memorize these guidelines. A little common sense will go a long way while floating the river. Just be alert, prepared for anything, and remember the most important rule of all—enjoy yourself.

Safety on the River

Once on the river keep in mind a few important rules for a safe trip. Don't go alone in a boat. Two people are usually needed to handle a boat safely. It is actually better if there are four people and two boats in your group. This way, if one boat runs into trouble, the other can help. Canoes designed for two people are best only for two, but a third person can ride in the middle if gear is limited. Johnboats can take three or four passengers. A kayak by design allows only one person.

When going through riffles or other obstructions such as log jams or low-hanging trees, have only one boat at a time go through. Wait until each boat is completely through, to prevent collisions and jams. Stay around until every boat is through, in case the last boat upsets. Everyone should keep watching ahead and all around constantly for obstructions above and below the water, or for anything else that could cause problems (animals, barbed wire stretched across the river).

Most rule books say one should never stand up in a boat. Conditions often dictate otherwise. When approaching riffles or obstructions, the sternman usually stands to better survey the situation in order to determine what course to take. Johnboats were designed for standing while casting or gigging. Obviously, standing must be done with care. If you have little or no sense of balance, don't try it. Otherwise, just keep your weight centered in the boat. After a while, you'll get your "sea legs," and standing up in a boat will be easy. The same holds true for leaning out of a boat. Just don't lean too far.

If you can't swim, or the water is very cold, wear a life jacket. Innertubes or life preservers should always be handy for spills. Even though much of the water you will float through is wadeable, there are deep spots made treacherous by strong currents around obstructions. So be prepared.

If you're out under the sun paddling in spring or summertime, don't overwork. Sunstroke (also called heatstroke), caused by the body's loss of fluids from overheating, can kill. Drink plenty of fluids and use extra salt if heavily perspiring. But since the Ozark rivers are mostly well shaded, you can usually stay in the cool shade of trees and avoid overheating.

By the same token, if you're on the river in the dead of winter with thirty-miles-an-hour winds blowing, don't exhaust yourself to the point that your body can no longer keep warm. Most people will never be out in bad weather, but then again, you might. A fair winter day can change into a freezing storm. If things go badly, beach the boat and walk to the nearest farm, which is usually less than a mile away. Telephone your friends to pick you up and get off the river there.

Dress appropriately for the weather. In summer, a wide-brimmed hat, sunglasses, and suntan lotion on exposed skin are your best protection. While on water you receive a double dose of the sun's rays from over head and reflections off the water's surface. It's quite painful to sleep on a sunburn at night.

In winter, wear plenty of clothes to keep warm, rubber gloves to keep hands dry, and rubber footwear. Several light shirts are better than one or two heavy shirts. You can remove clothing as you become hot from exertion and replace it when you cool off.

Besides avoiding trouble by your own actions, you must give some attention to problems offered by the river itself. Passing tree limbs catching on the boat can lash back and injure an eye or scratch your face. Sunglasses fulfill a double purpose for eye protection here. Cob-

Dress warmly for a float trip during the winter.

webs and wet leaves are annoyances on your face and down your neck. Floating under the trees, which are precariously balanced on the river, is not particularly hazardous but is unsettling to the nerves.

The only foliage offering injury is poison ivy. Poison ivy is easily identified by its three leaves extending from a central point. The irritating agent is in the sap, which is transferred to skin by crushing the leaves or handling a bruised vine. You can also get the rash by touching anything that has come into contact with the sap—paddles, clothing, pets—or from the smoke of burning vines. The irritant acts differently to each person because of individual skin chemistry. Since your own skin sometimes changes, you can be immune this year and get a rash next year. If you can't remember which plant is poison ivy, play safe and don't touch anything you are unsure about.

Dogwood, redbud, and other trees flower during springtime and summer, along with a hundred other plants. If you have an allergy you can bet it will flare up on the river. Either come prepared with medicine, or wait until fall to float. On the other hand, if you have a fall allergy, float earlier, when the irritant is not present in the air.

Animal life is not too great a threat, since wild animals fear humans and the strange sights and sounds man brings along. There is one poisonous water snake in the Ozarks, the cottonmouth water moccasin (Agkistrodon piscivorous). Most watersnakes are harmless, but many

Just hanging there waiting for the time when you're not looking are the tree limbs, ready to knock some sense into your head or break your fishing rod.

people confuse poisonous snakes with harmless ones and figure that every snake they see is dangerous. Unless you startle or corner a snake it will retreat. Don't try to kill a snake with a paddle, because it might be tossed into the boat on your backswing. Snakes can also drop into the boat from overhead limbs. Do your best to get the snake out without turning the boat over.

There's a story about a man who always kept a .22-caliber rifle in his boat to kill snakes. One day a snake dropped into his boat from a tree limb, and in a panic he began firing on it. He was shaking and the snake kept moving, so he used up his shells and never hit the snake. Pretty soon the boat was under water, and the snake swam out on its own, unharmed.

The soft-shelled, or snapping, turtle is another reptile that can cause distress if you try to corner it or kill it with a paddle. Its jaws are strong enough to bite off a finger or take a sizable portion of flesh from anywhere else. And once a turtle bites down on a paddle, it's very difficult to persuade it to let go.

Rattlesnakes and copperhead snakes might be found while on a short hike on land or camping out. Both are poisonous and prefer rocky ledges to hide under. These three snakes—cotton-mouth water moccasin, copperhead, and rattlesnake—are the poisonous snakes native to the Ozarks.

Other animals you might see are skunks, stray dogs, and nonpoisonous snakes. Nosy cows and mean bulls are sometimes a nuisance if you are in an open pasture. Insects such as mosquitoes, gnats, horse-flies, deerflies, biting fleas, ticks, and chiggers will be a problem during warm weather. A good dose of insect repellent will be needed. Re-member to reapply repellent after perspiring in the sun and after swim-ming. Check nightly for ticks and chiggers and soak them down in alcohol to get them loose. Get ticks off as soon as possible, to pre-vent infection. Don't pull ticks off, for an embedded head left under the skin can lead to infection. And don't squash ticks on your finger-nails. Germs on your hands will undoubtedly make their way into your eyes or mouth. Toss the little buggers into the fire and watch them pop.

Hornets, wasps, yellowjackets, and bees might be seen along the river but will mind their own business. On occasion you might see a hornets' nest hanging from a tree limb. Do not disturb it. Hornets can fly faster than a man can run, let alone a man paddling a canoe.

Leeches are sometimes present in mud and around water plants. They're after one thing—your blood—and once they set on you they are bound and determined to stay there. The worst thing about leeches is that they're painless and you won't notice them until you see them. Look for leeches while you're looking for ticks. Rub them with tobacco juice, rubbing alcohol or a lighted cigarette and they'll come right off.

Contaminated spring water is a problem near farms and cities. Sewage, barn lots, industrial wastes, fertilizer runoff, and sinkholes filled with rubbish will allow germs, disease organisms and foreign ma-terial to seep into the springs. In wilder areas the springs may be pure enough to drink, but recent studies show pollution travels long dis-tances in the Ozark underground water system. Therefore, it is safer to boil or chemically purify the water before using. Better yet, bring clean water from home. On an extended trip, take a walk to the nearest farmhouse for a friendly chat and a fresh supply of water.

Camping Overnight

About two hours before sunset you should pick a spot to camp. Gravel bars make fine campsites. They are close to the water, free of ticks and chiggers, and clean. However, tent stakes are difficult to se-cure in the gravel. If you are using a tent and cannot secure tent pegs in sand or gravel, tie a short log or stick onto the end of the tent rope and bury it in the ground. The additional weight will keep the ropes tight.

If there is a rainstorm in the middle of the night and the river rises, the gravel bar will be the first to flood. If that happens, grab your

A turn of the century camp on the James River. Courtesy Lillian Hall Tyre.

gear and head for high ground. In the morning reassess the condition of the river, and if it's too high, *do not* try to finish your trip. Find the nearest farmhouse, explain your predicament, and call your friends to pick you up.

Grassy areas on the bank are safe from high water and give softer footing and anchorage for tent poles, but they may be infested with crawling insects. Pick an area with a breeze blowing at night to keep flying insects away.

After selecting a campsite dig a firepit and get a fire started using only dead wood. There will be plenty of dead wood lying around and the landowner will take a more tolerant view of you if you don't cut down trees. If you use a gas stove, then you need not worry with wood unless you wish a campfire for the mood of the scene. Spread out your gear, but keep sleeping bags and blankets covered up, or the dew will leave them soggy.

Try to get supper cooked before the sunlight leaves. It is a lot harder to cook after dark with only a flashlight to see by. Clean up your utensils after you use them instead of waiting until morning. Sand or fine

Almost all men in the Ozarks were fishermen. Courtesy Lillian Hall Tyre.

gravel makes an excellent abrasive to scrub pots and pans, except on teflon. Put the next day's food away securely and burn or bury any food scraps. Tossing scraps in the bushes will bring night prowlers in search of food. It could be a skunk after your hamburger. Keep all your unburnable trash and any plastic in a trash sack. If you had enough room to pack it in, then pack it out.

In the morning, after you have cooked and eaten breakfast and cleaned up, break camp. Reload your canoes as carefully as at the beginning of the trip. Fill in the firepit and then take a last look all around. Is everything the same as you found it? It should be. Leave the river as clean or cleaner than you found it. Disrespect for property will lose the river to boaters, while courtesy ensures you'll be welcome again next year.

We have not tried to explain everything about camping, because there are many books and guides available on general camping and cooking. What we have done is explain the differences found in camping on Ozark rivers.

Joys of the River

Knowing how to do something is one thing, knowing why you do it is another. All the trouble it takes to get on the river, all the precautions to observe, and all the annoyances once there may cause you to ask, "Is floating the river worth it?" Before answering that, let's examine some of the joys of the river.

The rivers offer a calm retreat from everyday living—peace and quiet and the chance to be alone are the gifts of the river. But it is not lonely. In any supermarket or department store you may feel isolated and lonely, even in a crowd. You are restricted to be the same as a hundred other people surrounding you.

On the river, you are an individual. When you face a problem you make your own decisions and are free to act as you see fit, accountable for your decisions immediately. Everything depends on what you decide. When you face riffles, do you go left or right? Take a chance in a log jam, or get out and portage? If your decision was correct the reward is a smooth ride. If not, the river will flip your boat over. The river judges everyone swiftly and fairly.

Because of this, you learn something about yourself on the river. You find out how well you can make your own decisions. If you break your last paddle five miles from the takeout point you can't just let someone else handle the problem or quit and go home. Not until you finish the last five miles. Only your own resourcefulness can get you

There are many places to pause along the way.

home. Do you repair the paddle with a stick and rope? Whittle a sapling into a pole to guide the boat the rest of the way? Get out and pull the boat through the water? Or use the camp shovel as an improvised paddle the rest of the day? You must decide on some course of action and finish the float.

Besides yourself, you also learn a great deal about your partner. Facing the problems, discomforts and minor dangers on the river, you see how he or she reacts. Is she as level-headed as you thought? Or does she panic at every little crisis? Can he or she also find joy on the river or only boredom? Does he appreciate what the river has to offer, or long for the comfort of anonymity in crowds?

Back home, someone is always trying to sell you something, but on the river nature reveals her secrets only to those who have the patience, curiosity, and understanding to look for them. What you seek is the order and balance that only nature has and that man seems to have forgotten. Squirrels play in the treetops, hawks and buzzards circle overhead, and fish splash about in the water. Dragonflies hover in search of insects, snakes glide gracefully through the water, cutting a V to trace their path. A fragrance of flowers drifts over the water, caves in bluffs open their black mouths to the river and bees hum in search of pollen.

Rounding a bend to view a colossal stony wall beats all that Rome has to offer in monuments. Startling a blue heron or white crane into flight or following a flock of wood ducks down the river all day is ten times more interesting than watching nature shows on television. With TV, you are merely an observer. Not on the river. There you are the actor in the real thing. Sit quietly, and the river will play her orchestration of sight and sound, taste and touch. All senses come alive at the dip of a paddle blade.

Is it worth it? Without a doubt, *yes!* The rivers are worth the time you spend on them today and the effort you give to save them for tomorrow. No amount of exclamations can state it forcefully enough.

Stalactites form from water dripping slowly from the ceiling.

Mysteries of Caves

Hidden in the bluffs along the rivers are the hundreds of caves, quiet, dark, and mysterious. Their openings, usually masked with vegetation, rather discourage the passerby than invite him as the sparkling rivers do. But the lure of the unknown has always tempted many persons into their depths. Although the caves have not played as great a part in the lives of the people as the rivers have, they have become a showcase of the results of what the people have done to the earth. Studying its depths reveals to us the interdependence of earth and man.

Nowhere on earth can we realize the awesome age of our land better than in the exposed depths of the caves. It is as if the earth is giving us a brief view of its ancient beginnings by allowing us to trespass briefly into its inner being. The profound quiet seems to indicate a dead atmosphere. But most caves are alive, building and tearing down, one drop of water at a time, slowly, endlessly, and forever. The caves hold the secrets of the region's origins for those who can read the signs displayed in the rugged country, the pitted surface and honey-combed underworld. They contain the reasons for the high water table and plentiful springs. Reading the knowledge the caves reveal in their black depths can give us a better understanding of this Ozark land which has sustained the generations before us. The underground passages reveal early signs of the damage past and present generations have done to the land above. The plentiful and easily accessible Ozark caves are an open showcase allowing knowledgeable and concerned people to see what is happening to our land in many parts of the nation.

The Geological Story

About four hundred million years ago, the Ozark region was the floor of a warm, shallow sea. The sea was abundant in hard-shelled marine animals known as brachiopods. The brachiopods lived their life span in these waters, and when they died, their shells floated down and left deposits on the ocean floor. The shells, made up of calcium carbonate, were compacted by the enormous pressure of the water into hard rock layers. The continuing life cycle of these animals over the ages left very large deposits of calcium carbonate, or as it is commonly known, limestone.

The pulsating earth alternately uplifted the entire area above the warm waters of the sea and dropped it back under the ocean several times.

The Ozarks are surrounded by lowland plains on all sides. In the beginning the area was a broad, asymmetric arch. The eastern and southeastern slopes are steep, with the northern and western flanks gently sloping into the western plains. The abundant rainfall and the rivers began to erode the plateau into deep valleys and hills with as much as seven hundred feet difference in relief. Most of the hilltops in the Ozarks are about the same height. It is the valleys that vary in depth. This erosion by rivers left the Ozarks with a rugged topography. However, some areas of the Ozarks were more resistant to, or have not undergone as much surface erosion, thus leaving flat, rolling prairie lands like the Springfield Plateau, which is formed of younger Mississippian limestone.

The bulk of the Missouri Ozarks are on the Salem Plateau, formed of perhaps less water-resistant Ordovician dolomite, which has undergone more relief changes caused by uplifting and surface erosion. This dolomite is from a thousand to two thousand feet thick.

As one drives through the Ozarks, descending from the high prairie-like areas in the Salem Plateau into the river valleys, one can see along the exposed bluffs or highway excavations the different strata of the Ordovician dolomite rock, from the more recent Jefferson City strata

down through Roubidoux, Gasconade, Eminence, and Potosi formations to the basic granite, which is exposed in a few places such as the
shut-ins, Elephant Rocks State Park of the east central Missouri Ozarks,
and the Boston Mountain Range of the Ozarks in Arkansas. It took
millions of years for this geological cycle to form the Ozark hills, perhaps the oldest geological formation of any size in the United States.

Caves develop in limestone or dolomite, and most of the rocks in
Missouri are limestone related. The Pennsylvanian limestones of northern and western Missouri are too thin to support any substantial development of cavern systems. But the thicker Mississippian limestone
of the Springfield Plateau of southwestern Missouri and northeastern
Arkansas and the Ordovician dolomite of central and eastern Missouri
constitute an ideal environment for the developing caverns. This fact
is evidenced by the more than twenty-five hundred known caves in the
Missouri Ozarks alone.

Surface water drainage is also a key factor in the development of
caves. The Ozarks tend to be a dome, with the water drainage spiraling
from the top around to the base. A drainage map of the area shows
the flow of rivers from the east-west divide that runs roughly through
Webster, Wright, and Texas counties of Missouri. The river flow is
generally in three directions from this area: north (Niangua and Gasconade rivers), south (Current, James, and Eleven Point rivers), or east
(Jack's Fork and Meramec rivers). Of course the drainage depends
largely on the slope of the surface, the stage of erosion the land happens to be in, and the small areas of weak outcropping rock.

Caves are formed when water from surface runoff, rivers, or rain
seeps through the initial layer of topsoil and mixes with carbon dioxide
and carbonic acid formed from plant growth. This material produces
a chemical change in the water, and it becomes somewhat like a mild
acid. Some of this water is taken up by plants, but, if the source of
water continues, as it does in a rainy season, the acidulated water will
begin to seep into cracks in the limestone.

Slowly, the acidulated water dissolves the limestone, enlarging the
crack in the stratum and at the same time dissolving a path downward.
It will continue dissolving its downward path through the porous rock
until it meets some resistance, for example, a layer of rock with a certain content of chert or sandstone. The cherty limestone is more resistant
to erosion than the layer above it, and the acidulated water cannot dissolve it. Therefore, the water then begins to spread horizontally, dissolving passageways in the rock. This is how some cavern systems can
join with others to form a larger system, perhaps on different strata of
rock.

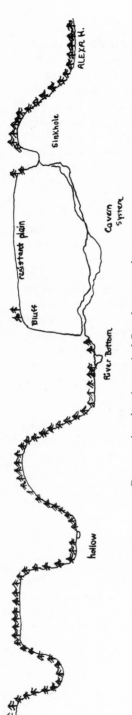

Cross section showing typical Ozark topography.

Acid water
dissolves
passage

Passage
gets
larger

Deposits
form

Water continues
eating away at
walls and ceiling

Ceiling
falls

Sink hole
covered with
vegetation

Some sinks
hold water

Stages of cave development from youth to old age.

The acidulated water continues to enlarge the passageway. It spreads horizontally and runs out a bluff where a river has cut a deep valley into the countryside, forming an opening. Some of these openings are too small to crawl through, others are eighty feet high. The development of caves in height, depth, and length depends upon the resistance of the limestone or dolomite, the eroding strength of the acidic water, the thickness of the formations, and the joint development (vertical fractures) in the layers of rocks, or bedding plane.

Caves are constantly growing because of water erosion or earth movements. Sometimes a cave can open up into a new system of caverns by a movement of the earth's crust in an earthquake or tremor. There was a bit of cavern activity during the period of the Alaskan earthquake. One cave that we visited had opened up to a new branch of caverns during this period. When we were there, this system had just recently been explored for the first time, and we could still see the footprints of the first explorers.

An important factor often overlooked is the relationship of the forests of the Ozarks to its geology. The dissolution of the rock to form springs and caves as a result of the water's acidity is greatly enhanced by the presence of a forest cover that actually helps increase the flow of streams in the Ozarks. The forest cover slows down runoff from rainfall better than a grassland covering by allowing more water to soak into the thin soil. The leaf litter carpeting the ground increases the acidity of the dissolving water passing through the rock.

Cave Deposits

Most caves have water dripping from the ceiling. This water is surface water which has seeped through the topsoil and through the rock into the caves, still eroding and changing the features inside. Caves with the water dripping or running in the form of a stream are referred to as live caves. Caves without water are dry or dead caves.

After many thousands of years, after the water in the cave has found its way to the outside, the water level recedes. But water continues to come in through the cracks and through the openings. It still drips from the walls and the ceilings. The water moves through rock, becoming concentrated in calcium carbonate. When the water makes contact with the air in the cave environment, there is a release in pressure. Carbon dioxide is then given off, and some calcium carbonate is precipitated onto the ceiling as the droplet of water slows, collects weight, then drops onto the floor area. The rest of the car-

Drops of water flow through the inside of the soda straw and out the hole, which is the same size as the drop.

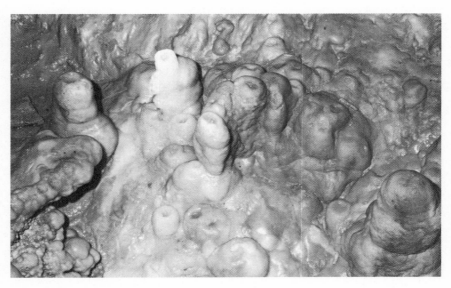

Water falling from soda straws forms interesting deposits on the floor.

Draperies.

bonate is deposited on the floor or moves on through the cave by way
of a stream.

The dripping water inside caves forms many interesting, beautiful,
and fascinating deposits called dripstones. All cave deposits are made
of material from the four main sedimentary formations: dolomites, limestones, sandstones, and shales. Some temporary deposits are also made
out of clay or mud. The more common dripstones are stalactites, stalagmites and columns.

Stalactites are formations coming down from the ceiling. A calcite
curtain may form from the dripping of water from the ceiling of a cave
where a crack has been. The simplest type of stalactites are the soda
straws, which are straw-like formations hanging from the ceiling. Soda
straws may develop if the water drips very slowly. The calcium carbonate is on the outside of the droplet of water giving the hollow soda
straw condition. The hole is the size of a drop of water.

Another common dripstone in a cave is draperies. Draperies are
shaped much like the draperies in a house, but not with such regu-
larity nor with such rounded and smooth corners. Some draperies start
from the wing-like expansion of icicle-shaped stalactites. Starting on
the wall of a cave, they drip down the sides, forming a sort of blade.
This blade then builds a vertical ridge, with the width the highest at

Columns are formed when a stalactite and a stalagmite join.

the top. During the whole process the thickness of the blade stays the same. By shining a light through the drape you can see the growing procedure it has gone through. You can see the metals, iron or magnesium oxides, that the water has carried down the side of what used to be a very common and very beautiful dripstone. These deposits even have a ghost-like appearance.

Stalagmites build up from the floor of a cave. They are formed from the excess drip of the water off a stalactite. The extra water runs off the stalactites and hits the cave floor, building up a sort of mound from which, in the future, a stalagmite will form.

A good way to remember which is which is that the word stalagmite means that it *might* join the stalactites. The word stalactite means that it is joined *tight* to the roof of the cave. Another way you can remember the difference is in the spelling. The G in stalaGmite means ground and the C in stalaCtite means ceiling. Or a humorous saying may help: "When the mites come up, the tights go down."

A stalactite and stalagmite often join after many years of constant dripping of the stalactite. When they join, they form a column. Columns often grow to be enormous, sometimes as wide as they are high.

One of the most delicate and fragile of the secondary calcium carbonate deposits are the helictites, which range from the thick, the size of a pencil, to the very frail and thin, the size of pencil lead. Helictites lower from the ceiling and are crooked in every direction. They are not true dripstones, because a helictite in its development follows a slightly different method of depositing the calcite than does the soda straw or stalactite. There is not enough water moving along it to form the usual heavy droplet of water that is seen on the end of a soda straw. For this reason helictites do not have to contend with the weight of the water droplet. Rather, the crystal structure controls the development of the helictite and it may go up, down, around and into—or whatever direction the crystal patterns demand—until there is a sufficient weight of water to cause it to form a droplet. Then a helictite may become a stalactite and go down.

Rimstone dams can form from any irregular surface. Water builds up on these irregular surfaces, such as the rugged edges of stalagmites, stalactites, drapes, or even sediments of mud or gravel, or irregular surfaces on the rock floor. The calcium carbonate solution in the water builds on these deposits, causing a dam. Then whenever the water flows over the edge, it forms a ripple or a rim, creating a stone dam.

As water slowly trickles down cave walls or floors, it builds another kind of deposit, a ripply stone surface known as flowstone. Flowstone starts as a thin coating on the wall and floor of a cave, but when layer after layer is added, it looks like a waterfall that is frozen solid. It may cover mud on the floor that is then eroded away, causing the flowstone to become a free-hanging shelf.

In shallow pools the calcite may fasten itself to very tiny single pieces of sand. As water slowly drips into pools, the grains turn round and round. New layers of lime are added, and the sand grains become cave pearls. The pearls grow until they are too heavy to be turned in the puddle. The scientific name of a cave pearl is oolite. Cut in two, it would look like a tree cut in half, with many layers of lime through it.

As beautiful as the cave pearls are the anthodites, thin needles of stone that cluster on cave ceilings. These fragile white spikes are not often found in Missouri, but if found, one should not touch them, for anthodites grow only one inch every several thousand years.

Sometimes water traveling down through the cave dissolves and leaves behind other substances beside limestone. In many caves there are curving stone feathers and flowers that look like tiger lilies and roses. These cave flowers are made of gypsum, a white mineral that is softer than limestone.

Johnson's Sink is an example of a cave whose ceiling, weakened by years of water action, has fallen in.

Sinkholes

Water erosion is the most important factor in the building and also in the destruction of a cave. The cycle of erosion is divided into three main stages—youth, maturity, and old age.

The first stage, youth, is the birth of the cave. The limestone in the earth soaks up the water, which then eats its way through the limestone, forming passageways that go off in many different directions. The water usually, after making a passage, exits by forcing its way out of the side of a hill or out of the ground in a spring.

The second stage is the time when the cave accumulates its deposits. The calcium carbonate gets into the humidity of the cave and gathers on the ceilings. Deposit such as stalactites, helictites, stalagmites, and draperies start to form from the dripping of the water. A cave has reached maturity when they are formed in their proper proportions.

The third and final stage is old age. This is the stage in which the stream in the cave takes its toll. All through these three stages the cave deposits have been building up. But the water in the stream has been also tearing down the limestone walls and ceiling. As a result, sometimes the roof of the cave falls in, making a sinkhole.

The Ozark peneplane is full of sinkholes. A region that has many sinkholes is known to geologists as karst topography. In our immediate area we can go a mile in any direction and find a sinkhole or shallow depression.

A sinkhole is a surface land form, not a true cave. Most sinkholes, though, have a cave attached to them at some point. Sinkholes are found mostly in undissected parts of limestone regions, although many square miles of the region are completely without sinks. Many of the sinks found are several hundred feet across and fifty to a hundred feet deep. There is a shallow sink in Lebanon that is about one mile across, as well as a deeper sink where the Osage Indians formerly held council meetings.

These sinks gave early settlers of Missouri the first indication of the presence of important minerals such as lead and iron. Today they are often used for dumping places for old junk cars or other discarded material.

These sinks form an important factor in the drainage of the area. Surface water runs into these sinks as if they were drains in the street. Very few sinks hold water, so the surface water drains into them and then flows directly underground to enter the underground water table or join waterways in caves and crevices to form springs.

Many times people fill up or build over sinks, or use them as dumps. If they are filled up or built over, a plug is put in a source for underground water, causing the surface water, which would have gone underground, to run off into rivers. Stopping up enough of the sinks, as is done in residential areas of cities, can cause major surface drainage problems and deplete the underground sources.

Filling sinks with junk and trash, dead animals, or sewage causes another problem. Surface water continues to drain into these dumps. As the water seeps through the insecticides, cans, rusted iron, and other chemical and noxious agents, it carries the dissolvable waste into the springs and underground water sources.

The limestone dissolves so readily that water traveling through its passageways goes rather rapidly. Therefore, the filtering action that occurs in most subterranean water systems is not very effective in a karst condition. Rather than filtering out the impurities, as was formerly thought, the relatively unobstructed streams flow rapidly, carrying the pollution with them. In the absence of sunlight the cave water will tend to carry some bacteria that might be killed by exposure to sunlight in a surface stream.

The crystal-clear water trickling or gushing now out the Ozarks caves and springs is not any longer the safest water to drink. In some of the tight places we explored in caves we noticed a slight sewer smell, even though we were fifteen to twenty miles from a city.

The depths of the caves tell us more than what happened here twenty million years ago. They tell us what is happening now and what will happen in the future.

Just think through what has been written in this story. The rains come pouring down. The water goes into the cracks of the karst topography, into the earth to form a cave. The waters dissolve so much limestone the roof falls in. People like you and me throw dead animals, oil cans, and pesticides into these sinks. The water carries the pollution from this junk and trash through springs to the rivers and the lakes. Water containing the pollution continues to run through the ground to the underground water system. The geological structure of our land, which originally provided us with good water and beautiful scenery, can, by our not reading the signs, allow us to spoil everything.

The Ecological Story

Though many people believe it to be true, a cave is not an isolated hole in the ground inhabited only by bats or hibernating animals. Many animals do hibernate in caves, and caves are bats' favorite roosting places, but life in a cave is extensive, varied, and interrelated with life outside. The life forms range from bacteria and fungus through insects and up to larger mammals that come into the mouth of the cave for protection or predation.

Animals can be found in all parts of the cave. Some are found only in specific areas, while others range throughout.

The cave environment in which the animals live is fairly uniform, not varying significantly from season to season or from the front of the cave to the back.

Some of the outstanding features of the cave environment that differ greatly from the surface are darkness, fairly constant humidity, and constant temperature. Of these, darkness and constant temperature most affect the cave life.

Since the only sunlight to reach a cave's interior is at the mouth, the number of life forms found in a cave are automatically limited. There are almost no green plants, for sunlight is essential to the food-making process, or photosynthesis, in most green plants. The lack of sunlight limits the energy output in a cave, forcing life to use other sources.

Water is a necessity for almost all forms of life except perhaps bacteria and molds. Most animals can live several times longer without food than without water. Although caves are poor in food production, water is abundant in most caves, easily supporting the animals' needs. Humidity is high, the walls are quite damp, and water drips from the ceiling. Readings we took in a local cave showed the humidity at the mouth to be around 50 percent; at the center, 82 percent; and toward the back, 90 percent. Humidity can reach 100 percent. When a bat maternity colony roosts in the cave, fresh guano (bat manure) combined with bat respiration and urination can raise the humidity level from 60 percent to over 90 percent.

The level of humidity does not seem to directly affect the life in a cave. However, there are some so-called dry caves—not too common in our area—in which there is no moisture at all. Under these conditions, it is almost impossible for life to exist except for fungi and bacteria.

Besides high humidity, caves often have moving streams that provide a habitat for aquatic animals, which in turn become food for larger animals.

Another factor affecting life in a cave is its even temperature. Sunlight cannot warm a cave, except at the mouth. Even there it is noticeably cooler than outside in hot weather. Moreover, the temperature throughout the cave may not vary more than a few degrees winter and summer.

Readings taken in a cave showed the temperature to range from 52°F to 58°F. The temperature at the center was 52°F, but by the time we reached the back, it had warmed up to 56°F. These temperatures are fairly representative for caves in this area.

The ambient air temperature in a cave is nearly constant year-round. Tom Aley, owner of the Ozark Underground Laboratory, Forsyth, Missouri, said, "The reason it doesn't fluctuate is the rock surrounding the cave. The temperature of the rock is determined by incoming solar radiation. It will come to equilibrium with the average annual temperature of the area. So temperatures in a cave are determined by the rock. The temperature of the rock is determined by the location of the cave, so it is colder in caves in Wisconsin than in Missouri, and colder in caves in Missouri than in Texas."

Barometric pressure has little effect on cave life. Nevertheless, we checked it to see another of the differences between the cave environment and that in which we live. Standard barometric pressure is slightly over 30 inches, but readings we took were slightly lower than this, ranging between 29.5 and 29.54 inches.

The life existing in the cave can be divided into that which uses the entrance temporarily, that which makes the cave its home but feeds outside, and that which is dependent entirely on the cave ecology for its existence.

Of the temporary dwellers of the past we can include Indians. From archaeological research it seems evident that the Indians did not make permanent homes in the caves, but used them as temporary hunting camps. At least that is true of the Osage Indians who lived in villages in winter and went on hunting trips during the summer. The cave entrance provided shelter, protection, and running spring water, as well as a site for burial of the dead.

Man's contribution as an inhabitant to the cave life cycle was of minor importance. But many animals continue to use cave entrances

Cavers look carefully before they step in order to avoid squishing cave life. The ecology is so fragile that even indiscriminate tramping will upset it.

as the Indians did, for protection, a temporary home, or a food source.

Mammals like the pack rats, foxes, skunks, opossums, groundhogs, and raccoons are often in caves. The fox may make his den in the protective blackness of a hole dug in the clay of the cave floor. The raccoon visits the cave to obtain part of his food. The cave challenges him to find his food in the darkness. He eats fish, crayfish, salamanders, or anything else he can catch, going all over the cave to hunt for food.

Some birds use the natural openings and holes in the cave entrances and bluffs for their homes. Flycatchers and other cliff-dwelling birds such as pigeons roost in cave entrances where the insect hunting is good.

The best-known permanent cave inhabitant that feeds outside is the bat. The bat is probably the most read-about cave animal in the world, and also the most misunderstood. Superstitions abound, and because they operate only at night and because a very few species feed on blood, the whole order has been given a bad name. Most bats are very beneficial, eating thousands of insects and doing no harm other than scaring unenlightened people.

Because they like darkness, caves are a natural home for them. They

A disturbed big brown bat may look ferocious, yet is really gentle.

are the main vertebrate animal that commonly lives in totally dark parts of caves. They live there by day, leaving at night to hunt food, which is not blood as some fear, but insects and fruit. Tom Aley claims that his colony of 150,000 bats eat a thousand pounds of insects a night— a far sight more than most birds, even martins.

Bats are usually divided into solitary or colony living types. In a ten- by twenty-foot section of a cave ceiling there may be as many as 155 bats per square foot. Or in another cave there may be just a single

These colonial type gray bats, sometimes found in numbers of a thousand to fifty thousand in a group, give the cave wall a "fur coat" until disturbed by a noisy caver.

bat. Their hind feet are modified for clinging. Toes bend inward with sharply curved claws, so that the bat can hang upside down for hours, dangling from the rough surface of a rock with no muscular effort, even after death.

Bats have their young in caves. The females separate themselves from the males and go to special nursery rooms in the cave, where the young are born and nursed. Adult males do not enter. Young bats mature quickly, learning to fly in one month. By the end of summer the nursery colonies are deserted.

Some bats hibernate, living on stored body fat. Other bats migrate, using caves as their motels along the way. They stop off to sleep for a couple of days and then are on their way.

Bats are beneficial to man because of their destruction of thousands of flying insects. Although they have eyes, they do not need them, for they have a natural radar emitting high-frequency sounds inaudible to humans. The echoes from these sounds tell them what the object is. They can distinguish between echoes from insects, trees, rocks, and rain.

Another benefit of bats to man, and especially to the ecology of the

The cave cricket can be found in most dark, damp, cool places. It will move out of the cave every forty-eight hours to obtain food. Sometimes they are found by the thousands on cave walls. Their long antennae make it difficult for predators to get close.

cave, is its guano or manure, which is used as fertilizer. Tom estimates that his bats convert their nightly catch of a thousand pounds of insects into two hundred and twenty pounds of guano.

It is this guano which directly or indirectly supports the remaining animal life in the cave.

There are many kinds of insects and other very small animals which make their home in caves. But cave insects such as flies, crickets, mosquitoes, and gnats are not like the everyday kind found around the house. These insects are unique in that they have adapted to the darkness, being found not only at the entrance, but all over the cave system.

Spiders may feed on insects that come near the cave wall, or on mites living on the bat guano. Their web is unseen until hit by a light source of some kind. When that happens, the web takes on a silver-plated effect from the moisture accumulated on it. The web itself is beautiful to the human eye, but to the eyes of an insect, it means a quick death.

There are many different kinds of flies in the cave system, from the common house fly to fruit flies. They feed on other insects, bat guano, and dead animals.

The crickets that inhabit a cave are well adapted to that life. Over

What looks like a worm caught in a spider's web is a very unusual animal sometimes found in a cave. The inch-long larva will develop into a fly. It spins a web
to live in until maturity. The larva is completely transparent. The color seen by
an observer is its internal organs moving.

These flattened back to front isopods are scavengers in the shallow cave streams.
The legs and antennae are used for finding food and places to hide from enemies.

With its eyes fused shut and appearing like only dark spots, the grayish color of the Ozark Blind Salamander gives it a ghost-like appearance when light is reflected back from the flash of the camera. Since the salamanders live under rocks, be careful when walking in caves.

the years this small insect has developed long antennae that give the cricket a high degree of sensitivity to any type of movement and air and temperature change. Their diet is about the same as that of the fly. The cricket is a migratory insect, migrating in and out of the cave every forty-eight hours. It feeds outside, but leaves its droppings in the cave.

Mosquitoes and gnats are different from the flies and crickets because they are found at the entrance near light. Female mosquitoes must have the blood of animals in order to lay good eggs. Thus, they could not survive entirely in the darkness of the cave. But there are varieties of these insects that can be found anywhere in the cave that there is a food source, in the twilight zone and even in total darkness.

Several aquatic animals feeding off insects are part of cave life, too. Salamanders, like other animals, have adapted to cave life inside and outside. Those at the entrances are colored and can see. These little amphibians are beautiful, coming in a variety of colors, from the common cave salamander, which is orange with black spots, to the blind white salamander.

Of these two salamanders the blind white cave salamander is the most interesting. Over hundreds of years this little animal has adapted to the cave environment. It gets no pigment in its skin because it gets no sunlight. It has no eyes because it needs none to see in the darkness. This salamander mates and raises its young in total darkness. The Ozark blind salamander feeds on insects and almost any animal that is small enough.

Salamanders have a unique way of protecting themselves when roughly handled. They may secrete a milky fluid through the skin that is poisonous to some animals.

The blind white crayfish is another animal dwelling in total blackness. This crayfish has no pigment or sight, but has very long antennae that are very sensitive to movements in the water. It gets its food by preying on animals that fall into the water. It and the blind cave fish (only about two inches long) can detect any slight movement within or on the water from several feet away.

Molds and fungi in a cave are decomposers, growing on guano, dead animals, wood, string, or anything they can cling to and obtain energy from. They are white, since they produce no chlorophyll. They in turn become a grazing ground for some other cave inhabitants.

In absence of sunlight, the energy source above ground, a cave's basic food energy source is bat guano. This guano does not contain as much energy as sunlight, but does have roughly the caloric value of beefsteak. In some caves one can see guano piles several feet high underneath favorite roosting places.

If it were not for the guano deposited by a cave's bat population, the cave would be nearly devoid of energy input. Nearly all living things in a cave depend either directly or indirectly on the guano for life. Molds, bacteria, and fungi live directly on the guano for life. Many cave insects such as mites, crickets, and flies also receive nourishment in this fashion. Animals such as cave spiders feed on other cave inhabitants that derive their nourishment from the guano.

When guano falls into the water in a cave, the microscopic plants, animals and bacteria derive nutrition. These in turn become food for larger aquatic animals such as isopods and amphoids. And these animals become food for salamanders that become food for raccoons.

Bats and other inhabitants or predators that die in the cave are treated no differently by the living inhabitants than is the guano. They simply become another source of energy, supporting the continuing life cycle.

The life in a cave does not lead a danger-free existence. Besides the constant threat of predation, there are other threats to cave life.

One of these dangers is the disproportionate depletion of guano in many caves where the supply is being used up faster than it can be replaced. Since guano is the cave's main energy supply, the cave would soon be unable to sustain life if it were gone.

The main factor contributing to guano depletion is the general decline in bat population, brought about by natural and human causes. Flash floods in caves wash out the guano. Collapses and increased molestation of the bats' roosting places by cavers, researchers, and sightseers decrease the number of bats.

Another danger to cave life is the common practice in many parts of the Ozarks, and probably in other parts of the country, of dumping trash in sinkholes. The pollution from the dumps goes into the underground streams.

Tom Aley estimates that he has done more groundwater tracing than anyone else in the United States. Tom developed a process by which he stains Lycopodium spores. He then releases them into a stream system or into the ground, either directly or by injection. He can pick them up later using calibrated nylon netting.

Lycopodium spores are approximately thirty-three microns in diameter. (About 850 laid side by side would equal an inch.) However small this may seem, they are about ten to fifteen times larger than most bacteria. A study made at the Underground Laboratory showed that only 25 to 30 percent of a virus injected into the ground that came out in a cave stream was in virable (potent) condition. Obviously, the Ozark sub-surface is not a good filter.

When it rains, bacteria and viruses are washed from trash in a sinkhole into the ground, traveling through the subsurface stream system. If the bacteria come out in a cave stream, they pose a definite threat not only to the cave's aquatic life, but also to groundwater used for drinking. Aquatic life is killed, a vital link in the cave's food chain is broken.

Life in a cave is not in a separate unrelated world, but is so intertwined with the surface ecology that any alteration of water drainage or depletion of a species or change in a surface form can endanger the delicate balance. Almost all the animals in the cave are adapted to life in darkness, just as we are adapted to life above ground. Major disturbances such as the collapse of the ceiling of a cave might destroy them, for many of the animals who had adapted to the dark, damp, consistent cave situation could not survive in a new environment.

Even such seemingly harmless activities as trampling through a cave threatens its life. Tom said, "It changes the nature of the sub-strata. It squishes animals. To me it's one of the most damaging things you can do to the ecosystem in a cave."

What happens above the cave is reflected in the cave, affecting the food supply, water supply, or other environmental conditions within the cave. What happens inside the cave affects in many important and subtle ways the environment and life outside—including that of man. Careless and destructive use of caves that discourages bat colonies, for instance, can upset the entire food chain, which may cause over-population of insects. Or wholesale use of chemicals on the surface may pollute the underground, which in turn affects the outside by contaminating ponds.

Therefore, caves become showcases to give us better insight into what is happening to our environment and its possible effect on our future habitat.

The Human Story

From the time earliest man first entered the Ozarks area up to the present day, its many caves and sinkholes intrigued him. The caves' importance and appeal has remained, basically for the same reasons, even though our civilization is nothing like that of the early Indians. Through thousands of years and still today, caves have provided man with protection, some of his material wants, and a source of mystery and wonder.

Perhaps protection was the most evident use of caves by the ancient Indians. Throughout the years man has used caves for protection from the weather or enemies. Though modern man rarely lives in caves, even today there could hardly be a fisherman, hiker, or hunter who has not taken refuge in a cave when caught out in a storm. Besides protecting him from physical harm, caves have protected his belongings. Because of their inaccessibility and defensive positions, caves have also provided concealment from human enemies from marauding tribes to modern lawmen.

An easy access into the riches of the earth, caves have always been a source of some of man's material needs. The fresh cool springs flowing from many caves often determined locations of homes and villages during Indian and early pioneer days. Caves have provided easy access to clay and stone, saltpeter, iron, lead, and other minerals. Today, because of early man's habitation, they are a source of a different kind of richness—the artifacts left by vanished civilizations.

The deep, dark, inaccessible parts of the world that can be glimpsed in caves have always created mystery and excitement in the minds of imaginative and adventurous people. For the Indians they were ideal for tribal and religious ceremonies and for burial places. Today the hidden depths of some caves remain the only areas left unexplored in the Ozarks. Discovering new sources of knowledge—perhaps the most exciting adventure of all—is being experienced by individuals and groups on field trips underground. The wonder and mystery of caves, of least importance to ancient man, is perhaps the most important use

of caves to modern man, though his needs may revert to the first primitive need—a shelter for survival in the event of atomic disaster.

Caves hold many secrets that challenge modern man. Perhaps the most dramatic use of caves now is the archeological research being done in them, for untouched caves hold the best sources of information about the early Indian civilizations of the Ozarks.

There is ample evidence that various Indian families and small groups in different archeological periods inhabited the caves in the Ozarks during all seasons from as long ago as ten thousand years. The habitation was intermittent, seemingly for short periods, such as over the winter or as a temporary hunting campsite.

The ideal cave was in a bluff with a rock overhang that protected the area below. It would have a spring in it, located near the confluence of two streams, providing easy travel access and greater water supply. The mouth of the cave would face the south for the most protection against winter winds and the most warmth from the low winter sun. It would overlook a valley or open area that would provide good hunting practically on the "door step."

The Bluff Dwellers who lived in northwestern Arkansas about the beginning of Christian times used caves for the center of their activities. Preserved in the dry mouth of some caves are stone and bone tools, pottery, and impressions of perishable articles such as woven mats from which we can recreate their culture. They lived in the mouth, protecting themselves from the wind and cold by mud-plastered skins or mats. Blocking off some of the recesses and holes, they used the cave for storing their food. They also buried their dead there, usually in the twilight zone.

Caves containing Indian artifacts often have extra dirt piled in the mouth. Over the hundreds of years between sporadic habitation these south-facing caves could have been filled with dust from the prevailing southern wind, covering up evidences of earlier tenants. But since the dirt is piled so regularly, some people think the Indians carried it in, either to cover the dead or to cover up their trash instead of cleaning it out. Whatever the reason, digging deeper often results in finding new ash beds, which are remains of fires, with tools, pottery, and other artifacts of prehistoric peoples close by.

At the time of the advent of the white man in America, the Osage Indians controlled the Ozark area. Until the eastern tribes were deported west and challenged the Osage territory, the tall, graceful, and powerful Osage Indians reigned supreme.

There were never great numbers of Indians in the Ozarks. At the treaty of 1808, when the Osages sold their land on the Ozarks plateau and moved to Kansas and Oklahoma, there were only seventeen villages.

The Osages probably did not use caves except for campsites while on hunting trips, because they lived in rounded lodges built of poles covered with hides. Their villages were in open areas like the Springfield plain and the prairie where Lebanon is located. However, they did make some use of sinkholes in their ceremonies.

The Wyota Village, which existed for centuries on the site of present-day Lebanon right beside modern I-44, was probably located there because of the nearby sinkhole. The Osages believed their ancestors were sent by Grandfather the Sun to care for the Sacred One—the earth. They called the sink "The Hollow of the Sacred One's Hand." According to their legend, there was a narrow doorway which led into a huge dark cavern. Therefore, their village was near this sink, which is shaped like a huge bowl, where they held their tribal ceremonies with pomp and dignity as befitted such descendents of the sun.

Young Osage men also did their courting there. The young maiden would go to the sinkhole and sit quietly. If he chose her, the young man would come sit beside her.

Today, part of Lebanon is in a huge shallow sink about two miles across. Its lowest point is this smaller sink that was the ceremonial place of Wyota Village. There is no entrance now to the fabled cavern of Indian legend, though generations of children have dreamed of being the one to discover it. Today the Sacred One's Hand is filled with old foundations, beer cans, and excess highway fill.

One of J. W. Davis's hobbies is searching for Indian artifacts. He finds many of his points and stones in open, freshly plowed fields near a cave. He searches hidden crevices and sifts through loose dirt in the mouths of dry caves. When asked if he ever found anything really valuable, he said, "No, the Indians in the Ozarks were poor. I've just found points and stones cut for different purposes. Some are for scraping skins, breaking bones open for the marrow inside, some for knives, tomahawks, and points for arrows. I find lots of bones where they buried, mostly arm and leg bones. I've found hundreds of human teeth, sometimes five or six in a shaker of dirt, also dog and coyote teeth, and bear. Some had holes drilled in them like they used them for ornaments."

Though the early pioneers did not use caves as much as the Indians, caves still had an influence in their lives. They often built near caves for the convenience of the spring water and for storage of milk and other perishable foods. Some easily accessible caves were used for sheltering stock and machinery.

Pioneers discovered evidence of the Ozark mineral wealth in caves. It was soon known that there were supplies of lead, iron, zinc, and coal in various areas of the Ozarks. Today the eastern section has extensive lead and iron mining operations. Fallen sinks and caves have exposed stones man needs, such as granite and limestone. An organic product often mined is bat guano. It is obvious from the many caves called Saltpeter Cave that this mineral was in demand from early days to make gunpowder.

Most early people did not have any desire to explore caves. Except when searching for mineral wealth, the early white man's use of the cave, like that of the Indians, stopped at the twilight zone.

But legends grew and were passed down. The dark unknown was there, tempting later adventurous youths who, with coal oil or gas lanterns, could explore farther and longer than earlier persons could with a burning torch.

At the turn of the century, caves became favorite gathering places for picnics and Fourth of July outings. The whole community would gather, bringing covered baskets of chicken, potato salad, ripe tomatoes, pickles, pies, and lemonade. Enjoying the cool breath from the cave, the ladies put out their dinners on the cloths spread on the rocks or grass. They added cold water from the spring to the sweetened lemon juice brought in a fruit jar. Everybody ate. The children played in the river while the young people explored the recesses of the cave.

Sometimes they were gone for hours, until just as the worried men set out to look for them, they would appear, dirty and tired, but exhilarated at having discovered still a different passage deep inside the earth.

When the automobile carried people farther away, local caves lost their appeal. At that time some caves were developed for tourists, drawing people from everywhere to the tours. Commercial caves such as Meramec, Bridal Cave, and Marvel Cave, to name only a few, still give visitors the sense of mystery and wonder caves have held for all the ages past.

Perhaps the most prevalent of the many stories and legends about caves used as hideouts are the legends about Jesse James. There have been true tales of outlaws and hunted men hiding temporarily in caves, but it is highly unlikely that Jesse James ever did. He had too many friends in the Ozarks who opened their homes to him.

Moonshiners, however, did use caves to good advantage during prohibition days, for two reasons. The obvious one was to keep away from revenue officials. But even before they needed to be secretive, men made whiskey in caves during the winter. The 52°F. temperature was not too cold for fermenting, and there was a handy supply of running water to cool the distilling coils.

In recent years the mystery of caves has intrigued scientists seeking the answers to some of our ecological and geological riddles. With growing concern about our ecology and increasing knowledge about our global ecological interdependence, it is logical that some of the answers must lie under the surface. Students and researchers from elementary school through graduate study and private scientific organizations are studying caves to unlock their story for the benefit of all humanity.

Many caves have stood for millenniums undisturbed. Compared to their existence, man's contact with them has been brief. But in that short time humans have managed to influence their ecological story just as the caves themselves have had a part in the human story.

Legends

Sam Bradford always had a story to tell. He used to tell us some of his favorites whenever we went to see him. He volunteered this story about a pioneer family and their use of a cave. Like good story tellers, he gave this rather widespread story a local setting.

Now this is a story about a family that moved here, one of the first pioneers. I've got my story because I got a piece here and a piece there and pretty soon it all fit together.

A family that had moved here long way back, when Lebanon was just a tiny little town, came in with two horses and a cow and some tools and household necessities. They went way back in the hills and settled, or squatted, as they used to say then, on a piece of land and began to farm. Well, there came a terrible winter, and finally those boys showed up in town riding two horses, with blanket rolls, no saddles just blankets, strapped onto the horses and they had some money. Nobody hardly knew them except they knew who they were. They were the family that had gone out in the hills. Now the towns-folk wondered what the boys were doing in town so the question was asked.

"Well, no place else to go."

This rose the people's curiosity so they dragged the story as to what happened out of the two.

"Well, Ma was sick. She was awful sick, and we ran out of grub and there wasn't any medicine, and it was so cold, that all we could do was just huddle."

All the heat they had seemed to be a fireplace. Those fireplaces were very inefficient. You have to poke it and warm on one side then turn around and warm the other side. The mother being sick, you see was in a bed and they had a terrible time keeping her warm.

And one of the older boys said, "Pa went to town and never come back, so we know he got into trouble somehow. We found Pa. He was froze to death in a cave. He looked awful peaceful, like he went to sleep." And he was frozen there in that cave entrance and when they got back their mother was dead. They didn't have any way to dig a grave in that very hard frosted ground, so they carried their mother and put her beside their father and walled up the cave with stone for their burial.

"Where are you boys going?"

"Don't know."

"Can't you stay? Why don't you stay on the place?"

"It ain't home. Ma ain't there, Pa ain't there. It ain't home."

"Well, what did you do with the cow?"

"Had to eat her a long time ago. Nothing left but the two horses."

"Where are you going?"

"Don't know. Someplace."

The boys left the very same day and were never heard about again.

The cave where the bodies were buried is still there and some of the stones covering it are still in place.

126 THE EARTH

Ralph Amos told this story, which he said had happened in a cave on his farm.

This story has been handed down from generation to generation since the Civil War days and that's how I know it. I have never heard the exact date of this happening, probably in the latter days of the Civil War, but I have been shown the exact place of the incident.

Two young men by the names of Depue and Ferguson left their army duties and came home. They had to hide out during the day and at night they went down to the Depue home. Their hiding place was a small cave. It was a large flat sand rock with a cut-back under it about fifteen feet off the ground. They built a barrier across the front for protection. I think they chose this particular spot rather than some of the large caves in the area because it was more comfortable and easier to defend. The authorities were searching for them constantly, and this cave wasn't known as well as the others.

The men would spend the day in their hideout and the night in the house with the family. The Union Army had sent out scouts to find and punish the deserters. The punishment back then was facing a firing squad. Finally the scouts located the deserters' hideout, but because of its protective position, they did not try to capture them during the daytime. The plan was to take them when they came out of the cave at night.

There were footpaths along the limestone bluff where the cave was that the deserters had to take to reach their families at the west end of the bluffs. The scouts positioned themselves along the path to trap them one night. The men came out after dark and followed the footpath to the house. Ferguson was in front of Depue and when they discovered their plight, it was almost too late for action. Ferguson was caught. Depue retreated along the winding footpath which he knew well. By luck or previous arrangement, a neighbor's boat was on Depue's side of the river. He crossed the river so the scouts couldn't follow and hid in a barn.

The scouts had an idea of the direction he might take, so they followed. They camped on the opposite side of the swollen river. Depue watched them very closely the whole night through, being very anxious for his friend.

The next morning, he guessed right on this, Ferguson faced the firing squad at dawn. There were ten guns and every man got one shot. That way no one knew who killed the victim. It was still dark enough that the two neighbor boys who saw it could see the blaze from the guns. The scouts then gave the boys permission to bury him.

They laid him out on an old oak door and buried him there in a shallow grave. There's nothing there but stones and two marks on the trees. There's very few people know where it is.

The scouts had an idea where Depue was, but they never captured him. He lived there for some years.

Part of the stone wall still stands in the cave where they hid out.

Other stories and legends about caves come from Myrtle Hough.

West of our home on Parks Creek across that big hill on the west there's a cave known as the Journegan Cave and that's where we had our picnics when we were children. This is a high dry cave, and along the north and northeast side of that cave there is a huge stone that looks just like a man lying there facing with his back in the opening, facing in the wall of the cave. My father always had so much fun. He said, "Now you just touch that and you'll hear a groan."

I never did hear the groan, but the other children'd touch it and step back saying they heard something. I think they just imagined something, but there was a legend there that someone had disobeyed the great spirit and was turned to stone. It was an Indian legend that had been passed down from generation to generation.

There's a cave on the Lambeth farm where they've been digging for treasure. My father was a traveling salesman. He was coming along there one time and across the river there was a lovely little valley and he took his horses out to let them graze while he ate his lunch. While doing this he heard someone coming. He wondered who they were, so he hid behind some bushes. They pulled up and took a big load of stuff into this cave. Now my father thought it was bars of gold, but I was telling my son and he said there was a still in there. He had been there with his geiger counter and found where they'd made whiskey by finding the metal barrel loops. My father still thought it was bars of gold.

I had seven brothers and any spare time they had, they wanted to go to the caves. My father was always warning them about this Howell Cave. He told us when he was a young man, and I always wondered if he was one in the bunch—he never said he was, but a group of young men went in one Saturday or Sunday and one of them in the group had a violin. And they kept going and this fellow that had the violin would stop and play to hear the sound—the echoes. But he got lost from the rest of them and for nine days they searched for him and he played that violin. As he became weaker and weaker the violin strains became lower. But sometimes they would be under the music, sometimes at the side, sometimes they'd be at the top, but they never did find him. So my father always warned the boys when they'd start that this was true. He'd urge them to be sure and take things so they would guide themselves out. Of course, they didn't have string. They just had coal oil lanterns then. I remember them taking corn stalks in. When they'd come to an opening, they'd lay the stalk down pointing the way to go.

They hunted for this boy for nine days. They would hear him from all sides. Of course, they didn't have any means to drill down and work like we do today. They'd just hunt for him but never finding him.

And then one time when the boys went to the cave they found a rock with a man's hat on it that was nearly decayed. They searched for the violin but it was so many years past that it would have been gone. They wondered if it wasn't this man's hat.

The boy was lost about 1850 or earlier. My father was a daring fellow and I just wonder since he urged the boys to be so careful, if he wasn't in the group when the boy was lost.

Moonshiners

Emmitt Massey shared with us a story of a cave that people had been in and out of many times before it was ever discovered there had been moonshine made there. Back during prohibition there were a lot of stills in operation. Sometimes they were known about, but the owner of this cave didn't know there had been moonshiners in his cave until his neighbor threw a birthday dinner and Emmitt, along with his friends, discovered it while walking down the river path to the party.

In my younger years I was always prowling around the cave. That is, me and my friends would be down to the caves and mess around in them. There are two caves in particular along the river that we had been in before many times. The lower of two caves was the one we found moonshiners in.

Me and the boys were on our way along the river to a birthday dinner when we stepped inside the lower cave and found some fruit jars in plain sight. Well, naturally we had to investigate, so we went on back in the cave to the small opening that opened up into another good-sized room. We crawled through, and there was a barrel setting there just full of fresh mash.

Now them moonshiners, they went to a lot of trouble to keep from being found. The only way they could get a barrel into that back room was by taking it apart outside and crawling through with the pieces, and then putting it back together inside the room. There were several places where fires had been built and some old mash had been dumped out right there in the room. I don't suppose they worried too much about their smoke being seen when distilling the mash. The wood they used for fire was probably oak or hickory which didn't make a lot of smoke and there's openings all up and down the bluff that the smoke could get away.

Well, you take a bunch of kids, they're always up to something. We saw that mash and then one of us found a can of kerosene they used to start fires with. Naturally, we just poured that kerosene into that barrel of mash. Then in a day or two after that birthday dinner a bunch of us went back near the cave and we found where they'd dumped that mash outside the cave near the river. Now I don't know whether we ruined the whiskey or not, but I bet it had a heck of a kick to it. And I don't know who made it. I can remember back after that when we'd see those moonshiners go down through the field to the cave.

Moonshining wasn't as bad for caves as one might think. All those sour mash dumpings sometimes had some unexpected side effects. Besides adding to the food source for many cave inhabitants, they also helped get rid of some undesirable cave life.

There is a cave a few miles from Stoutland that was commonly called Rattlesnake Cave. It is a large cave that used to have so many rattlesnakes in it that anyone that dared to venture into it ran the risk of getting bitten no matter what precautions he took. Moonshiners were always looking for a place where no one would dream of finding them. What better place could there be than a cave full of rattlesnakes?

This cave was perfect. Not only would no one venture there to search for them, but there was plenty of cold running water to cool the distilled alcohol and also, the cave's temperature was ideal for fermenting the mash. The moonshiners were safe. In fact, they were even safer than they knew, for after they began operating, the rattlesnakes disappeared! Some think that the commotion scared them off, but I think they just simply left in disgust when their home was turned into a souse house. That shows just how much smarter snakes are than people.

Bat Cave

Gene Chambers of Conway, Missouri, was outside his house waiting for us by his pickup as we drove up January 9, 1975.

"Get in and I'll take you yonder to the cave," he said pointing across the river bottom field. We could see through the bare trees lining the river to the bluff on the other side. About half a mile away, we could make out the huge inverted V that was the cave opening.

Facing backward as we sat on a bale of hay, we rode in the pickup in the opposite direction from the cave. Gene started up the hill, out of the bottom. "We have to go around the road to the bridge," he explained.

After about four miles of twisting through the hills and going through a couple of gates, we found ourselves bumping along a very narrow trail squeezed between the bluff and the river. Tree branches slapped at us, the four-wheel-drive pickup tilted dangerously toward the river, and once the wheel hit a log hidden under the leaves, knocking us sideways at least two feet closer to the river bank. With all four wheels pulling, Gene made a run up the short, steep hill to the cave's mouth with us hanging on and ducking as best we could.

"Lots of people get stuck on that road," he explained after he turned his truck around in the spacious, level—but muddy—mouth of the cave. "I've never had no trouble myself to speak of. One night when I come over here gigging there was so many cars in here there wasn't no room to turn around. There was nothing to do but back out. Not a one of them would even try it, it being night and all, but I got my flashlight in one hand—we had no back up lights then— leaned out the open door, steered with the other hand and backed her the whole way back to the gate. I've had lots of experiences like that.

"We've owned this cave, me and Dad together, for a long time. He bought it in about the year of nineteen and nine—no before that. It's been in the family from that time on. It belongs to me now since my parents passed away."

"I'll bet you're glad you have the cave on your farm, aren't you?"

"Oh yeah. I enjoy owning it. I go to town every once in a while and people will say, 'I was in your cave Sunday.'

"But the trouble with caves in this country is there is no way getting to them. If I'd had any inlet to this cave I'd been a millionaire a long time ago. There's lots of ways I could have made this paid off. But you can't get nobody in here and you can't do nothing about it the way she's located way over here. I've just let her set here and used it for nothing in my lifetime. I don't guess I'll ever use it for anything, for I can't.

"I had to dig out the trail here to the cave myself. There was just a path here along the bluff. We dug it out with mules and an old road grader. I don't know how many different times and days we went sweeping up here with them ole mules and that ole grader. Before that you couldn't get nothing in here without coming a-foot or down the river. Now, even though the road is grown up some, you can drive machinery and a pickup clean up to the mouth and back in the cave to where it gets dark, like we're doing now.

"This is known as Bat Cave. It's well loaded with bats and the manure from them bats is the best fertilizer in the world. In the period of time before Dad bought this place there was a bunch of men that had a contract to buy that stuff out of here.

"They crawled up on them ledges and raked her down. And I suppose they wheelbarrowed it down to the mouth and sent it on a boat down the river 'cause there wasn't no road up there then. They couldn't haul it down in a wagon. They had to go down the river or carry it in a bucket or sack down a path. There was a path you could walk on foot. That was all, and you were lucky if you didn't fall into the river on such a narrow path.

"They worked at it for a month off and on, taking that bat manure out of there. It hadn't been bothered then for no telling when, never, maybe, and it was really loaded back in there. They got a lot of it. They carted it out of here and took it down the river to that gate where a wagon could come. That was before nineteen and ten, 'cause that's when I was born.

"I go back in the cave once in a while and I'm thinking of doing it again this spring. Just around the corner there and up on a shelf is where a lot of the bats live. The manure falls off that shelf back on the ground. I can back the pickup right up there pretty close to it—and I have many a time—and haul it out to put on the garden. You can't buy fertilizer at the store as good as that is. No use trying it.

"Me and Dad hauled it out of here on our tractor with a rear end scoop. We hauled five loads out of here one spring and put on our garden. We didn't notice so much difference that year, but the next year—I mean that garden fairly went wild. Now it really went.

"I wouldn't be surprised if there aren't less bats here than used to be. I suppose people interfering with them, they've got kinda backward. They've got further back in the cave on us anyway. I've come over here many a time of a night and if you turned a light on you just about had it. They'd hit you right in the face. Shut your light off and let them calm back down. They do come out of here and come clear over to the house in the summertime. I've had them get in the house. We had an idle flue over there and they built a nest in there and just filled that flue full. We didn't know they was in there. They got to coming out that flue into the house. And ever night or so we'd have another bat. We'd get him out, and next night or two we'd have another or two. Come to find out they was a-nesting in there in that ole dark flue. Had to clean it out. And they'd come from here. They're aggravating. It just scared our women to death when they got in our house."

"Except for the bat manure, was the cave used commercially in any other way?"

"I remember there was a couple of men in Conway that made a contract with Dad to grow mushrooms. They made several beds of mushrooms back there away from the light. Hot beds, you know. They planted and worked them all summer. When they started in we only had a path up through here. The road we just come up the river on was made then with a pair of mules. Me and them two men made that road. They worked all summer on this road and the mushrooms and never did get nowhere with them. The mushrooms wouldn't grow. It was too cold in here was their trouble—what made them have to quit.

"You see right over there just around the bend in the dark is where they made them hot beds. They'd be eight to ten feet long, just like us old farmers used to make sweet potato beds to raise plants to set out. But they just didn't do any good."

"This sure is a big cave."

"This is the only cave on my farm. I think it's one of the biggest in this county—the biggest I know of, anyway. I've had as high as five or six automobiles in here at one time with room to turn around.

"I used to store machinery here some. I run out of a machine shed over at the house so I got to using this old lad for backing my machinery in. It wasn't a very good shed because, see, there's water dripping. It's too wet. If you wanted to lose your paint on a brand new piece of machinery, leave it over here one winter and you didn't have no paint. So I got to taking my best stuff to the house and eventually built me a shed up there, but I left an old cultivator right over there and an old corn planter here. I come over here one day and they was a-setting right down there in the river—just a tongue of that planter sticking out. A bunch of kids pushed it over in there. So I hired a man with a log winch to pack his winch up here and pull that old planter back out of there. A little while later I come back over here and the old cultivator was a-setting in the river. Well, I couldn't pull it out myself. So I just tied it on behind the tractor and its on over the hill by the house now. Except my binder. It's setting right over there in the water. I had it setting here right in front of the cave. And kids, you know, they got to playing and they rolled that thing off over that hill there, and I can't get it out of the river with nothing I got. I expect the wheels are broke too, one of them is off. It's past using. There's no more use for it now anyway, for people quit them. It's a good old binder and it'll just set there and rot down. It's been there fifteen years I guess.

"I don't object to nobody coming over here. The only thing I object to is the way they treated my machinery when we had it over here—push it off in the river. And that old binder, they'd shoot it full of holes and break sprockets off of it with rocks and stuff like that. I had to quit using the cave over here for machinery, and it wasn't a fit place no how. It was too damp.

"I used to put in a lot of time here in my younger days, picnicking around. People'd come here and want to go back in there and see that old cave. I took them back a few times. But I'm not much of a hand to go back there where you have to lay down and crawl. But a lot of guys did. I ain't a-going to do it. I don't care what kind of lights they got or what they ain't got, I ain't going to lay down and crawl back in one of these things. I just got so far and I quit.

"I used to be over here at least once a week when I was a boy up till I was married—spent practically every Sunday over here with a bunch. This neighborhood was full of young folks and we'd picnic around over here. But time as you get as old as I am, the old rocking chair's got you down and you don't do none of that picnicking. You set right there in that ole rocking chair and go to sleep.

"About all the cave's used for now is when a few people come over here picnicking around. You can see by them tracks around in there that there's been someone over here not too long back. I hear them over here once in a while in the summertime. It'd be a bunch of young lads, I suppose. I'll see a fire. But, you can hear them from over at the house, and it sounds like a cyclone. They're just having a picnic over here. And a few fishermen come down here in the winter, gigging.

"If I could use this or had it where I could use it for stock, why it'd be worth its weight in gold to me in the wintertime for protection for stock. But you see, the river's in the way. I can't use it. It's just a comfortable temperature for stock. And they come here in the summer to get rid of flies.

"When I was grading this road back in here we got stuck up. So I went back to the house to get my pair of mules. They wasn't used to coming in here and they wasn't no way in the world I could beat them in this cave. They was afraid of it. They wouldn't pull twenty-five pounds on my truck. I went up here to the neighbor's and got another pair and put four mules on and they all four done the same thing. Wouldn't pull nothing. Well, I took them all off and I got ahead of my mules and led them right into this cave. I just stopped and let them stand about ten or fifteen minutes. That cool air just felt so good to them, and they seen they wasn't going to get hurt, so their excitement got over with. I drove them down there and hooked on to the pickup, and they like to tore it in two bringing it into this cave. I mean they brought it in here right now, too. And from that day on, as long as I had that pair of mules, I could start up that road and ford the river and they'd just start walking faster. The further, the faster. They'd come a-trotting right in here and the minute they got in here, you could throw them lines down and get off and they'd stay there all day and never move a muscle. Just stand there. Comfortable—no flies on and there wouldn't be a one get on them anymore—just cool in here. But I had a time, first time, getting them in here to learn them mules.

"Yes sir, lads, this here cave has seen a lot of action, yet has stood here just a-setting most of the time."

Cave Crawling

Spelunking is the hobby of exploring caves. Unlike speleology, the science of exploring caves, spelunking, or cave crawling as it is more commonly called, is mainly for amateurs who enjoy caves for beauty and fun. This definition fits our group of *Bittersweet* cave crawlers. Almost all staff members have gone to at least one cave, in groups as small as four or as many as eleven. We first started during a very cold winter spell and continued cave crawling all the rest of that year and into the next.

In this period we have seen a great variety of caves, since there are more than two hundred caves in our county alone. We have gone down in sinkholes of all types and have explored small cave entrances that blossomed into huge rooms covered with intricate formations. We have explored caves that have huge entrances that dwindle to small passages in a few hundred feet and explored others that are filled with so much mud and water that we had to crawl and wade. Even better, we have explored caves where we could walk upright hundreds of yards without crawling or getting wet.

George Kastler, graduate of our high school and now state naturalist, was with us at all times. Since he has mapped many of the caves we visited, he knows about the caves—their dangers, their pleasures, their distinguishing formations and their locations. George was always there to give a helping hand, to explain a particular point, or to give reassurance when everyone was tired. He gave us the opportunity to learn about the many natural caves of the Ozarks and to experience the excitement of discovering a new world in our backyards.

George pointed out that to make the cave crawling experience more enjoyable and safer there are preliminary preparations and courtesies to be followed. These are locating the cave, checking weather conditions, asking permission, having a partner, notifying others where you are going, and preparing the pack.

The first preparation is to find the best route to the cave. As we get ready to go, we check maps to find, as nearly as possible, the exact location of a cave. If we know the general area where a cave is located,

Some cave entrances are high in a bluff.

it is much easier to find. We also consult the maps to determine whether the cave is approachable by car. If it isn't, we have to estimate the walking distance to it.

Also, just before we leave, we check the weather report. In the winter, we need to know the chances for snow, not because it will affect cave conditions, but because a fairly heavy snow may make the roads and trails leading to the caves difficult to traverse.

After the snow season passes, rain can present problems. The rains can cause the rivers that are outside most caves to flood. In rainy weather, a river or branch can rise so rapidly that a cave entrance close to the riverbank can be submerged in a few minutes. The water level inside the cave may also be affected. When it rains, the water absorbed into the ground begins to filter through the bedrock. It will work its way down farther and farther until it finally seeps into the cave. Once in the cave, it begins to collect, causing the water level to rise.

The speed at which the water collects in a cave depends on many things. If the bedrock above the cave is already wet, groundwater will not filter through as fast as if the bedrock is dry. The size of the openings through which water filters down also has an effect—the bigger the opening, the more water will seep in.

A prolonged, slow rain, such as a spring rain, will cause the water level to rise, but it will rise only to a certain point and stabilize. After it reaches that point, any additional water will simply run off, because the bedrock will be too saturated to let any more water seep into the cave. Therefore, in rainy weather there is not much danger of one of the spelunker's worst nightmares—a flash flood inside the cave. For us the prolonged rain means only mud that makes the going a little harder. However, if the cave has a lot of sinkholes in its watershed, there is still the chance of fast-rising water.

The situation is different in late spring and early summer. The bedrock is much drier and the weather much more unpredictable. A light blue morning sky can become grey and heavy with clouds by noon. And if it starts raining hard, like two inches in hours, the water can go through the bedrock like flour through a sieve. This can cause some caves in the area to fill up completely in only a few minutes. Obviously, this predicament would be very dangerous for anyone caught in the back of a cave when it starts to fill up. Therefore, we keep careful watch on the weather, and if conditions look favorable for this situation to arise, we cancel our trip.

In addition to checking weather reports and maps, it is important to get permission from the landowner for all caves on private property.

If we are allowed to go in, we are careful to close gates, respect all property, and refrain from littering.

A fundamental rule in cave exploring is never to go alone. We are always sure to have a partner along, for the dangers of mishaps are greatly reduced by going in groups. For example, if someone falls and injures himself while descending into a sinkhole, the rope around the waist will not help if there is no partner above to pull him up and go for help. In muddy caves it is especially necessary to have a partner. If someone happens to get mired in a mud hole, he can always call on his partner to pull him out. Or, if one gets separated from the rest of the group, they will be able to locate him much more easily if they have several people to help look. Another advantage of caving in a group is that if everyone gets trapped or lost together in a cave, the chance of panic spreading is greatly reduced. The greater the number in the group in case of accident, the more likely someone will start searching for them quickly.

This leads to another important safeguard. Before going into any kind of a cave, large or small, it is important to notify someone, giving him an approximate time of return. George made this part clear. "One of the first rules of safety is, be sure someone knows where you are going—*exactly* where. And if you anticipate making any changes in the plan during the day, let someone know. You say you're going down to Twin Bridges. Well, in the Twin Bridges area there are close to a good dozen major caves. Counting some of the smaller ones, you've got close to thirty-five caves. If someone should get lost or hurt and you don't come home, someone will come down and try to find you. Where do they start looking? Course they'll look in those obvious ones first, where people tend to go, but suppose you're off in one of those little jobbies somewhere?"

To reach most of the caves we visit we have to walk at least half a mile, so we need packs to carry our food and equipment. Although a few of us use large hiking packs, we do not like them because of their bulkiness in a cave. Instead, we favor smaller packs that are more mobile. However, their size limits what we can put in them. For those who have cameras, this means leaving some equipment at home. Our photographers usually limit themselves to one camera body, two lenses, and a flash. Sometimes we take a tripod, but it makes the going much more difficult. Along with the camera equipment, we put extra lights in the pack and an extra change of clothes—shirt, pants, shoes, and socks. The remaining space is stuffed full of high-energy food that doesn't take up too much space, such as candy bars, canned soft drinks, and sandwiches.

Once all the preliminaries are out of the way, we are ready to go. When we arrive at the site of a cave, we usually have no trouble finding the mouth, especially when George is with us. However, if the underbrush has grown up, if some landmarks have changed slightly, or if the area is covered with a new snow, it is necessary to relocate the exact position of the opening. The fastest and simplest way to do so is to disperse and walk through the woods until someone finds a small stream of water crossing the trail. Since water runs out from the openings of many caves in this area, all we have to do is follow the stream toward the bluff to walk right into the opening.

George has another way of locating new caves. Many caves "breathe." That is, a current of air is always moving in and then coming out again. A cave with a fairly large mouth will expel air hundreds of yards outward. Cave air doesn't feel or smell like other air; it feels damp and cool and smells of bat guano and mold. Since this air is carried outward from the entrance of a cave, it is actually possible to "smell out" a cave. We all thought this sounded incredible, but George insisted it was possible. In fact, he said that he has smelled out caves from as far as three hundred yards. He would drive down country roads in areas that have bluffs, rock outcroppings and other evidence of cave formation, stick his head out the window and sniff. If he caught the scent, he would follow his nose to the mouth of a new cave. It takes an experienced person with a gifted nose to be able to do this, but it is an accurate and interesting way to find new caves.

After finding the cave entrance, we walk into the cave a few yards. Then we stash our packs in a hidden dry place where we can pick them up on the way out. Before going farther into the cave, we unload from our packs anything we want to take with us—cameras, film, lights, extra batteries and maybe a couple of candy bars. We do not carry our sandwiches and drinks back into a cave. Instead we usually come back to where we stash our packs to eat lunch.

In a cave we need light foods that give quick energy because of the constant physical exertion. Candy bars, with their high sugar content, give a quick energy boost to anyone who is tiring. Sandwiches are good when one is in a cave long enough to require a meal. Water in caves may not be safe to drink. While some of it is clear and looks clean, in the Ozark karst formations seepage from dumps and sewage systems can contaminate the water. Therefore, we carry all our liquids with us, preferring canned drinks to thermoses because a thermos is more likely to break.

We found out early the value of George's insistence on safety and how important it was to be prepared. As we made our way into our

Cave entrances vary from narrow fissures . . .

first cave, each of us with just one light, we spread out too fast. We had a line of six people spread over two hundred feet. Even though we arrived in a group, it did not do anyone any good if we didn't stick together, as Robert McKenzie found out.

"I sat alone in the pitch-black passage wondering what would happen. The flashlight's once-bright glow had quickly melted into the darkness of the cave when I had been stupid enough to drop it into a large pool of muddy water. That was the second mistake I made. The first was that I dropped back from the rest of the group to sneak in a few more pictures. As a result, I was left behind in the dark when I dropped the light.

At first, I had tried in vain to find my way out of the maze of rock and mud. But each direction I crawled yielded only another wall of coarse rock. Only after my futile attempt at escape and my initial panic subsided did I realize my helplessness. I was nothing without my light; I could see nothing—no shadows, no reflections, not even the smallest pinpoint of light. I couldn't even tell if my eyes were open or not. I lost my sense of direction and all sense of time. I was in a lost dimension. The absolute darkness made my mind wander as the seconds ran into minutes and then, seemingly, into hours. Stifling the urge to panic, I forced myself to sit down and await the return of

. . . to thirty-foot massive arches.

the others. After what seemed like hours, but was actually only fifteen or twenty minutes, they returned and found me. This experience in the darkness made me realize that a light source is the most important single tool for a cave crawler."

From our experience, strong three-cell flashlights are our first choice for light because of their compactness, reliability, and availabiliy. But even flashlights need some maintenance. Batteries in the two-cell lights run low after about four hours. Since we are in some caves longer than this, it is necessary to take along several extra sets of batteries, as well as extra bulbs for the flashlights in case our bulbs either burn out or are broken. Through experience we have learned that nothing can be kept dry in a cave unless it is in a watertight container. Therefore, we put all our extra batteries and bulbs in plastic bags. The only major drawback to the flashlights is that their light is too directional. Since they do not spread light well, most of the caves would have existed only as small spots of light except that we corrected this problem by using a much better light source.

This other source is a gasoline lantern that spreads a bright light over a large area, enabling us to see small details more clearly and to focus our cameras more easily. A disadvantage to the lantern is its bulk and weight. It cannot be taken into some very small passages simply because there is not enough room for both it and us. Another disadvantage of the lantern is the danger of falling and breaking a more expensive piece of equipment. Therefore, George is the one who carries the lantern, since he is more sure-footed than the *Bittersweet* staff members.

Like the flashlight, the lantern will not burn without maintenance. On long expeditions, George always brings along extra gasoline. If we take the extra fuel into the cave with us, George is sure to have it in a tightly stoppered, unbreakable container to prevent spilling it and contaminating the water.

Although we don't use carbide lights, George warned us of the precautions involved in using them. Since carbide combines chemically with water to give off light and heat, it is important that anyone using it should keep his extra carbide in completely watertight containers. George told us a story about a man who carried a small packet of carbide in his hip pocket while crawling through a cave. Forgetting the carbide's presence, he began to wade a small body of water. When the water reached his thigh level it contacted the carbide and of course, began to emit light and heat. George said, "It didn't take him long to get out of those pants!"

George also warned us about dumping used carbide in caves. Left

George Kastler is prepared for any emergency.

in a cave, carbide can poison animals and eventually work its way into the water table. Used carbide should always be stored in a separate container and disposed of properly outside the cave.

A secondary light source is very important in a cave. If Robert had had an extra light source when he was trapped in the dark, he would have been in no danger. A small flashlight that fits in a pocket makes a good back-up unit. However, if you are in a group that has several lights, a box of matches and some small candles serve well as emergency lights.

Cave crawling can be safer and more comfortable if the caver is dressed properly. A hard hat is probably associated with caving more than any other item of clothing, and for good reason. Hard hats protect against low ceilings, hard falls and overhanging rocks difficult to see in the semi-darkness. They really do help insure safety. However, many people who go cave crawling will not wear one. Their usual explanation is, "Oh, I'm always very careful, and besides, I can sense when my head is getting near the roof."

"I admit that I didn't think a hard hat was necessary," Robert said, "until a recent incident far back in a cave made a believer out of me.

"We had worked our way to the back of the cave some eight hundred yards from the entrance. As usual, George made us find our way out without his help. He would always give us a five-minute head start and then lag behind the group, never saying anything until we found our way out.

"Becoming impatient after a few minutes, two boys and I decided to go on ahead of the slow-moving group, searching for daylight on our own. After the sounds of the rest dimmed behind us, we came to a fork in the passage. We scrambled up a large clay bank that leveled off on top rather than wade the three-foot-deep waterway of the other channel. We walked on the slick mud about a hundred feet when we heard the others behind us walking in the water passage below us to our right. Evidently we had come the wrong way. Since we didn't want to backtrack to the fork, our only way down was to climb down the fifteen-foot, forty-five-degree incline. The ceiling ran parallel with the incline about four feet above it. By sitting on the edge of the incline and placing my hands on the ceiling, I could, in theory, lower myself down to the bottom. It would not have been feasible to try to slide to the bottom because I'd have hit the wall. So I sat on the edge looking down the slick mud and dug my heels in at the same time my searching fingertips found refuge in the gnarled ceiling. Slowly I began to let myself down.

"It was an agonizingly slow process—find a hand hold, then drop my feet and dig in my heels, then lower myself. Each time I did this I came a foot closer to success. But after four times, my fingers were beginning to tire. With aching and almost numb fingers, I began to lower myself again. Then suddenly I was shooting toward the bottom and the wall in a blur of speed. Instinctively I threw my hands in front of me and waited for the crash. But my hands never touched rock! Instead my head was snapped violently backwards. A projecting ceiling rock had knocked me flat on my back, sending my hard hat and flashlight flying in different directions. I sat up slightly dazed, wondering if I was still alive. My hat, upside down in the water, was floating out with the current, while the flashlight was giving off a dim glow three feet under the murky water. I gingerly examined my head. I wasn't hurt. Feeling rather stupid, I retrieved my hat and my now-dead flashlight, uninjured except for a slightly bruised ego and a deformed hard hat.

"This incident made me realize the great importance of head protection in a cave. I for one will never go into a cave without one."

Choosing the right pants and shirt to wear in a cave is not too difficult but is important. The main advice is: don't wear anything you expect to keep clean. Most of us wear washable cotton shirts, preferably long sleeved to protect elbows and forearms when crawling into narrow passages lined with sharp deposits. We found, after crawling into many wet places, that flannel becomes very heavy when wet.

The trick in choosing pants is to get some that are not so new that they could be ruined, but not so old that they will fall apart. One of the girls had some bad luck. A quarter of a mile into one cave she suffered an embarrassing rip-out in her pants that hindered her mobility the rest of the day. The majority of our group select heavy denim jeans that take a lot of punishment without coming apart. Even more durable than jeans are the strong, water-repellent G.I. field pants.

In cold weather it is necessary to wear extra clothing on the way to and from caves. This extra clothing, which usually consists of a heavy coat and a cap, can be worn outside in the cold and wind until reaching the mouth of the cave. We then leave the extra coats with our packs in a dry place at the mouth, since coats are not needed in the 55° year-round temperature of the cave.

Proper footwear is almost as important as proper head gear. Tennis shoes would seem like a logical choice, but actually they are not for some caves. They do not offer enough protection from sharp rocks or hard falls, and they don't always stay on your feet. There is nothing as disconcerting as stepping in mud and drawing out a shoeless foot.

Boots are the answer. Besides staying on feet better, they offer added protection. Ankles are protected from bruising jolts and gravel cannot work its way into boots as easily as into shoes. Rubber boots are good because if they fill up with water the heat from your feet will warm the trapped water and thereby keep your feet warm. However, in some caves ordinary rubber boots are not enough. When the mud is waist deep and covered with six inches of water, fishing waders keep the spelunker moving. But when we use waders, we have to be very careful to keep from snagging them on the sharp rocks.

Gloves are optional. Some people feel naked without them, while others cannot stand to wear them. Gloves do protect against the rough cave environment, especially in the event of a fall; however, some of us do not like them because they take away our sense of touch, something we feel is necessary to enjoy a cave. If gloves are worn, though, they should be leather work gloves, because cotton gloves become heavy and clumsy when wet.

When leaving the cave, especially in cold weather, or any other time to be more comfortable and to protect car seats from cave mud, we change into clean, dry clothes, wrapping the clay-covered wet ones in plastic bags. We pack everything back in our packs and put on our jackets, ready to trek back up the bluff to our cars. We check once more to be sure we have carried out all empty cans, dead batteries, and all our trash.

We leave the dark world just as we enter it, stealing only a few pictures to explain and document the beauty, excitement, and personal growth each of us experience in the limestone caves of the Ozarks.

2. THE PEOPLE

Though it seems to us today that life in the hills at the turn of the century must have been hard, no one who lived through those times thought much about their lot. Rose Lowrance said, "We raised lots of fruit on the farm and corn and oats and wheat. I guess you wonder how we done it all. They come at different times—wasn't all jammed up together."

"We thought nothing of having to work, " Warren Cook said. "One thing that's happened to us today is that we've become so conscious of creature comforts that we don't want to do anything that takes too much effort."

"The women have always done their part," Rose said. "In that day and time they worked in the field just the same as the husband did. They worked together. I remember when we lived near Seymour, Mother would always take our clothes down to the James River and do our washing. We'd always leave our big kettle down there and do our washing and not bother about water at the house. We washed on a board and boiled our clothes in a great big iron kettle with legs. We'd put our clothes in there and stir them with a paddle. They was clean too!"

Children did their share, sharing in the responsibilities of making the living and caring for the family. Next in importance for the child was getting an education in the one-room school within walking distance of each child. Though the need was recognized, some children weren't able to take full advantage of the schooling. Johnny Starnes said, "I went to school down at Brownfield. It was an old log school. I didn't go over just about one month and I had to go to work and never got to go to school no more at all. Now they just had these old blue spelling books was all they had. And you just had to get up and spell. I stayed the head of all of them while I went."

Mary Moore's family responsibilities prevented her from going to school very much. "I just went to the third reader. I didn't get no education and I didn't get to go all the time when I went. My mother

147

worked lots and we didn't make no money. Well, now lots of times she had to keep me at home to take care of the little brother."

They worked, they played, they studied, they worshipped. They grew up, raised their own families and grew old. "You can live a long, full life," Ernie Hough said. "They ain't nothing to that at all. All you've got to do is in your mind. If you think you're getting old, then you will get old. If you think you ain't getting old, and you want to stay young, then you think young and don't never think you're old. You can either be an old young man or a young old man."

Just Some of the Little Experiences of Growing Up

I Knocked That Snake's Head Square Off Its Shoulders

Interview with Iva Bradshaw, Eldridge, Missouri, December 18, 1977.

I was born in Dallas County, Missouri, in 1888. I lived on a farm practically all my life. I was the third child in my family.

When I was growing up on the farm we all worked together to help make a living. Everyone that was big enough had to go to the field and work. While I was so small that I couldn't get out and do work, there was babies in the house, and I'd stay and watch them. I remember one time my mother left me there to take care of the babies and fix the beds. She didn't get her beds made for they was planting corn. They used to have big feather beds, you know. I got the feather bed off on the floor and thought I'd do a good job with it. I made it nice, but it was so heavy and I was so small, I never could get the bed back on the bedstead, and it was laying in the floor when the family came home for dinner.

But as I got older, I started going to the fields. When I was nine and Henry, my oldest brother, was eight, Dad bought us a jenny. There was seven acres in the little place that we lived on, and Dad rented ground around other places to make the main crop. That jenny was for me and my brother to tend that seven acres around home. We did. We tended it. We took our double shovel and plowed that seven acres and raised a right nice little batch of corn out of it, too. Yeah, truck patches and such things. When Dad'd hook his team up, we would, too. Why, I could hook them up just as good as anybody. We had some mules that was just three years old and they was kind of mean. I was harnessing up the jack strop one day and a mule kicked me on the leg. Oh, I thought I was ruined! But I got him and he never

149

tried it anymore. We just kept plowing every year till I was thirteen.

Us kids used to play lots. We'd get into some mighty big things. We'd go up on the hillside, throw down some rocks, and they'd get to rolling. We'd take big steel wagon wheels and they'd go for a quarter-mile when we'd get through with them. I'd make my own dolls. I'd have to get maybe a corncob or something like that and stick arms and legs in it and fix them up.

We played cat and mouse. We'd get in a ring and hold hands. There'd be one inside and that was the mouse. The cat would be on the outside of the ring and he'd run around and go between the arms of two of us and we'd try to catch him.

We'd make playhouses and build up on the hillside. I'd like to go up and see if I can't find the place where we'd take rocks and build up walls. In the summertime we lived where they was a creek and they was a big flat gravel bar where we'd build a little log house just about two by six—we'd build us a chimney and a fireplace and everything. We'd go to the field and get corn and stand it up in front of the fireplace and we'd bake that corn. Dad always had his meat in the smokehouse and we'd go up there and get meat, too. Lots of times we'd eat our dinner down there on that gravel bar. Mother wouldn't call us to home 'cause she'd know we was there cooking and eating ourselves.

Mother learnt us how to tie a hang knot. They used to hang people and she could tie a hang knot. Us kids made a plan to hang Rob—that was my brother. So we took him to an old barn where there was rafters and led him up on the scaffold. We sung the song mother learnt us—the song that they sung when they hung these fellers. It said, "My name is Charlie Guiteau, My name I'll never deny. For the murder of James A. Garfield, I'll meet my scaffold on high." Well, us kids had him up there with the hoodwinks on and the rope around his neck. But when we got to singing that song, we got to crying. That's what saved his life because we'd a-broke his neck just as sure as we'd a-pulled that rope.

I remember one time we heared an awful noise down in the potato patch. I was the leader, so I said, "Now you little ones stay back and I'll go see what it is." It made the awfullest noise. I got down there and it was a snake a-swallowing a frog. Oh, he was making the peculiarest noise ever, and I hollered and told the kids that it was just a snake, not something that'd hurt us 'cause we could kill it with rocks.

I never was scared of snakes. I tried to kill every one that I'd see and I've killed a lot of them. I've lived places where they was real bad snakes. I remember one time we went to the graveyard to see a grave and coming back they was a copperhead snake going across the road. Well, it was just before it got dark and they'll shine, just like brass, and the kids got out to kill it, but they didn't kill it, and I just got out and picked up a rock and throwed it and knocked its head square off its shoulders.

I've said a lot about what we did, but we wasn't always working or playing at home. We went to school. We didn't go but three or four months a year. That was the longest term we'd have. Sometimes we'd take two months in the fall and then two more months in the spring. When it got too cold, we'd stay at home. I always loved school.

I Plowed with an Old Red Steer and a Wooden Plow When I Was Nine Years Old

Interview with Ernie Hough, Lebanon, Missouri, June 28, 1977.

I lived right down the river from Orla about a mile and a half. I lived on a farm of two hundred acres. It would have been a farm when we got it cleared. We had an upland farm and then we had a farm on the river, too. They was about one-half mile apart. We growed everything there—wheat, corn, oats, just about everything you wanted to raise.

Now I know, or I think I do, that I would be the only one in Lebanon that ever plowed corn with a steer. My neighbor got behind with his work, and I was big enough to plow, eight or nine years old. My dad told me to go over there and help him. I plowed with an old red steer and a wooden plow. They was an iron bolt come up from the foot piece of the plow and through the beam. Then the shovel on it was iron and the rest of it was all wood. Everyone had horses then and they had horse collars, harness and everything like that. We put a horse collar on this old steer and a set of old chain harnesses. Of course, they had to be upside down. And then I had a halter on him and rope tied on each side for driving reins. If he wouldn't go where I wanted him to go, I'd have to pull him around with the rope and when I wanted him to do anything, I'd say "gee" or "haw." If I said "gee" he turned to the right. If I said "haw" he turned to the left. I plowed corn with that old steer, and I bet you ain't nobody else ever done that.

I never lived too many different places. I lived at home from the time I was born on July 2, 1882, 'till I was twenty-three years old. We had an eighteen-foot-square log house and a kitchen. We carried our water from a spring for drinking, cooking purposes, and all. We didn't have no baths and running water and stuff like they have now. All the running water we had was a branch of the spring running down. But we had a good spring. And we had a house over the spring where we'd keep our milk and stuff.

But then later we had a well drilled up close to the house. We didn't

"Now I'll tell you about some of my boyhood stuff."
—Ernie Hough.

use the spring very much after we did. We used the well water to water our stock. We had horses in the barn and we'd put a hand pump in that well and we'd pump the water in a water trough for the stock to drink.

Now I'll tell you about some of my boyhood stuff. We'd camp out and we'd go hunting. A whole bunch of us would get out in the woods. We'd have our dogs and maybe we'd tree a possum or something like that. We'd build up a fire and cook eggs—have a big meal.

Of a night most of what we'd catch would be possum. Some coon, but possum was what we was hunting for. Skunk, we didn't mess too much with the skunks.

I like to hunt coons, but if you didn't have a real good dog that understood what he was doing it never was very much fun. He never would get one of them up a tree. Most of the dogs would get a coon's trail and trail it and bark, and Mr. Coon, he stayed ahead of that all the time. But if we had what we called a silent-mouthed dog, when he got on the track he never barked, only went just as fast as he could and first thing you knowed he was right on that coon and the coon didn't know he was there. He wouldn't go too far and we'd never find him till he caught that coon. Maybe he'd be a fighting it and we'd get there and see the coon and dog fight. It took lots of dogs. The dogs had to understand what they was doing or they couldn't kill a coon.

There was lots of wildlife. You had to watch that nothing got the chickens. The foxes wasn't too mean about that, but owls—there used to be a lot of those night owls. If they found a chicken around there they'd catch it and carry it off. You'd have to watch about them more than fox and mink.

We had minks along the river and they'd come up to our place. One night we had an old hen and two chickens with her on the roost. That blooming mink came up there and killed every one of them there chickens and a turkey. When they got into your chickens they just see how many they can kill. We never trapped for them, but we finally got the dogs after them. They'd tree and we killed them. They're not too big. They're kind of slim.

It wasn't all work. We had lots of entertainment, more than you'd imagine. I'll say I'd be, oh from fifteen on up when I went to parties. We'd have play parties and I don't hardly know how to tell you how they played them, but anyhow, we never danced or nothing like that. When we had a dance, we wouldn't do nothing but dance. But at a play party we didn't dance—we sang the singing games. We had quite a lot of fun.

I'm going to ask if you know anything about candy breaking? We got different colors of stick candy. We'd break that in two and put them in a dishpan. We'd cover them up and you would get somebody to draw candy with you. The one that you had chosen would reach in there and get a stick. If you didn't match her, well that was it, but if you reached in and got a piece that matched her candy, you got to give her a nice sweet kiss and squeeze her around. It was fun.

We used to have box suppers and then we would have a cake for the best looking girl. The men and boys would put up some money as votes for the girls. Usually two would run against one another. Everyone would take sides with a penny a vote. The girl that had the most money got the cake.

I worked in a country store when I was a young kid and saved my money. I bought me a buggy, and we had a good matched team. I could go get these gals where some of the others couldn't. I had a team and buggy and the storekeeper's son had a buggy and team, and we was about the only two who did.

I think religious training is important. I sure do. It's very important. The way you're raised and taught up to about fifteen or sixteen years old, that's the way you will generally go. If you're living in a family of religious people, you will be too, just as sure as night. Of this I am certain.

My folks trained us kids—taught us to be religious. My folks are all religious but very few I knew that wasn't. Of course, we didn't have no big fancy churches like they got now, and I don't think we needed them. They'd make a church out of brush—brush arbor they called it. They'd meet in August. They'd have a camp meeting and they'd go there and stay—just bring their food and stay there for several days at a time. And boy, of all the shouting you've ever heard in the world, it was done. They had big times. Of course, they don't do that now and some say it's better, but I don't know that it is. I like to hear people sing and shout. They'd call young people up to what they called the Mourners' Bench—they don't never have that anymore. And they'd pray and sing with them. And they'd pray for themselves, and maybe they'd be two or three, three or four of them converted. And I think that ought to be more than what is now.

Back when I was a boy all those old folks, their word was their money. When they told you something you could depend on it completely. Don't you think now that some folks will tell you something and kind of get a little of the advantage on you and then don't do what they tell you? I don't think people is more so dishonest than they used to be, but there weren't as many people as there is now. Back when I was a little boy the population was pretty thin. People all knew one another a whole lot better than they do now. And you knew people from farther around. Lots of people live here now, or maybe in a little larger town, and they don't even know who their next door neighbor is. Well, it wasn't that away back when I was a youth.

But most folks now I think is pretty honest. And all the young folks growing up here like you are now, I think, well I just think so much of them I don't know what. Just to see them strive so much to get ahead. I like to see young folks out marching with their bands. I think that's wonderful. I sure do. And of course, there is a few bad young folks, but not any more than they always was. They was a few that was just a little unruly it don't make any difference how far back you go. I think, considering everything, we have got a good element of young people. I sure do. I think they're just tops.

I Used to Hunt and Fish An Awful Lot

Interviews with Homer Massey, Lebanon, Missouri, May–July, 1978.

Many of us are fortunate enough to have grandparents to recreate for us their childhood days. I listened for hours to my grandfather, Homer Massey, tell of his growing up on a river farm the oldest of two sisters and two brothers. — Vickie Massey

I don't know where or when I was born. I was there, but I can't remember anything, but I'm satisfied I was there. I tell people I am like Abe Lincoln. I was born in a log cabin and still live in a house that was built before the Civil War. I was born near Orla, Missouri, on September 5, 1907. Georgia Beard Massey and Walter Massey were my parents.

There were five of us kids in the family. Arthur and I worked together all the time, but Ralph was younger. Isabell and Gladys was both girls. Gladys never did work out much and helped Mother a lot. Isabell was a tomboy. She was everywhere doing nothing.

We had to raise our own living then, and nearly everybody would have a milk cow or two milk cows and make a big garden and have a bunch of chickens. Everybody in our family had a flock of chickens. We milked several cows but we did it different then than now. We didn't have what you'd call dairy cows. They were shorthorn—red polled cows and something like that. Most people wouldn't have no big dairy herd, but they'd milk all the way from seven to eight to a dozen cows. They'd let the calf nurse, depending on how hard up they were, enough until the cow would give the milk down. They'd milk that, separate it, feeding the milk to the pigs. We either sold butter or sold cream—sour cream.

One of the big things they had back then was a bunch of turkeys to pay the taxes with. A forty-acre farm would have three or four turkey hens and raise twenty-five or forty turkeys.

I went to grade school at a rural school known a Stony Point, and it lived up to its name. At Stony Point there wasn't any outhouses.

"When I was a kid, our family never went to town more than three or four times a year."—Homer Massey.

It was on top of a hill. The girls went down on one side of the hill and the boys went down on the other. We never peeked—we got shot for that. Well water was what we drank. We drawed it up with a bucket and a rope. When I first started school one dipper did for everyone, and then they got particular and in three or four years everybody had to have his own drinking cup. They had these little folding cups then, and we'd dip it out with the dipper and pour it out in a cup so everyone wouldn't be drinking out of the same dipper.

We took our lunches. Our mothers would fix them. Later it got where we could buy lunch pails, but then it would either be a gallon syrup bucket or a zinc bucket. Mother'd put a paper down in it and the lunch down in it and put a dishcloth over the top of it. Most all of the lunches was fat meat and biscuits and a glass with butter and molasses in it, and you'd stir them up.

Ed Simpson owned the land where the school was located. The school property was fenced off with a rail fence, but it rotted down. His hogs—he didn't feed them too good—learned that the kids would throw scraps and things out up there. Once in a while the kids would come to school, and the others would be playing ball or something. They'd be in a hurry when they got there to get into the ball game, and they'd set their lunch down there under some big hickory trees close to home plate. Once in a while when somebody'd set their dinner down there, Ed's old sows would get it and eat it up. Kids was pretty good, they'd chip in and all of them eat together. They'd spread the dishcloth out and everybody's eat what they had.

All the year till frost everybody went barefooted to school. We just had two pair of shoes a year. Get a pair in the winter and then in the spring of the year when they got kinda ragged we got a pair of what they called Sunday shoes to wear through the summer.

I don't ever remember my dad taking us to school the whole eight years I went, and we had a mile and a half and a river to cross. It was hard to cross the river in the winter the first three or four years up until 1915. The first three years I went to school we had a footlog that we had to walk. It was a big sycamore log hooked to another tree on the other side with a log chain. They had a two-by-four up on the side of it and a cable run through them so we could walk that log. Once in a while one of us would slip off of it. I remember falling off of it into the river one winter and it was real cold, too. But it was over a riffle, so the water wasn't too deep. In '15 they build a swinging foot bridge. It landed on top of a bluff on one side and had high posts on the other end. Two big cables held the welded wire sides and a bottom. There were boards on the bottom to walk across on.

Many times the roads would be muddy and bad. As far as we lived from town [seventeen miles] in the wintertime Dad and Mom would come into town at Christmas to do Christmas shopping and pay taxes, and they may not be back in Lebanon until way in the spring. In the wintertime when people would go to town to keep their feet warm some would take their dog and tie him in the wagon. Then they'd put a quilt around him and their feet. Others would use heated rocks in the wagon to keep their feet warm. When I was a kid our family never went to town more than three or four times a year. As a kid, I probably never went to town but once a year. My parents had to buy salt and some of the supplies we'd need that the rural store didn't carry. It'd all come in barrels. The rural store didn't carry a very big inventory— just the necessities of life—rope, pulleys and buckets, and everyday clothing. There wasn't a big variety of that. When they went to town, they'd take maybe a load of wheat in to sell, but a lot of people took their own wheat to the mill to make flour. We had those little old grist mills out in the country. They would have a post office at every one.

All the flour mills were located on the streams where they had water power.

The men wore overalls and blue denim jumpers for jackets. The women would probably knit a wool sweater to go under it. I remember when I was a kid at home mother knit all of our socks and gloves and all of our sweaters. All the women wore a great big long dress that came down to their ankles. It was usually heavy cloth. They had calico, gingham, and cotton cloth they made their dresses from. Always a split bonnet in the summer to keep the sun off to keep them from getting sunburned. It would have been a disgrace for a woman to have been out in a pair of pants.

Of course, most of the time your transportation was pretty well horseback or buggy. Lots of women rode horseback, but they rode a side saddle. They had the old-time fox-trotting horses. All the better farmers had two things — a good stock dog and a traveling horse. There were horses that could carry a forty-pound saddle and a two-hundred-pound man ten hours a day on any kind of road.

In the fall of the year all of the better farmers would have a set of ice shoes set up for their saddle horse and usually a set for one team. If there came a big ice, then they could drive them and get around. The shoes were just like the common horseshoe only where the toe turns down they'd make it longer and sharpen it. The blacksmith would heat it and beat it out to a point. All the horseshoes were made different than they are now. They had a heavy cork and a heavy toe on them. The men that rode regular usually shod those horses and in three or four weeks, they'd have them reset and let them wear them another three or four weeks before they had to have a new set on them. But six to eight weeks was about as long as them "using" horseshoes would last.

We worked hard but we had fun too. We hunted and fished, played baseball. In the summertime, baseball and swimming, and there would be areas there at the river or creek or ponds, and we'd gather there and swim. Baseball was one of the biggest athletic games.

I used to hunt and fish an awful lot. Back in the early days we didn't have any game laws, though we did have hunting and trapping seasons. In fishing, anything was legal back in the thirties all the time. Trapping was the way the kids got their spending money. They'd set rabbit gums [homemade wooden, box-like baited traps with trapdoors to catch live rabbits]. There were times, some of the better times, in cold weather, when those rabbits would bring about a quarter apiece, but most of the time they were about a nickel or a dime. We had a world of rabbits. It wasn't anything to have fifteen or twenty rabbit gums and catch eight or ten rabbits overnight in them. Mink and muskrat fur was high. The first mink I ever caught in a trap was about 1918. Dad shipped this mink hide in a bundle of furs he and Uncle Arnett had, and the pelt brought forty dollars—almost the value of two cows! That was the biggest mink I have ever seen in my life.

They'd have parties and lots of square dances. Some of those boys could really dance a tune, too. I didn't think there was a joint left in them. They'd have house raisings and husking bees. That was where they'd get in and help someone build a new house and they'd help a guy get his shock fodder out.

People would get together in revivals, too. Morgan church was Baptist and Fairview was Methodist. They'd have their big revivals and instead of being a week like they are now, they'd run two or three weeks, and they'd have church usually in the morning and then at night—two sermons a day. They usually got a pretty good turnout.

They'd have a few annual picnics that'd last for a week. It was kind of a homecoming for people who had left home. They'd come home for that annual picnic and some of them would even take wagons and tents and stay around the picnic a week at a time and camp and cook. They called them celebrations. Stoutland would have one, Lebanon would have one. Bennett Spring would have one.

At the celebrations there was lots of drinking and fighting. If people had a grudge there's where they always went to settle them. I remember a picnic at Smittle Cave on the Fourth of July. That morning Dad was binding oats and we got through about ten-thirty or eleven. Mom got an early dinner. I saddled my horse up and when I rode up, I never got off my horse. I must have sat there on him for forty-five minutes—the reason I stayed on him was because the crowds was ganged up. I watched four fights before I ever got off and tied my horse up. I said they would fight to settle an old grudge. If some feller's hogs had been eating your corn up and you hadn't fixed your fence, you got on to him because his hogs eat your corn up. Whichever was the best man whipped the other one.

Back in the twenties they began to get radios. When I graduated from high school, we had to have head phones to listen to one. Uncle Arnett got the first radio I can remember. That was before we got electricity—it run off a battery. He got it in the fall, and that winter every Saturday night it was about like going to a big picture show. Everybody gathered in his house to listen to the radio. They'd sit around and drink black coffee and smoke home-grown tobacco. It would get so thick that you couldn't cut the smoke or breathe either. Never heard tell of cigarettes then. Everybody would go.

Although crime existed, the reasons for it and the types were very different from those of today. Many people marked their property very well, or locked it up to prevent temptation.

Nearly everything had a mark or a brand on it—hogs and cattle both. Back then when they had free range you had to fence against the stock. If you put out a corn crop and somebody's hogs started getting in it, it was your responsibility to fence his hogs out instead of him taking care of them. In the spring of the year a lot of people would brand their cattle and put a bell on two or three old gentle ones. Then they'd just turn them out in the woods and let them go. Maybe there'd be some big spring or river or a natural pond—they didn't have ponds for them to go to water then. Wherever they were getting water, the owner would go over and put out salt. Sometimes they'd turn them out and never see them anymore either. Stealing would be as bad as it would be now. People more or less knew everybody's brand. When they gathered these cattle up in the fall come feed time, it'd maybe be six or seven miles from home, but if one of my cows or one of my steers was over in someone else's area, they'd lot it and call me and tell me.

'Course stealing in that day and time was different than now. Now they'll steal automobiles and gas and other parts of cars, but back then the biggest things they stole was either chickens or meat or grain. If you stole any kind of chicken after dark it was a penitentiary offense. I forget how many chickens you had to get in daylight before it was a penitentiary offense! What made meat such a terrible thing was we had to butcher all our meat in the winter time and cure it, enough to run till the next winter. Lots of families, especially in what you might term the poorer families, wouldn't have hogs enough to run them till the next year. Nearly everyone had a lock on his smokehouse. If they couldn't get that then they'd steal chickens. If they had some chickens or a sow and some pigs and nothing to feed them, they'd steal grain to feed them.

Youngsters were given much responsibility at young ages. My uncle Arthur and grandfather shared a lucrative hog business when they were still quite young.

It was in 1916 when Grandpa Massey gave me a registered Poland China gilt, and I haven't been out of hogs since. There have been two different times when the cholera got me down to where I just had one old sow live through it. At that time he gave me one and Arthur one. The first litter of hogs I raised I took to Morgan and sold to Fred

Indermuehle, who was a shipper out of Morgan to St. Louis. I believe it was ten pigs I raised, and since we did the milking, Dad gave us the milk to feed to our hogs. We sold them to Fred for twelve cents a pound, but they brought us almost two hundred dollars. We thought we was rich!

Back down this side of Morgan about a mile and a half there was an old man by the name of Frank Smith. On our way there we saw an awful pretty white sow and eight pretty pigs. We talked about buying them. On the way home we asked Frank what he would take, and he said a hundred dollars. So we bought her and the pigs. The other sow hadn't farrowed yet, and since we were milking the cows, we had plenty to feed her with, but when the other sow farrowed, we didn't have enough to feed all of them. Dad told us, "By jove, you boys are getting so many hogs around here you're going to have to buy your feed." We done a lot of slopping. We went to buying shorts [a ground wheat product] and mixed them with the milk. When we got ready to sell them hogs, both litters, the hog market kind of broke. We got just about two-thirds as much a head on them as the others had. Both litters brought about three hundred dollars where that other litter had brought us around two hundred dollars. We didn't get rich quite so fast in the hog business once we had to go to buying shorts.

To live then everyone pitched in and helped one another with necessary chores. Be it the family or the neighborhood, the tasks had to be done so the people wouldn't starve. The work may have been a little hard and tedious, but once winter hit, no one regretted their varied summer or fall labors. According to Grandpa, no one who put forth an effort to survive ever starved—his neighbors wouldn't let him.

In the fall of the year when we'd butcher a beef, there was no way to keep it, and so then we'd go out and peddle it out among the neighborhood before it would spoil. Some would butcher a hog in the summertime. They called that pickling it. They'd cut up the meat and put it in fifteen or twenty gallon stone jars full of real hot brine. That's about the only way to keep it. Before they got ready to use it, they would have to soak the meat to take the brine off.

We raised all our beans. We used to pick them in a sack and keep them around the house. Us kids would play with the sacks of beans and that would wear a lot of them out of the hull. They lay around for two months there until they were wallered out of the hulls. Then we'd take them outside on a real windy day and throw that sack up to let the beans out and the hulls would blow out. Then we'd pick the beans up. We didn't have gunny sacks. They were nearly all big cotton sacks—heavy cloth—even heavier than denim. They called them grain sacks, and they'd hold two to three bushel. It would be nothing for a family to have two of them big grain sacks full of dried beans.

We also raised our potatoes. A lot of people didn't have cellars or anything to keep them in, so they buried them. They buried apples and cabbage. They'd dig a trench and poke the cabbage down and leave the root sticking out and cover it with dirt. Apples would be put down in a pile of straw. Take maybe a half a load of apples and start dumping them in a pile. When they got what apples they had to go in one pile, they'd cover that with straw real deep and then they'd cover all that with dirt maybe six or eight inches deep. Then they'd set a shock of fodder around that dirt. In the winter when we got ready for a bucket of apples, we'd dig a hole in to where these apples were and run our arm back in there and get a bucket of apples, or potatoes, the same way. We had dried peaches and dried apples besides what we'd can.

Dad used to have a big cane patch, but the neighbors would come in when it was time to strip it to make cane molasses. They'd maybe come and work all week stripping cane for a gallon of molasses a day. They used it for sugar to make cookies, cakes, candy. One of the parties we had was to have a molasses candy pull.

A lot of people raised tobacco. Dad raised a tobacco patch nearly every year. He didn't even use tobacco, but he'd sell it.

A big percent of the corn was shocked back then because they had to have the fodder for roughage to get the stock through the winter. It would take us all winter to get it out, because when it was warm and dry, we couldn't handle it because all the leaves would break off. It needed to be in case [tough]—froze or damp. Old man Schneider, a German, said that was the worst trouble with the people in the Ozarks—they'd work all fall to get their fodder cut and put in a shock and they wore the fodder out getting the corn off to save it for the winter! He just fed his stock the whole stalk, grain and all, to save time and labor.

Wheat was drilled like it is today, only the equipment was a durn sight smaller. In that day and time there was more wheat growing than there is now. Once in a while there would be some old-timer who would cut some with a cradle, but most of them had binders that would tie it in bundles and then they'd shock it. Actually we drilled more wheat back then than they do now because it took less labor than corn. The demand for wheat for flour for human consumption was more. The yield wasn't very high, averaging ten or fifteen bushels an acre.

Attending high school was difficult for rural kids. Often they had to move to town, going home when it was possible. Such was my grandfather's lot.

There was only fifty-four in our graduating class. Half of them were residents of Lebanon. There were only about twenty-seven or twenty-eight of us rural kids. Some would work for their room. All four years I went to school I shared a room and we done our own cooking. I believe we had to pay four dollars a month. We had to do our own laundry, too, if we couldn't get back home. They just furnished a room. We even had to furnish our own furniture, our bed and stove, table and chairs, a work table. Anyhow there was four upstairs rooms and there were eight of us boys up there. Each pair lived in their own room with a separate kitchen, with a gas stove. All the electrical equipment we had was just the lights. No electric skillets or coffee pots or anything like that. We'd take the majority of our food from home. In the wintertime the roads would get bad, and sometimes we wouldn't even get to go home for three weeks. There were times when it would be two or three weeks—I'd run out of money and groceries both and walk home. There were several of us from our neighborhood in high school, so someone from home would manage some way to take us back in to school. If just one of us got back home, he took back groceries for all of us.

To pay for their room and board most students had to have a part-time job. The first three years I worked in the school library. We had to pay our own tuition then. At that time it was four dollars a month. The class day had eight, forty-five-minute periods. Ordinarily we only had four courses and were supposed to have four study periods. Most of the time there were four of us working in the library and we worked two periods a day for our tuition. I also worked a Roy Davis's, a grocery store where I delivered. The better grocery stores that day and time nearly all delivered groceries there in town. Roy had a hack and a pair of little western gray ponies. I'd work on Saturday and after school. At that time I knew where about everybody in town lived.

Another job I had with the school, we'd take chalk dust—I don't know what it was, a white powder—and stir it up with water. We'd go to town and paint the sidewalks instead of putting out pamphlets like they do now. We'd paint signs on the walks at crossings—Lebanon versus Crocker in basketball or baseball or whatever activity it was.

Grandpa took a test to qualify him to teach after graduation from high school and a summer of college. He continued teaching for several years before he had any more college.

I taught my first school at Stony Point—sixty-five dollars a month and I done the janitorial work. When school started I was eighteen and taught six or eight that were up, I'd say twenty or twenty-one. The older ones would come back to school—they wouldn't take what you'd call a full course. The only thing the boys studied was mathematics. We had one of the old-time math books called *Milnies Math*. There were two books of it, a lower grade and an upper grade. The upper grade started back with about what children nowadays would do in their seventh grade, and it'd go plum through high school—geometry, trigonometry and so on. Probably not as deep and detailed as it is now, but it covered all the fundamentals. Most of those kids would come only until they finished the book. A lot of times they'd start when school started and maybe they'd get through it in three or four months. Then they'd drop out. The rural school was much larger than what they are now because there were so many people in the rural area. I taught both my sisters, Gladys and Isabell. I had all three of my own children—Robert, J. W. and Thelma. Your dad [Don] went to half of his school with his mother. They were just the same as the others. They weren't any more problems.

I taught school long enough to have three generations of four families. In thirty-five years I only had two parents come on me because of their children. When they came to make their complaints, I told them I had a certificate to teach school and I had a contract to teach that school, and if they were going to teach it, for them to get a certificate and a contract and they could have the job. I was never bothered with either one of them anymore. For thirty-five years school teaching was my vocation and farming was my avocation. Now then it is strictly farming.

In the meantime, while I was teaching rural schools, the Thirties Depression hit. I was teaching school and one year I taught I was supposed to get eighty-five dollars a month, but I only got thirty because people couldn't pay their taxes. I got the warrants, but I never could get them cashed because they couldn't pay the next year's money out on back debts. They had to keep it to operate on. Since they didn't get enough money that year to pay it, I lost it.

I Must Have Been a Little Bit of a Tomboy

Interviews with Katie Lowry, Lebanon, Missouri, November 2, 23, 1976; January 25, 1977.

I remember the little things. I can remember when I was a little girl and my dad was clearing some trees out of the yard. He fastened a chain on a log and was dragging it in. I guess I must have been a little bit of a tomboy, 'cause I was with him an awful lot and I thought to myself that would just be a good thing to ride on. I was sitting on that log just having a good ride. He happened to see me and I never will forget what he said. "Doggone you little fool! That will roll over and kill you." Oh, that was funny. Those words I never will forget.

Did I tell you about the time I got on a two-year-old horse my dad had? Well, I wanted to ride it so bad, but no, they wouldn't let me. They didn't know it, but I got it and I rode it around in the enclosure around the barn. Then I persuaded my brother to help me. He was ten and I was fifteen. I told him, "Let's tie a rope around its neck and you lead it." We went to the back side of Dad's forty acres. My brother was deathly afraid of a horse, I don't know why. I wasn't. Well, it just went fine going down there. Then coming back, why the silly thing started to trot and that scared my brother. He turned loose of it. The nearer the horse got to the house, the faster it went. Mom and Dad were still at the dinner table where they could look out the window. Just as the horse got in front of the window, it started to turn and off I went. Oh, they thought I was killed, but it didn't hurt me. I would have gotten on it again. It looks like I still like to ride most anything. Ricky, one of my great-grandchildren, took me for a ride on his motorcycle two years ago. I lived over on the hill at that time. Rick came over on his Honda and he said, "Grandma, how about you riding over to our house with me?" And I did! That was before I got in this walker.

I was born the tenth of March in 1894. My mother and father were raised in Hamburg, Germany. My father must have been eigh-

"I remember the little things about growing up."—Katie Lowry.

teen years old when he came over here and worked for the farmers in Iowa. His father in Germany had a secretary, and that was my mother. One day he said, "Margaret, I wish I had a picture of you from the shoulder up for my birthday. She had it made and what did he do? He sent it over here to my father and said, "This is the girl I want you to marry."

After that my dad went back to Germany. I guess he was there about eight months when they got married and come to America. Momma had one of those bright, shiny pianos she sold to make the trip. She thought she would see Indians and excitement. But she said it wasn't so exciting on that boat. When they came across, it was so stormy my dad would tell her, "It'll be all right, it will pass." But he had to tie her in the bed to keep her from falling out. And sick, oh, she said she was sick.

But they came over here, and in a year or so they found out I was on the way. So they went back to Germany and that's where I

"I always just think what's to be will be, and what the future holds, we cannot see."—Katie Lowry.

was born, in Hamburg. Then they came back over here and finally stayed.

I think I'm pretty dumb because I don't remember the German language, although I couldn't talk English until I was seven. I can count in it to fifteen. I didn't forget that—ein, zwei, drei, vier, funf, sechs, sieben, acht, neun, heute, elf, zwolf—something like that. But that's all. I don't remember the letters.

My mother already knew the English language when she came over here, as well as French and German. My dad really didn't learn English till he came to this country. I don't think he learned it in school in Germany like Momma did because he got better all the time. He was kind of Dutchy. The young folks used to laugh just to hear him talk.

My father brought my mother to the farm—a little farm he had rented up north. She was so afraid of chickens that my dad had to set the old hens because, as she called it, they tried to bite her. Finally, when she did get used to the chickens, she had a nice bunch of white pullets. One morning they all lay on the ground, for a weasel had cut their throats and sucked their blood—they won't eat the carcass. Another time my dad had a cornfield that come up close to the house. Momma had an old hen and a bunch of little chickens that would run around the cornfield. Then one night they just didn't come back. Something had caught them. Things like that Momma had to put up with and she didn't know much about it. She had a lot to learn.

When we came down to this part of the country my father had started to Arkansas because he had a good friend there who said, "Land is cheap and it's good, but it's a little hilly." My dad fixed up a covered wagon. That's the way we started out.

I must have been about three and a half or four years old, and I can kind of remember that because I was afraid they would lose my dog. I thought so much of my dog because my dad made him a little dog house. My mother would put a quilt over it. I'd ride that old house and pretend like my dog was my horse. I don't know what made me like horses so well.

Anyway, I can remember that they got as far as Lathrop, Missouri, where we stopped with some people who were German, too, and you can't imagine how nice they were. They let my dad put his team in their barn and invited us in the house. They put me in a little bed that had slats kind of like the little beds they make now and I remember sleeping there. I remember they had pancakes, bacon, and molasses for breakfast. Then they told my dad why didn't he just go on and get settled and they'd send me and Momma on a train.

He got as far as Lebanon, where he met a man who told him, "You don't want to go to Arkansas. I can sell you a farm lots cheaper than you can find down there. It's nothing but hills down there." So my dad took his word for it.

Momma and I got on a train and those people we were staying with didn't have no children and they wanted to keep me. They said they was well-to-do. That was an unreasonable request, but anyway I can remember that I just hung to Momma's coat.

I remember riding on that train. I was scared to death. If I remember right you could look down in that toilet stool and see the tracks. The people could drop diapers or anything right on the tracks!

The little place my dad bought was so poor, it wouldn't raise beans. It was in the Dry and Dusty area. It had the right name! I hated dust. I hated dust on my feet and on my hands. I thought when I get married, how in the world will I ever stand flour on my hands? That is true. That's what I thought. But I soon got over that, because I helped Dad plant potatoes. He was so particular. You know how they cut potatoes up? Each piece has to have one or two eyes for sure. He would have me to stoop down and put each cut piece down so they come right up. Of course my hands got dusty doing that, but I thought, I'll fix that. I'll just spit on my hands. And I made it worse! That's just some of the little experiences of growing up.

My dad had a lot of rabbit traps and he taught me how to kill a rabbit caught in a trap. He said, "Now you just take hold of that rabbit's hind feet. Take him out and when you get to his head, just knock him on the back of the head." Oh, I just simply thought I couldn't. One day I went down there and it wasn't a rabbit. I reached in there and it felt different, so I ran to the house and told him I thought maybe it was a young bear. I guess he didn't know what it was, but it was a possum. Anyway he shot that thing in the trap. He wouldn't pull it out while it was alive. Then he took me over to some people that lived pretty close and asked them what it was. They told him, and they told him it was good to eat. Why, he told them they could have it. He wouldn't eat it himself.

When we lived in the Dry and Dusty area, we lived by a dirt road—the Springfield Road. Now it's called 66 or I-44. The first thing I can remember was a man with a monkey and a little grinder. He'd have that as a little act and we'd give him, not much because we didn't have much in those days.

I think I'd went to Dry and Dusty school two years when my dad bought a farm on the other side of Lebanon. We always said that it was just like moving to another state for the soil was so different, so much better.

When we first moved to that place I always felt sort of haunted. Right down the hill from the house, the people who owned it before us had dug a well eighty feet deep and they had to go around boulders. The next day they let their son down in that place with a sort of wheel. But during the night the well had formed a gas and when he got down so far he passed out and fell on down. He'd hit one boulder, then the other when he fell. It killed him. Then to get the body out they had to find somebody that would go down there. They started to let one man down, but he jerked the rope and wanted them to take him back out. He was passing out. But there was an old man who offered to go. He went down there and tied that body to the box and brought him out.

They filled the well up after that, but all the time we lived there that spot would always sink down. Then my dad would put on more rocks and stuff and fill it. I can still see where it was. Every time I looked down there I felt haunted.

I was blessed with a good mother. My father was good to me, too. I always helped him saw wood and helped him stack hay. My dad was afraid of height. Momma told him one time, "You're just a coward to put that child up there to stack that hay." But he'd tell me just how. I was just a little bit afraid. I didn't much like it. But he would always talk so nice how I always helped him and so forth and so on, so I didn't want to disappoint him. I helped him do things like that.

I'll say he thought I was pretty fine, too. I don't know you girls, your religion or anything. I know you believe there's a God, which I do. I'm a Christian, but I remember after I was married when Hugh and I went to a tabernacle meeting and were converted. My father-in-law was a Christian and always taught in Sunday School. Now my dad never did believe, I'm sorry to say. When my father-in-law met my dad he told him about our being converted. My dad told him in his German way, "She was always good. She didn't have to get any better." Wasn't that something nice for a father to say about his daughter?

We had a neighbor who I really didn't like, but she hired me to help her before I got married. Twenty-five cents I would get a day. But a man only got a dollar a day in those days, and with a team he got two dollars. In those days they would make rows of corn three foot apart, then crossways four foot apart. Each cross place was where you planted corn by hand. She hired me to plant corn for her. I dropped it, just two in a place. I guess I overlooked it but there was three kernels in one place. And you know, she made me come back and pick up that extra grain of corn!

I would also help her with the bees. She had fifty hives of bees and a row of peach trees. I used the smoker. She would fix me up with some of the boys' old pants and tie them tight around my legs and I had a hat with screens.

The smoker looked like a tin can, but it run to a small point where there was a little hole. They'd fill that full of rags. Those rags were not supposed to blaze. They would just kind of smolder and make smoke. There was a thing underneath you would kind of pump and somehow or other it'd make a terrible smoke. The bees just couldn't stand it.

She was supposed to give me half a gallon of honey for doing that. I'll tell you why I didn't like her. I just loved honey. There was a knife laying there and I took just a little dab of honey and ate it. She looked at me and she said, "I'll give you your honey." She bawled me out.

Another time I took my little sister with me over there. On the way home there was a mud puddle. You know how water stands in tracks? There were little pollywogs there. Some of the pollywogs had their legs and I was trying to explain to her that they would finally be big frogs. So later that old woman told Momma that she ought to teach us to come right on home and not be fooling around along the road. She didn't know that it was all right with Momma. You know I just couldn't hardly stand to look at her. After I married I had an old pet hen that I named Meely because that was what we called that old woman and the hen actually favored her. That's part of growing up, really.

When You Work Together It Works Out Pretty Good

I Married a Farmer and, Oh, It Was Rough

Interviews with Katie Lowry, Continued

I was almost seventeen when I married. I decided maybe that would be the best. And I guess it was, in the long run. I've ended up with a wonderful family. Hugh, my husband, was always good to the children. He was good to help me with them, dress the little ones, and get them ready for breakfast. You just think of the good things when you get older. We had our disputes too, but they didn't amount to anything, really.

We had three children. The little one who is the baby, she was born in 1928. My other daughter was born in 1921. And my son was born in 1913. So he's way up there. Poor guy. I just think he looks like an old man. I have five grandchildren and nine great-grandchildren.

I married a farmer and oh, it was rough. I've helped my husband saw wood rather than for him to hire someone and have to pay them back. And I'd help him in the hay—I didn't mind it. I was used to it, for I helped my dad like that. But I had always said when I was growing up that I'd never marry a farmer. But you get ambitious, and when you work together it works out pretty good.

When I met Hugh, well, I claimed boys and they claimed me before then, but we had been to a Christmas program and Hugh asked me for a date. I hadn't ever been anywhere, because my folks didn't like for me to tag along with other couples. Hugh and I kept company until that fall on the twenty-third of November we were married. Let me see, is today the twenty-third? What do you know! Today's my wedding anniversary. If my husband had lived we would have been married sixty-six years today.

Hugh had two sisters. When we was going to get married one of them and her husband was going to go with us to stand up with

173

us. We had my husband's horses, which were young and frisky—and cold—and a buggy with three seats. My husband and I sat in the front. His sister's little boy was with us and he said, "What are we going to do?" His father said, "Hugh and Katie are going to jump the broomstick." When we got there the preacher performed the ceremony and went through it just like he should. And the little boy said, "Well, Momma, when are they going to jump the broomstick?" Of course, that caused a big laugh. But that was about all there was to that. We drove back and my mother had dinner ready for the whole bunch. Then they had what they called the infare dinner. That was the next day at my husband's home. Everybody was there and that was Thanksgiving.

When I first got married, oh, I was kiddish. It come a big rain and I would pull off my shoes and I'd go down there and wade the water and come back by and pick a green apple and eat it. Grandma Lowry would just swear that I would die. And she said, "You must have a stomach made of iron." I guess I did.

I'll have to say Hugh's mother had to be a pretty good lady to take in a sixteen-year-old girl. But then I did just what she wanted me to do. She would lots of times sit down and tell me about her life. It was interesting. She was something. After we built our little house she thought Floyd, my son, he was a little guy, she thought he was just about it. She about spoilt him rotten. She always had a piece of ham meat for him and she was never too tired to go to the cellar and get him a glass of milk.

We always got along, but I was used to helping at home. My mother-in-law did the cooking. I did the dish washing. I always thought, well when I get to cooking for myself I'd do so and so, but the only thing I knew to cook was apples. My mother had a great big square pan and I would cut those apples that baked real well in two and take the core out so I had a great big square pan filled with those apples. Then I put a little water in the bottom and filled the cavity with butter and sugar and a little cinnamon. Oh, they were so good! I'm going to make some again soon some day. And fry potatoes, I could fry potatoes, oh boy!

But my mother-in-law did all the cooking while we lived with them. She always baked cornbread. She had to be different. Hugh had an unmarried brother that lived at home, also. He and his father wanted thin, crusty cornbread. My husband and his mother wanted thick cornbread. So she had a big square pan that fit in the oven. And she always stirred her cornbread with her hands and she kind of fixed one side of it thick and the other side thin.

My father-in-law wanted what he called red-eye gravy. She would fry ham and then she'd pour the top grease off and put it aside. The goody, you know, the brown part, she would put water in that and make it so it would be kind of red and she put that in a separate bowl. Then my husband and his brother wanted what they'd call white gravy. It would almost stand alone. So then she'd pour the grease back in the pan and she'd make that, too. She was really all right.

When we was first married it was the twenty-third of November, but they were still making molasses. They had a molasses mill. And, of course, you know how people are like that. They get so tired of working at that for maybe several weeks. But I thought it was fun and I would just feed that old molasses mill. They let me do it, and when the juice was all squeezed out, then there was that big molasses pan that had sections. They had some sort of long-handled thing. Maybe you've seen them in pictures. Haven't you? You don't know anything about anything like that? Oh, that's a shame. You've missed it all. It's like a scoop that had an edge to it and a handle. This juice, when it cooks it foams up, and you have to dip that foam off. If you dip enough of it off, why then it will be real clear. Have you ever eaten molasses? Well, you've not missed all of it then.

And also I remember when Hugh would sow grass he would stand in the back of the wagon. They didn't have the things to sow like they do now, the tractors and stuff. But he would stand in the back of the wagon and he had a bag full of seed and a sort of opening in the bottom. They'd turn a wheel and it would just send the seed flying. I'd drive and he'd do that. And I was always afraid he'd fall out.

My mother-in-law was a Christian. When we lived there she wouldn't let nobody play cards, and I had to hide my Finch cards. My husband was just like her. He didn't want me to have them. And I hid them. But he chewed tobacco, though. I knew that before I married him, so I didn't have no reason to fuss at him about it. But, my mother-in-law, oh, I don't think my father-in-law ever took a bite of tobacco that she didn't gripe at him.

I can remember my husband was going to be real nice. He bought a spittoon. He didn't like it because of the way it sounded whenever he'd spit in it. I don't even like to talk about it. Whenever he spit in it, it went plink! So he said, "Well, I'll fix that thing. I'll fill it with ashes." That got soaked full. It got caked down and he couldn't get it out. That old thing sat back where he never touched it. He had to use something else—a bucket. But I couldn't get after him because I knew he had to have it. They can have worse habits. So I always just think, "Well, chewing tobacco isn't the worst thing."

We lived with my husband's folks the first year, almost until October. And oh, it was the coldest, wettest October you ever saw. I remember us trying to move into our little new house. I thought it was a mansion then. It just had a big living room and an addition for a kitchen. And then a front porch and a back ell porch. We thought we were pretty well off.

I spoilt my husband. I would help him plant potatoes. Well, that was no more than right. I would help him dig potatoes because I was afraid he would leave some of them. And when it come to gathering corn off the stalk, he would take two rows and break the corn off. And I could do it just as fast as he could and I could take the down row, too. That's blowing on myself. That's not very nice. I spoilt him and he thought I had to help him with everything. I was ambitious and I went along.

I've lived on a farm all my life. When I was growing up at home I thought, oh, I'll never want to live on a farm because Germans thought children just work. I learned to work and I appreciated it afterwards, but I thought it was terrible. It was my dad's hunger to have a farm. He got sickly then and he had to go to the hospital. You see that so much. People work so hard. My own husband did that. He worked so hard and then something happens and you don't get to enjoy the retirement years in the home.

And that's another story. My husband worked in the hay field in 1936 and he had a sunstroke and he just never was well after that. The children even had to go with him when he went to the field. He was afraid to go by himself because he didn't feel good. In his later years he just didn't get to enjoy his home. That happens to lots of people, even to women.

After my husband passed away I lived there alone for some time. I had a big old shepherd dog. He would bark of a night and all at once he would be still. I couldn't imagine what it was. It scared me. I wondered if someone would maybe hit at him and make him shut up. So I got real brave. I could always use a rifle. I took my rifle and I thought, well, I'm going out there and I'm going to see what's going on. And the dog had a possum on the ground and he would fool around with it. When it would sull he would give it up—he wouldn't bark no more. But just as long as it would fight at him, why he would bark at it.

But I kept a rifle. I said that nobody would scare me. If they got to fooling with the door, Wham! I'd take them. But nobody ever. . . . There was a drunk man came to my house. I seen him coming towards the gate. He kind of acted funny. I always kept my doors hooked.

He rattled on the door and I couldn't understand him. His tongue was thick. I told him, "You must be of a different nationality. I can't understand you." He started out to the gate and then he come back and that scared me. I kept my gun handy and he went around to the back and rattled the back door. He finally left.

I told my son-in-law who lived here about it. He went to town and said that drunk whoever it was, if he fools around there he is going to get into trouble. She keeps a gun. And he just sort of warned them to stay away. That drunk never did come back no more.

I was still living there alone when my eyesight started to get kind of dim. I would buy those little old ten-cent eyeglasses, spectacles, or whatever you want to call them, at the dime store. I would get them just a little stronger and a little stronger until they run out. Then I went to the doctor and he said I was forming cataracts. I went on a little while. I had some kind of magnifying glasses. In 1962 my daughter Eunice took me to Springfield to an eye specialist, and they had to operate and remove the cataracts.

I went back to get the stitches out after so long. The doctor said, "Hold your head back, let me see." He said it kind of rough. Eunice was sitting on the couch, not in the same room, but where she could look in. The doctor was rough when he took those stitches out and I'd grunt, and Eunice fainted. He had to lay his tweezers down and go pick her up and lay her on the couch!

God did make it possible that I could see. I can remember before the operation I couldn't tell a tree from a house. If I can just always do this way and not be bedfast. You know, I've been told that it's a great privilege, but it does make me feel bad to take up the time to get this old. There's just been so many young people taken out of this life that are needed. They have families and it makes me feel bad every time. Ah, well, that's all I got to do now. Just think about all those things and look out at all the pretty things God has made for us. Oh, it's wonderful. It's wonderful I've got that privilege and can see real good.

I lay and count my blessings. My grandson passed through here and said, "Grandma, how are you doing?" I said, "I'm doing fine sitting here counting my blessings." I have more time than anything else. I have to get up at five o'clock as old as I am. The folks say to if I want to eat breakfast with them, and I do want to eat breakfast with them, so I get up.

I wrote to a friend from my school days. I haven't seen her in years, so I told her I would send her a picture. I said I don't look a bit like I did when we used to be together. But that's okay. That goes with life, doesn't it? I've learned to accept it. I just don't worry about anything, only if I think some of the children are sick. That's when I worry. I always just think what's to be will be. And what the future holds, we cannot see.

And I appreciate your coming. I just love company, I love people, and my mother—I guess I'm just like her—she loved people. My dad always was just a little bit distant. I guess it was his brogue difficulty. It's just things you pleasure. I couldn't tell you how much I enjoyed your visit.

I Know What It Is to Work and I Don't Mind It Somebody Had to Do It

Interview with Iva Bradshaw, Continued

My third husband was on the jury and he stayed away at court a week. When he came back he took the measles. He died, and that left me with the two little boys—one just a little over a year old and one a little over three years old. After he died—we had our crop and my oldest boy that was home was thirteen and the other was nine.

Then I had to take my horses myself and go out in the field, but I did. I'd always plowed at home when I was a girl. So I said I could make it. I had a sister that lived close to me. She said, "Sis, what are you going to do with all these children here? How are you going to raise them and make a living for them?" I said, "Well, I'm going to make a living for them, and they're going to eat."

We ever'one worked. All the kids were big enough to work but the two little boys, and my daughter was big enough to take care of the little kids so that I could work. My oldest boy could do a lot of plowing. Then the other boys would come in and help me out with the plow. I tended seventeen acres of farm in one year beside the truck patches. I know what it is to work, but I don't mind working. I enjoyed it.

I remember one time I'd worked all morning putting a beam in a double shovel plow. I'd broke it out. I'd worked all morning to get it fixed up, so that evening me and my oldest son was going to hook up and go out and plow corn. We got out there and the horse got scared and run away. All that was left of the double shovel was the new beam I'd just put in it. And it was split. Half of it was in the ground and half was laying on top. So there was my work all morning for nothing.

Then once the horses started to run off with us before we was in the wagon. We'd plowed with them all day and we thought they was so tired that they wouldn't try to run off, but the dog reared up in front of them when we got to the gate, and they just wheeled and run.

"I was always good and stout. I never hated to do anything."—Iva Bradshaw.

Lester said, "Mom, jump!" So I just jumped out of the wagon and broke my foot. There I was with a broke foot and a crop, so I had to lay low then for awhile. But it soon healed up. Oh, I just had one thing after another like that to happen to me all my life.

Now I've used all machinery to work in the field with, but a wheat binder. I've cut hay. I've cut grass with the cradle and bound it. I had about three acres of good oats and couldn't get nobody to cut them. Ever'body was so busy you couldn't hardly find anyone for a good job, so I just went down and bound them myself with my girl to help me. She stayed with me and she could bind the same as I could. John was eight years old, but he kept the plow, too, same as she would. On the days I'd have to wash, one would drive the horse, the other'd hold the plow.

I've had three houses to burn in my life. Our first house that burned, I don't know how it ever got afire. We wasn't at home when it got burned. The second house that burnt was Ed Bradshaw's. I married him. We lived together six years. He went to build a fire with kerosene and set the house afire, and it burnt him so bad that he lived eleven days and died.

After he died, me and John and his wife bought this house. Or anyway he bought it and I lived in it. I stayed with them about ten years. Then I went back home and stayed at my old home place just over the hill. That was the third house that burnt down. The flue burned out. It was just ready to fall in when I happened to see it. I was washing the dishes by the window. There was snow on the ground and the water was a-melting and coming off and it was red water. I said, "Where's that red water coming from? I guess it's just melting around the flue and is red."

And it seemed my fancy made me go and look anyway, so I just went to the stairway and opened the door, and oh, it was just a-popping and a-cracking upstairs where it had got afire from the flue upstairs. I called to John and said, "John, get over here as quick as you can. My house is afire." It all went down, anyway. That was three years ago.

I don't do very much now. I have pieced no telling how many quilts. I bet I've made five hundred quilts in my life. When my house burnt I had forty-five quilts that I was a-making for my kids and grandkids. It was about the only thing I had of entertaining myself after I got the crop gathered and brought in. Before the boys got grown they helped me get in my stuff. As they got grown, maybe they'd be married, but they'd come in and give me a day's work. We'd work it all in. We got by.

I was also a midwife. I've had lots of experience delivering children. I expect I've delivered two hundred children in my life. I've delivered two still babies and two sets of twins. Sometimes I got paid. Sometimes I didn't. I'd just charge two dollars. They oughtn't have minded to pay me money, but they didn't always. I'd take whatever they gave. I've took secondhand sheet iron for delivering a baby. Yeah. I made them happy, anyway.

One winter there was a shower of babies. I was over at my dad's when my sister was having a baby, and the doctor come and he said to me, 'cause I was handy with sick folks, anyway. "Well," he said, "it looks to me like some of you women is going to have to help me out with so many of these babies here this spring." I said, "Well, I'll do my best." And he said, "I'll see you through it if you'll take over." So I just began. I kept a-getting better and I had more, nearly, than I could do. Busy all the time.

I went down here to Phillipsburg to a place to deliver a baby.

It was snowing and cold and the only way we could see was to get out and warm a toe-sack [gunnysack] on the manifold and melt off a space in the windshield. It took us quite a little while to get down there. The snow was about eight inches deep. They lived right in the timber where there wasn't no roads or anything. When we got there, the baby had already been born, so we had to turn right around and go back the same way we came. I was pretty near all night riding through the snow and timber.

I had to do my own doctoring for my children. I doctored them with pills, black draught—lots of black draught. That's where you use turpentine, kerosene, and skunk grease. I never paid out very much for doctor bills with my kids, for I could doctor them very well myself. If they had a cold, I'd just grease a wool cloth and put on their chest. One of my sons came in one night and he said, "Mom, I'm just a-choking to death with a cold." So I got up then and made me a poultice with the skunk grease, quinine, coal oil and turpentine, and the next morning his whole chest was blistered. I hadn't put in enough grease to keep it from blistering, but quick as that blister came off, it healed up. It was just the first layer of skin. He done all right.

Skunk grease is pretty good medicine, all right. I believe there's just a lot of remedies like that that beats the medicine they have today. In fact, we didn't have the money to pay out very much doctor bills—couldn't afford to have a doctor if I could take care of them. Of course, if it got bad enough, we got the doctor.

I've doctored animals, too. I've cured three horses of fistula. I used bark off a tree for wire cut. You just take the rough bark off and get that inside bark next to the tree, shave it off and put it in a big kettle and boil it to make an ooze out of it. I'd put kerosene and turpentine and salt and things in that and kept bathing his foot in it until it got all right.

I didn't ever have discipline problems with my family. Never had a child to be arrested or never had to go to the law or get them out of trouble or do anything in the world as far as the law is concerned about one of my kids, because I kept them busy when they was small kids and they kind of took up with it pretty good. Idle hands is what causes bad children, don't you think? After they got up big enough where they could work, I kept them at it till they was grown. After they was grown, they'd heared me correct them so much that they sure thought it was the truth. So they stayed with it and I've never had a bit of trouble. They've always been awful good children. They've helped me out in every way that they could, and I've helped them out every way I could, so I've not been amiss.

My best advice to you is to keep on with your work. Today a person can't hardly blame the children—a lot of them—because their parents don't put them out to do the work. They don't have to. They can hire it done with the prices they are getting for their work until the children don't have to do that. And of course, if a child don't have to work—if you don't teach him to—he don't know very much about it. You got to make him get into it. A lot of them are lazy and they'll never get up to do very much. If they know how, it wouldn't be no handicap to them if they ever had to do the work. If my dad hadn't learned me to work, I'd have starved my children to death, because I wouldn't have known how to take over and make a living as a widow woman. I was always good and stout, you know. I never hated to do anything. It didn't make any difference if it was my job, if it fell in my lot, I just took it over and done it, because somebody had to do it. And I said the good Lord took care of us in a lot of places, and when kids are kids, why, they're took care of. Yeah! I think that if the good Lord didn't take care of us, they'd be a lot of us lost a way early in life. And here as it is, I'm getting now just about ninety years old—will be in April. And, oh, I don't know, I could just go on and go on.

We Lived In a Little Place Called Freedom

Interview with Walter Niewald, New Haven, Missouri,
September 23, 1977.

My great-great-grandparents came over from Germany in 1856, along with the many Germans who began immigrating to Missouri as early as 1820. Like many other German immigrants to the Ozarks, they did not come directly, but moved in from other states. After a short stay in Illinois, they joined others who had already settled in central Missouri.

My ancestors settled south of the Missouri River in present-day Osage County near a little village called Freedom. They came to America to leave hardships behind. Here they hoped to start a new life in a country where liberty was guaranteed.

Publications in Germany at this time influenced many immigrants, including my family, with descriptions of the easy life in America—large green pastures and fertile soil in which crops flourished to supply every need. These writings painted an inviting picture of what America had to give them.

When my great-great-grandparents arrived, they found many things different from what they had anticipated. Before they had lush green pastures, they had to clear the trees. In the Ozarks the rocks and clay soil made the land very difficult to till, even after the trees were gone. Crop failures and hard times forced many people to return to Germany, disillusioned that America was not the dreamland of a new life. Most families lived from year to year on the hope that the next year would be better.

Despite the hardships they faced, my family stayed. Though they did not immediately recognize it, the hard work was worth the effort. The family was one unit, with each member working as hard as the other.

This family togetherness, shared with me by my grandfather's brother, my great-uncle Walter Niewald, is my heritage—Stephen Ludwig.

My maternal grandparents, Frederick and Mary Krueger, came over in 1856. They sailed from Bremerhaven, Germany, to New Orleans. They were on their way about thirteen weeks in their rickety sailboat when they got caught in a terrific storm. I believe it was the hurricane season and the boat was tossed around. The captain and the

184

*"My grandparents came
over from Germany in
1856."*—Walter Niewald.

crew had given up the ship. They didn't think they would ever land.
Three weeks after they were struck by the storm they were in the same
latitude as they were when the storm began. Their food and water ran
short—especially their water. They couldn't use the ocean water, so
they rationed it, each getting one-half gallon a day until they got into
the mouth of the Mississippi, where they could drink all they wanted.
Eventually they did land at New Orleans.

From New Orleans they went up the Mississippi on a steamer. I
guess they landed at St. Louis, where they disembarked from their boat
and settled at Maystown, Illinois, south of Waterloo. There they lived
three years, but they were sick with malaria. The doctor told them if
they didn't get out of there they would be under the sod perhaps in
another year. He suggested that they try to get into the hills of Missouri.
That's how they headed out this way.

So my grandfather started out in 1859 with an ox team and a horse,
with no idea where he was going. I guess he started out on Highway
50, which was then the State Road, but it wasn't much of a road because people weren't interested in the State Road but the roads to
market.

They got about seven miles east of Linn, near present-day Freedom, where he found a place along the Gasconade River where he could have what he grew without paying any rent for five years. But he had to clear so much every year. That was his pay. They had a very, very difficult time. The little cabin had just a dirt floor and a fireplace built of wood and daubed over with clay where most fireplaces were built of rock. They had no windows in the place. The cracks between the logs were chinked on three sides except the south side, for that was how they got their light. To keep the cold out they hung something over the wall.

Before they came over, my grandfather had a grocery business. It burned, but they had some money left. They spent that on their passage, and others that had people over here begged him to take them along, and they were going to pay him back when they got over here. But when they got over here, of course, they had nothing with which to pay back. So they went through tremendous hardship which we have no conception of today.

Price's Raid was through there in 1862. Price was a southerner sympathizer, trying to take the capital of Missouri at Jefferson City, but he didn't succeed. The women were to report any losses, violence, looting, or anything that happened to a Mr. Rhoades who lived on the old State Road. Something happened there, and when my mother and her sister went to report, they didn't know that the State Road was crowded with rebel troops. They finally got through to report, and then they were afraid to go home. They stayed as long as they could. Grandma Krueger was on needles and pins—didn't know what had happened to the girls. They finally got enough courage to go through the ranks of rebels. It seems to me it took about two or three days for the whole rebel army to get through. See, the roads were not highways, not like they are today. They were trails, you might say. Grandma and the girls were not molested otherwise. However, more of the soldiers did branch out from the State Road and came to the little cabin. Grandma had some money that Grandpa had sent home. She didn't know what to do with it, so she wrapped it in some old rags. They had a little smokehouse and she ran in there. She threw the money down and set an old empty barrel on top of it. The rebels ransacked the smokehouse and kicked the barrel over but they didn't pick up the old rags. The money was saved in that way, and no harm came to them otherwise during the Civil War.

Grandpa's last active duty was at Vicksburg, Mississippi. He had a lot of eye trouble, and he was put in what they called the invalid corps at that time. He didn't see any more active service and was mustered out in July, 1865.

I don't think they lived there in that place much longer. Incidentally, the log house was up on the hill, and the spring was down at the river a quarter of a mile, and they had to carry all their water up that hill. My mother often spoke of carrying that water before they moved on that farm where your grandpa lives. Well, near their new place down the creek about a quarter of a mile was a spring on the Liesemeyer place. There was no well there when they built their house. They still had to carry their water a quarter of a mile, but that was really some improvement. They didn't have to climb the old Gasconade hill. They could at least walk on level ground with their water.

My father, Herman Niewald, came over from Germany in 1866. He was the youngest of seventeen children and he followed six of his other brothers who had come over before him. They lived with some relatives at Drake, which was about seventeen miles from where Grandpa Krueger homesteaded.

There was a man living at Drake that had a special trade. It may have been the stone layer that laid up the outdoor oven for the Kruegers, but I'm not sure. He came by mule to the Krueger place to do some work and brought Herman with him. Herman became acquainted with Wilhelmine Krueger in the fall of 1868, and on January 27, 1869 they were married in the Krueger home by the Lutheran minister.

They made their home with the Kruegers and helped Grandpa run the farm. Herman and Wilhelmine had eight children. The boys were Emil, Henry, August—your grandfather—and me. I was born January 13, 1893. I was the youngest of the boys in the family and I didn't really know my sisters Lydia and Mary too well, because they were already married.

I Liked Farm Work

I was born too soon for the tractor. I couldn't even start one. As long as I was home we never had a tractor until 1918. We did all of our work with teams. See, when I was going to college, my summers were always spent on the farm. I liked that. The whole farm there was two hundred and eighty-four acres, less than half of that was tillable. We had a lot of woods and rocky hills.

Farms were not fenced in my early days. We didn't fence animals in, we fenced them out. The cattle would roam over large areas, and everyone lost some of their cattle those days. Fences were made by splitting rails, and this took a lot of rail splitting.

If a farmer wanted to build a barn in those days, he would usually get a sawmill on his place—saw down his own trees or have them sawed into lumber. That is what our neighbors did. They got a sawmill out there, hauled the logs in and had their lumber sawed. In those days they had more timber than money. If you wanted to build some small thing, it wouldn't pay to have the sawmill come over there, so they would cut their logs and haul them to the mill. Maybe they would have to haul them two or three miles and then get their lumber back.

I liked farm work, didn't matter what it was, driving posts, hauling manure, milking cows, I just liked farm work. They wanted me to be a minister but I didn't feel that way at all. My father would have been glad to send me to college, but I had no intention then. I wanted to be a farmer. I didn't make up my mind to study for the ministry until I was about nineteen years of age. Then I went to the Lutheran Seminary in Springfield, Illinois. It amazes me what those professors accomplished in the few years that they had us. I never saw the inside of a high school. In fact, the highest grade I was ever in was grade seven and I didn't know what I was in then. Then in five years they take us hayseeds and accomplish something. I still marvel at it.

Housewives Made Everything They Needed

Mother baked bread once a week, baking sixteen to eighteen large loaves in an outdoor over. The side walls were about two and a half feet high, with a clapboard roof over it. There were two openings, one in the top and one in the bottom. Quite a thing and that was used for many years. When baking we would light the wood in the upper opening to heat the fire brick on the inside. When we had the oven heated, we would rake out the coals and mother would put her hand there in front of the opening and she could tell whether the heat was right, or if not, she would wait three or four minutes to cool a little bit. Then she would put her bread in where the coals had been raked out, all the loaves at one time, close the front up with a board and in one hour the bread was done from the heat stored in the bricks. After the bread was out, we would put wood in the top opening and then it would be ready for the next baking. If we had extra wood we would store it in the lower opening to keep it dry. I carried a good many loaves in and out.

Housewives made their own yeast, too, in those days. They would take corn meal, mix it with some of the yeast that was left, to the right thickness, cut it into cubes, place the cubes in a thin cloth and hang them up to dry. Then when they would bake, they would take as many cubes as they needed for the bread they were baking. In the early days, too, if their yeast went flat or their fires went out, they would borrow a start of yeast or some coals to start their fires. My nephew tells a story he heard where the farmer took a wooden shoe to carry home his coals. The shoe burnt up before he got home—no shoe, no coals.

Most of our food was put up in gallon or half-gallon jars and crocks. We usually put up some forty gallons of apple butter. Apple butter was always put in gallons; blackberries and sauerkraut were put up in half-gallon jars. We always filled a barrel with sauerkraut, and then when it had fermented, mother would put it in the half-gallon jars. There was no spoilage after that. Pork was cured, hams and so on. There was no such thing as fresh meat during the summer unless you had chicken. Maybe when the threshers would come around we would butcher a sheep and have mutton, but there was no way of keeping it. There were no refrigerators and, strangely, nobody thought of canning meat in those days. They did put up pork patties, bake them good and done and then put lard over them. That would keep them for a long time.

A person wonders sometime how they got by. Of course there were some very lean seasons. There were parts of the year when we had neither fresh meat or vegetables.

One way of curing bacon was to hang it after being properly cured. It may have been there until July, but by that time it was getting pretty strong—"strong enough to pull a plow." But we did it differently. We would get a barrel of salt around butchering time. We would salt the meat, bacon and so on, and leave it long enough until it drew salt, then we'd take it out of the salt and hang it up for a month or so and then put it back to store in thick layers of salt. That is where the barrel of salt went. After it had drawn salt and had been hanging for a considerable period of time, you could put all the salt on it you wanted, because it wouldn't draw salt any more and it kept much better.

Our apples were dried in the sun. We never used the outdoor oven. We spread the apples on what we called drawers—clapboards nailed on two-by-threes or something like that. Then at night we'd stack the drawers one on the other and cover it all with oilcloth in case of rain or dew, to keep them dry. Apples would discolor if they got wet. The foods we dried were mainly apples, some peaches. The peaches we had were called "fence corner peaches," and you didn't have much left after drying. We grew apples by the wagonload as we had a large apple orchard. We never sprayed—never heard of that. We had mostly summer apples. Out of them we would make cider, dry some of them, and make apple butter. We gave a lot away.

Mother sewed quite a bit of our clothing, having a sizeable household. She didn't make everything like they did in the old homespun days, but made shirts and so on. I don't know if we could buy them ready-made in the stores or not. Everybody wore homemade shirts and pants. However, farther back they had the old homespun, as they called it, and they would also raise their own flax and treat it. They would run the flax through a thing with nails or sharp pins. They slapped it on there and got the threads out of it. It wasn't used in my day, but Grandma Krueger undoubtedly used it. In those early days of my grandparents, people had no money, and even if they would have had some, they wouldn't have been able to buy material. It just wasn't done that way. They had very scanty clothing, too. They had no underwear, the houses were cold, and you wonder how they survived, but they did. There was no rich Uncle Sam to back them up—"root hog or die" was the old saying.

The family had extremely hard times during the Depression. Your grandpa told me this himself. He said that they kept track of every penny that they spent during the year and they spent five cents for non-essentials. They bought a five-cent box of potted ham. Your grandpa, he went through the mill there. He really did. He put in an awful lot of hard work. They had some real rough times there, your grandparents, during the Depression and before that, too.

The men never left for St. Louis, but many of the young girls would go to St. Louis to get a job there. In the country, five dollars a month was top wage for a hired girl. Those that would go to St. Louis got twelve, fifteen, or eighteen dollars a month, so a lot of the girls would go to do housework in the city. Factory work and all that sort of stuff was not even dreamed of for women in those days. They all did housework. The men would find work in the country. It took a whole crew to operate a farm in those days. But there wasn't much left for the young unmarried girls but get a job in the city.

We Always Talked Low-German to Our Parents

We always talked Low German to our parents, and they always spoke German to us, but among ourselves we talked a king of pidgin English.

The people did carry on a lot of the old German customs. When we came here in the early forties to take the church at Boeuf, I didn't know there was a place in the United States where so much Low German was spoken, as here. Even the children would play ball in German —Low German. There are many dialects of Low German. In Germany one town wouldn't understand the people in another town, for they had a different dialect. High German is the universal German. Any educated person speaks or writes High German, but among themselves they keep up their native dialect.

When Luther translated the Bible he used the German of the Saxon Chancellery. Wittenberg is in Saxony, and the official Saxon language is what he used for his translation. Luther is generally regarded as the creator of modern German. Before that, every little principality had its own dialect and these people didn't understand those and vice versa—at least they had difficulty. All the preaching and teaching in schools is High German. Some think that High German is something that elevates you a little and Low German is a little lower, but that is not it. High German people lived in south Germany, the high country, the mountainous part of Germany. The Platt Deutsch, flat Dutch, lived down in the level part of Germany, so these were the Low Germans. The modern High German is the German of today and has been for over four hundred years, from the time of the Reformation. Among themselves they may talk Low German as we did, but all my reading was in High German.

My education began in German. I went to the parochial school at Freedom in the years 1900 to 1901. They didn't have English, for the pastor was an elder man from Germany. In those days English was not considered as too important. There were the English-speaking people, who were more or less a community. While there was never any friction or trouble, in a certain sense there was segregation. People of a common ethnic background were more closely knit together.

I did quite a bit of studying at home on my own. I did a lot of German reading, much more German than English. So the years went by. In 1912 I entered into the Lutheran Seminary at Springfield, Illinois. Never a dull moment. I liked going to school, but if I should choose between working on the farm a day or going to school, as far as getting real enjoyment or satisfaction out of it, I would have stayed on the farm. If I could have gotten an education without going to school, I would have probably never gone.

A church was started there in Linwood in a little log house. They worshiped there and a layman, Giedinghagen, from Mt. Sterling, would come over there and hold services. They organized the Pilgrim Lutheran congregation at Freedom in 1868, and my grandfather was one of the charter members of it. I think there were five men that effected the organization at that time. Then they bought a piece of ground about a mile north of Freedom, across Contrary Creek. They worshiped there in a tobacco barn that was still standing when I was a boy.

The German service was pretty much what they were accustomed to in Germany. The men and women sat on separate sides of the aisle, the elders sat up in front in the chancel and the children usually sat up in front. It wasn't a custom as now for families to sit together.

When I Was a Boy Everything Was a Big Event

In my days I would go to Hope, have four, five, or six sacks of wheat and exchange them at the mill for flour, bran, and so forth. That was the new way. The other way was the old way. You took your little pack of wheat to the mill, and you waited in line. You got there sometime before sunup and you wouldn't get started back home until late in the afternoon, because every little jag of wheat would be put into the hopper and ground, so you would get your own flour. In the old days you got exactly what you brought in. If you had a bushel of wheat, they would put that in and grind it — all in rotation like at the doctor's office, to await their turn. So it would take them a day. I remember they said they would leave long before daylight to get there early before the crowd. There would be so many before them that they would be sitting around there yet in the afternoon, waiting for their little grain to be put into flour. The miller usually took his share out. If you brought in a bushel of wheat, let us say, why he would figure so much flour you get, so much bran, so much chip stuff. His percentage was deducted from what you took home.

Then another thing that interests me a great deal was transportation. The only means of transportation was what each provided for themselves. They had either to walk, ride horseback, or hitch up to the old farm wagon. Later we got a spring wagon and I thought that was about the greatest thing on earth. We were about twenty miles from MoPac [the Missouri Pacific Railroad] and forty-five miles with no transportation except the Gasconade River. That was a pretty busy stream in those days, with three steamboats that I recall that made regular trips. There was the *Peerless*, the *Kingfisher*, and the *Wallace*. They would go up as far as Vienna — maybe they couldn't make it year-around but if they had water they would go to Vienna. Then in 1901 or thereabout, the Rock Island built through there, so that eliminated the upper regions of the Gasconade for steamboating.

The steamboats always fascinated me. How they could maneuver those boats with the little water they had at times was just incredible. They would make a sharp turn, then ring a bell, then reverse it, then forward, then backward, then forward, then backward. Sometimes it seemed like the big wheel was not more than thirty or forty inches from the trees and roots on the bank, but they would never get into them.

Also interesting were those early ferries at Mt. Sterling. I remember well when they poled that thing across. They had a long pole. Sometimes one man would handle it, but if the river was up a little and had more current, then there would be two. They would go where there wasn't much current along the bank, go up the stream a certain distance, they knew how far, then swing the boat around and push forward. That would land them at the landing on the other side.

The first automobile came in there about 1908. I would say the first automobile I ever saw was at the World's Fair in St. Louis, 1904. They had them on the grounds there and you had to pay for a ride. They were all driven by chains. You could hear the chains rattle farther than you could see the automobiles. Then out there, I would say maybe around 1908, Wesley Cox was the first one that had an automobile. He had a little old red Maxwell and he would scare people's horses and he even got sued for scaring somebody's team. The animals were definitely afraid of the things. They never had seen such a monster before, nor smelled one either. The fumes probably did as much as the noise and the color. Those were the days. If anybody would drive thirty or forty miles and didn't have to clean a plug or two or patch a tire, he had a real news story to tell. I went out with Emil and I don't know how many flats we had. We went to Feuersville Mission Festival, about seven miles from Freedom. We got pretty near the Gasconade River and had a flat, so we fixed it. Then on the way back he said someone else would like to ride with him in the car, and would I mind riding back in the buggy. I said no, anything to get out of that business of pumping up those tires. So when we were about two miles from the church there was Emil putting air in the tires. When you pumped up a front tire, you put sixty pounds, back tires you were to carry seventy pounds of pressure. That is no fun to pump up a tire to seventy pounds of pressure, even if it is only a 3½-inch tire.

About 1900 and for some years later, Freedom had the store and a blacksmith shop. Herman Linhardt opened the blacksmith shop about 1903, and August Gerschefske had the wagon-making business.

The Freedom Store in my time had a post office in the back. The store handled general merchandise. Coffee was shipped in barrels, also sugar and salt. Flour was sold in fifty-pound bags. Crackers were packed in crates. Herring also came in barrels, six large herring for twenty-five cents. Blue jean material maybe sold for seven or eight cents a yard, maybe less.

Kind of interesting, the post office there. See, Linwood, now known as Ryors, was the post office, about a mile from Freedom across Contrary Creek. Fritz Niewald wanted the post office at Freedom. He got a petition to call it Liberty because he was an immigrant and here he had liberty and because he was so elated with the American way. But that was not possible, because there was a Liberty, Missouri. The postal service told him he would have to choose a different name. I got this directly from Dr. Tainter, who was the dentist in Linn. He said poor old Fritz Niewald was really down, for he wanted his post office to be called Liberty. Well, Dr. Tainter said, "You can have the same connotation—call it Freedom." They sent back to Washington, D.C., and that is how Freedom got established in 1889.

Family life was much different—the family was a unit. You didn't have any place to go, so you stayed at home.

Some of the people got to be quite old, my grandmother Krueger got to be eighty-seven, and Grandpa seventy-eight. But if you go to an old cemetery today, you will see a child's grave for almost every adult grave—the mortality among children was very high compared to now, and the older ones too. Many died middle age and earlier, in their early twenties maybe. They knew no cure for appendicitis or whatever it was but fortunately the doctors were not too far away. They had to ride horseback or drive—most of them would ride horseback to answer calls. There were no telephones—like when I had that broken leg. A heavy gate fell over on my leg and broke it above the knee. They carried me to the house and then went for the doctor on horseback. The doctor came and it took three to set my leg—one to hold me down, Dr. Jett to pull my leg and me to holler.

In time of illness the neighbors would help. In case of severe illness, neighbors would come and sit up with the patient all through the night. I can think of a number of instances myself when I stayed with a patient overnight so that the family would get some rest. There were no hospitals at the time, except in the cities and in those days, the hospital was the last resort. If it was a matter of life or death someone might be sent to the hospital. For instance in 1906 Pastor Seidel was stricken with appendicitis on the way home from a preaching engagement. He was so sick he couldn't make it home, so he stayed with some people. The next day he did make it home, and then they had to take him all the way to Chamois—made a bed in the back of spring wagon—then by train to St. Louis, a hundred miles. His was a very serious case.

I still remember the first time I went to Chamois to town. I was about seven, and I never had seen a town. It was an exciting time. My brother, Emil, was going to town, and he said I could go along. That was a big event that was a lot more than going to the world series now-a-days.

Once a year we would get a barrel of salt. Whoever went to town would bring it along for when we needed it during the year, but there was no such thing as a family going to town. I guess those who lived within a few miles of town may have gone, but it was no pleasure for us to rumble the twenty miles into town from all the way out there and back unless we needed to. Your grandpa and I made a trip once. We started out at two in the morning and got back at ten at night—to Chamois and back. And mud! It started raining on the way in and kept it up, and when we started back the mud was stiff. It is hard on your team when the mud sticks to your wheels. If it is thin and sloppy, it doesn't retard you much.

You know how the farm at Freedom is off the beaten path, down in that hollow? People in town or where there is a little more going on would say when I was a kid there, "Don't you die of lonesomeness?" I couldn't see how anybody could ever be lonesome there. I never was lonesome. I had a good time.

On Sunday afternoon a bunch of us boys would get together and have the time of our lives—a lot better time than if we had gone to a big ball game. I mean more satisfaction in our own simple way. We would get together on Sundays and evening, especially in winter when the nights were long, visit the neighbors, and they would visit us, maybe play dominoes—something to pass the time away. Some Sunday afternoons we'd get together and play "sow." Each one had a stick and a hole [in the ground], with one hole in the middle of the circle. You take an old tin can and batter it up. That would be the "sow." I think you would try to get it into the middle hole. I think you could choose who was "it" after that. Each one is defending his hole in the ground. If you got it in there, then you were "it." Sometimes you would get a pretty hard bang across the shins with those sticks as you defended your spot. We got a lot of fun out of that, though.

Pete Hoffmann and I had an imaginary engine—parts of an old binder. He had a big bull wheel and we would pretend we were running the engine. You know, a little scrap of iron lying out there—each one had his engine. We were pretty small then. Things like that would while away hours if we had nothing else to do. When I was a boy every little thing, even crossing the river on a ferry or fording the stream was a big event.

I think my parents liked the area where they settled, and I think my generation was many more times contented than people are today. They had hard going, but there was real contentment. You know I often thought if I had my choice to grow up when I did or to grow up now when we have automobiles and all our modern conveniences and luxuries that people in those days never dreamed of, I'd take the old days. I don't think people growing up today would have the memories that I have of my childhood days and young days. To me, the standard of living is not how much you got, but how content you are with what you have and that you find real satisfaction in what you are doing. Now to me that is a standard of living. Contentment.

So They Say: Beliefs on the Land

People living close to the land may not be any more superstitious than others, but in their daily dealings with forces beyond their control, such as rain, floods, drought, some have learned to take some comfort in their beliefs of preventive actions to forestall or appease fate or "luck."

All of us have some beliefs we almost instinctively cling to. A lady claims she's not superstitious but laughingly knocks on wood to keep something bad from happening. The Ozark tradition has its share of these beliefs. Who is to say there isn't some truth in them, though they are not based on scientific fact. In difficult or fearful situations they provide a generally accepted guide for behavior. There are hundreds of beliefs that have been handed down through the generations as naturally as rules for social behavior.

We have collected beliefs as we've visited with people throughout the Ozarks. Some of these are generally known; others may be unique to a specific area. We've made no effort to sort them out to determine any indication of how commonly they were believed. We are merely telling them as we heard them.

At times many of us will cross our fingers or gasp if a mirror is broken. But in the Ozarks some people depend greatly on good and bad luck in everything from work to play.

The housewife is careful never to drop a broom so that it falls flat on the floor, and it is considered bad luck for a woman to step over a broom handle.

Don't sweep the dust from your house from the front door. You will sweep your good fortune away.

A person may go barefoot or shod anywhere, but it is tempting fate to go out of doors in one's stocking feet, or to walk in the house with one shoe on and one shoe off.

It is unlucky to spin a knife around on the table.

To spill salt on New Years Day is unlucky.

Very bad luck will come if you do any work around the house on the Sabbath.

Back luck always follows if you place a hat, or a shoe, or a rifle on a bed.

It is very bad luck to bring cedar or mistletoe into the home, except during the Christmas season.

Peacock feathers brought into the house are bad luck.

If you kill a cat, you will have seven years of bad luck.

It is unlucky to take the cat with you if you move to a new house.

Changing a horse's name is unlucky.

It is unlucky to light three cigarettes with one match.

To hear the shriek of an owl is a bad omen.

A crow on the roof is a sign of death.

If you see a dead red bird under a tree you'll have bad luck.

To dream of being thrown from a horse is bad luck.

It is bad luck to kill a singing cricket.

When you see a hollow tree in the woods while on your way home, you'll have misfortune.

If you marry in black you'll wish you were back.

When walking with a friend across a bridge, never walk side by side.

Wearing green to a christening brings bad luck to the baptized child.

Bad luck will follow if two people pass a tree on opposite sides. The only way to break the bad spell is to say, "Bread and butter" and retrace your steps.

If someone hands you a pocket knife, be sure you hand it back the way it was given to you, with the blade in or out. Otherwise bad luck will come your way.

A death in your family will result if you buy new clothes to wear to a funeral.

There seem to be many more sayings for bad luck than good. Perhaps one should take every precaution to avoid the bad, but the good will come without one's expecting it.

To have water spilled over you is lucky.

If two or more people go fishing together, they must all cross the fences at the same time if they are to have good luck at catching fish.

The woman who happens to get her first glimpse of the new moon unobstructed by foliage considers herself lucky.

A button received as a gift is always lucky no matter what the color.

To find your initials in a spider web near the front door of a new home is a sign that you will be lucky as long as you live.

It is an omen of good luck if a bee flies into the room.

To see a white cat on the road is good luck.

A three-colored cat can bring good luck, but most cats don't.

The left foot of a rabbit killed in a cemetery is considered lucky.

It is lucky to take a horse through the house.

Seeing a live bluebird under a tree is good luck.

Putting clothes on accidentally wrongside out is good luck.

If you have a splinter in your finger, when you get it out, rub it in your hair and you'll have good luck.

It is lucky to have your bed facing east.

Because weather plays such an important part in an agricultural community, it is logical that there are many sayings about the weather, especially rain.

In dry weather all signs fail.

If you see a whirlwind coming toward your house, it is a sign of rain.

A whirlwind going into the sun is a sign of rain.

If the whirlwind goes toward the branch of a stream or any water, it is also a sign of rain.

A dog lying on his back is a sign of rain.

Another rain sign is when a tree turns the bottoms of its leaves up.

It will rain when dogs eat grass.

If it rains on your wedding day you'll cry that many tears.

In the dry summer when a spring goes down into the ground, watch it, for when it comes back up it will rain.

If you hear crickets on a warm summer night there is a rain coming.

But when you hear a frog croak in the morning on a cloudy day, it won't rain.

If a rooster crows after he goes to bed, he'll wake in the morn with a wet head.

Chimney smoke that blows toward the ground indicates rain.

If it rains, snows, sleets, or hails while the sun is shining, the weather will repeat itself at the same time the next day.

If you use for firewood in your house a tree struck by lightning, then your house will also be struck by lightning.

Coal burning with a hissing noise means bad weather.

A lot of crickets in the summer mean you'll have an early winter.

The day of the month on which it first snows determines the number of snows that will fall that winter.

When fire coals spark, it will soon snow.

A cat sitting with its tail toward the fire is a sign that a rough winter is sure to follow.

If it thunders in February, it will frost in May.

Since everyone is interested in food, it is a logical source for traditional sayings.

Don't plant peppers when the signs are going up, or you'll have all foliage and no peppers. The "signs" refer to signs of the Zodiac as shown in almanacs.

Any true hillbilly will never burn walnut shells.

Never pass a piece of bread on a knife. A quarrel is sure to follow.

If you do not cut your bread evenly, you will never be rich.

You will have money in your pocket all year if you eat black-eyed peas or cabbage on New Year's Day.

Eating the crusts of bread is supposed to make you pretty or make your hair curl.

It is bad luck to dream of eating cabbage.

Never let the supply of salt get too low. If you do let it run completely out, it means a whole year of poverty and privation for the family.

A woman mixing a cake should always stir the batter in one direction. If she stirs it first one way and then another, she will spoil the cake.

Thunder and lightning cause milk to sour in a few hours, even in the coldest weather.

Washing your face in water in which eggs have been boiled will bring warts.

Animals have always been part of our life, and many people, even today, feel that animals have a special significance.

If a bird flies into your house, there will be a death in the family.

Take off your right shoe and turn it upside down to drive away a screech owl.

Crows sitting in a field are a sign of good weather.

If a cock crows near a door, it means the arrival of a stranger.

When a cat washes its face, it means company is coming.

A horse is worth a hundred dollars for every time he rolls completely over.

Bad weather is on the way when ants are very busy.

You will never live to hitch it again if your plow trace comes unhitched at night while you are turning your mule at the end to take out.

If a girl sees a red bird and can throw a kiss three times and make a wish before the bird disappears from sight, her wish will come true.

A live snake put in a barrel of cider will keep the cider from spoiling and keep it sweet.

If you kill a spider in the morning, you will kill the spirit of one who had entered its body while it was sleeping.

If a duck egg is taken into the house after sunset, the egg will never hatch.

When a rooster crows in the night, you'll have company the next day.

Colts must be weaned when the sign is in the thighs going down. Again, meaning signs of the Zodiac as shown in the almanacs.

Don't castrate cattle when signs are going up. Do it when signs are going down.

Children were a prime importance to their parents and the region as a whole. It was important to bring the child up to be a healthy, intelligent person and as lucky as possible. Many beliefs pertain to raising children, and many others to love and marriage.

People who have moles on their feet and hands will have plenty of children.

If the mother-to-be reaches too high, the umbilical cord will wrap around the unborn baby's neck and suffocate it.

If a child is born in the night, he will never see spirits.

It is lucky for a child to be born when the moon is full.

A baby should be carried upstairs before downstairs, so that it will rise in the world.

The baby will be a good singer if you crack the first louse found on his head on the bottom of a tin cup.

Never toss a baby up in the air. If you do, it will cause him to be feeble-minded.

To keep a baby from being sick, bathe it in dirty dishwater.

A cat, if allowed near a baby, will suck the child's breath away.

Don't step over a child. It will stop the child from growing.

A nosebleed is a sign you are in love.

A finder of a four-leaf clover will be married within a year.

A girl who refuses to be kissed under the mistletoe will die an old maid.

Don't give the man you are engaged to a pair of slippers. You will never marry him.

If your apron strings come untied, your absent lover is thinking of you.

If the second toe of a woman is larger than the big toe, she will henpeck her husband.

Itching is an everyday thing and most people don't give it a second thought. But even itching is the basis for some special beliefs.

If your head itches, you are going to take in riches.
If your nose or your thumb itches, you are going to have company.
If your right hand itches, you are going to shake someone's hand.
If your left hand itches, you are going to receive money.
If your feet itch, you are going to walk on strange ground.

What are your thoughts after you've had a dream? Do you laugh at them, or are you frightened of what could happen if they should come true? Many of the hill people out of the past did believe things resulted from dreaming, and for all we know, dreams may really foretell unexpected or future happenings.

To dream of your future husband or wife, walk upstairs on three successive nights without speaking.
If you tell a dream before breakfast, it will come true.
To dream that the leaves fall to the ground yellow means that there will be an epidemic in the town.
If a person dreams of a woman, it means that he will have happiness. If, however, her hair is disheveled, it means there will be death in the family.
Dreaming that a tooth is being pulled without starting blood, means that some member of the family is going to die. If it's a back tooth, the person will be of medium age. If it's a front tooth, the person will be young.
If a person dreams that he is eating white grapes, it means that it will surely rain the next day.
To dream of blood means that nothing will happen.
To dream of snakes brings bad luck.
If a person dreams that a large sore breaks and the matter is discharged, it means that he will be able to settle up all of his debts.
To dream of a leafless tree means it will rain the next day.
To dream that a certain man attired in his finest clothes is in a company where the others are not so attired means that the man is going to die.
If a married man dreams that he is being married and sees himself attired in his wedding garments, it means he is going to die.
If a person dreams of a river, it means that something stands between him and his wishes.

Have you ever been asked the question, "What does this mean?"

Some of these beliefs may answer your question.

If on your way you catch a falling leaf, it means a year of happiness.
A broom standing in the corner of a room means a stranger is coming.
If a hairpin falls out, someone is thinking of you.
Singing before breakfast means you will cry before supper.
If you trim your nails on Sunday, you will be sick before the next Sunday.
Stepping over a grown person is a sign of a death.
If you point at a funeral line, you are next to die.
If you prick your finger while quilting, be careful not to get any blood on the quilt. If you do, you'll cry a tear for every stitch you sew.
When you find the hem of your dress turned up, kiss it and you'll get a new dress.
If you go in one door and go out another you're bringing company.
If your right eye jumps, you are going to cry, but if your left eye jumps, you are going to laugh.
Dropping a spoon means a child will soon visit.
Dropping a fork means a woman will soon visit.
Dropping a knife means a man will soon visit.
The number of white spots on a person's fingernails will indicate the number of lies he has told that week.
A person whose second toe is longer than their big toe is the boss of their family.
Don't cut hair in the dark of the moon or it will cause baldness.
If you cut your hair while the moon is growing, your hair will grow faster.
An iron ring around the wrist will give strength.
Sneezing on Sunday means the devil will have you all week.
If you drink three times in three minutes from any Ozark spring, you will come back for another drink before you die.
A girl who drops her comb while combing her hair is due for some sort of disappointment.
A woman who sews after sunset, or who pours water on a window-sill, will be poverty-stricken all her life.
You will have money all year if you receive money on New Year's Day.
A sputtering candle announces a stranger is coming.
Somebody is talking about you if your ears burn.
To have cold hands is a sign that you have a warm heart.
Many Ozark natives believe that whatever a person does on January 1 is an indication of what he will be doing all of the year.

A pimple on the tongue is the result of telling a lie.

If you see a star before dark, spit over your left shoulder and your wish will come true.

It is said that misfortunes always come in threes. This is especially true of household mishaps.

Sleeping directly in the moonlight will cause you to go crazy.

A leather string tied around the wrist will cure rheumatism.

A dirty sock worn around the neck on going to bed will cure a sore throat.

To cure chicken pox, lie down in a chicken house after the sun goes down and let a black hen fly over you.

To keep from catching whooping cough, wear a scarlet cloth around your neck when a canary sings cheerfully.

To cure an asthmatic child, measure his height against a tree, bore a hole in the tree at that height, and place a lock of his hair into the hole. When the child grows past the hole, he will have no more asthma.

To prevent or cure arthritis, wear a copper bracelet or chain.

Carrying a buckeye in a pocket will also help rid the body of arthritis.

If a woman eats strawberries excessively when pregnant, her child will be born with a strawberry birthmark.

Eating a black cat boiled to death in the water used to scald the hog will improve nocturnal vision.

3. THE LIVING

"No other generation will see such improvements or changes as my generation has lived through," said Homer Massey. "We went from the horse and buggy days to the moon. When I was young, seven or eight miles an hour was a fast speed to get somewhere. I guess they go up in the thousands of miles per hour in those rockets."

The changes that have occurred in the lifetimes of our older people are not just in speed of transportation. "It's a faster world all the way around," Homer explained.

We get our basic necessities like water and food so quickly and easily that we cannot conceive how it was to haul in and heat enough water just to wash the dishes. As we look back at all the time and effort spent in getting three meals on the table each day, we really begin to count our blessings. Probably three-fourths of a woman's time used to be spent raising, preserving, and preparing food and cleaning up afterwards.

Big families were the rule when making a living on the land. Feeding extra people was not too much of a problem, since the family raised most of its food. Very early the children helped with the many jobs and chores on the place, contributing to the family living. Their job was simple. They were to grow up and get what education they could. The girls were to learn to keep house, make garden, care for poultry, and raise children, while the boys had to learn farming or a trade. Then, when in their upper teens or early twenties, they were to marry, make a living, and raise their own families.

Children were expected to help with the work. Since the whole society was based on the work ethic, nothing was looked down upon as much as laziness or unwillingness to work, because working, for people close to the earth, was absolutely essential for those who wished to survive.

Many hands certainly did make the work go faster and much more pleasantly. The mother and her girls would all go to the garden to pick tomatoes, even the toddler, minded by one of the younger girls who couldn't pick very fast, anyway. Boys eight to ten years old would accompany their fathers to the hay field, or plow corn. In families where the father died, small boys would help their mothers make the living.

Mary Moore said, "I drove a cultivator—drove the team for my boy to plow for two years. Well, now, he was too little to plow the corn and drive the team, so I drove the horses while he held the plow. When we'd get done plowing, when noon'd come, we'd go to the house, and he'd take care of the horse and feed the hogs."

Iva Bradshaw was grateful to her parents, who had taught her to work in the fields as a child, so she knew how to make a living for her children as well as keep house when she was left alone. Katie Lowry's childhood experiences made it possible for her and her husband to make their farm support them.

Hard as their lives seem to us, these people have no regrets. Rose Lowrance said, "There's not a lot I'd change about my life—I guess some little things. I always worked at everything—never got too hard for me to try. I enjoy working. I've done lots of hard work of ever' kind, even help get wood—saw wood and have it for winter."

"I come from a long line of farmers," Warren Cook said. "It's hard work. I guess that's the reason everybody had big families back then. Parents could work the boys and the girls, too."

"The women have always done their part," Rose continued. "In that day and time they worked in the field just the same as the husband did. They worked together."

Working with the family or with neighbors, it was all the same. Rose remembered, "When we had a good crop of fruit, we'd invite our neighbors, telling them we were going to have a peach cutting or apple cutting. We'd build a scaffold out in the yard. We'd all get together at night and first we peeled the fruit and cut them off the seed. Then we'd cut that fruit and put it out on that scaffold and turn every piece the way we wanted it for the sun to hit it first, and then leave it there until it dried. I do that yet. That's the way we had our fruit. We'd go out in the woods, if it was in the woods as it usually was, to pick our gooseberries and wild raspberries and things like that, and can them for our winter fruit to make pies out of, usually. Sometimes the menfolk would have a contest to see who could eat the most green gooseberries. It wouldn't take many for me to balk on."

Keeping busy and socializing were both taken care of. Whenever possible, neighbors would get together to help get the work done faster, making a sort of party of it. Butchering the winter's meat supply brought both men and women. The neighboring women and girls often made outings of blackberry picking in July, and everyone looked forward to making molasses in October.

An especially fun time for the young people was cornhusking time which often turned into a real party. There were prizes for the fastest huskers. But the most fun was to find a red ear of corn or one with a red cob. If a boy found that ear, he chose a girl to kiss in front of the others. If a girl found the red cob, the first boy that saw her could kiss her.

As they worked with family members and with the neighbors, they never forgot their other partner, the earth. As the people reminisce, they show pride in their own strength, know-how, and ability to work with the land to make it support their families. The earth responded, furnishing them with a means of livelihood and supplying them with the means to get their water, food, clothing, and household needs. In their need and ignorance and greed, sometimes people took too much from the land. Sometimes they worked together in perfect partnership.

"By the time I came along in the early 1900s, all the bluestem grass which grew under the big trees was gone."—Warren Cook.

The Land Will Make You a Living
If You Let It

Use It Up, Wear It Out, Make It Do or Do Without

Warren Cook, Republic, Missouri. Interviews April 17 and June 13, 1978.

The subject you had in mind was the change of farm life, farm style and practices and so on. We might understand it a little better if we backed up a little bit to see what caused the changes and what was happening at the same time and the same way all over the region. I think the basic answer to that is to some extent where the people that settled in the given area or neighborhood originated from, for they brought their practices with them. It happened that I was born on a farm in Newton County. A goodly number settled in that area came via Alabama, Tennessee, Kentucky. Then the other thing that made the difference was the terrain and the cover of the area which the people settled, because the soil and the cover—the growth that is there—had something to do with the farming that they would do regardless of where they originated, because they had to fit their activities to the land.

I would like for us to spend a little more time in trying to visualize what this southwest Missouri area looked like when our people came in here. Now remember that the whole country had some kind of cover, either woods or prairie grass out on the prairie section, but in the hills and rolling terrain it was woods, but it was not the type of woods that we see today. When my family, in 1836, moved to the old place I grew up on, they could see for a mile or a mile and a half through the timber. Savannah, in other words, open timber, large timber, good timber—walnut, white oak, black oak, post oak, chinquapin, with good grass cover under it. In some areas further south there was pine. So the clearing of the land then was an altogether different approach than we have now.

The accomplishments they made here show how frugal our forebears were, how they improvised, and how they were real good conservationists, although we think about it now, saying, well, they slashed the forest down. They actually didn't destroy very much of the wood. They utilized most of it for houses and furniture, fences, fuel, and even tools.

The reason we have this brush and weed trees, that I call it, in our woods now, is that the big trees were removed, and they didn't try to replant any kind if tree in place of it. Then by intense cropping year after year, they depleted the soil. Trees that will survive on less fertility than the big oak trees and walnut trees and so on will move in—that's the blackjack, post oak, scrub post oak. We call it scrub post oak because some of the land is depleted to the point that it won't even grow a good post oak tree now because it's washed away or overcropped or burned over—all of those things have happened to it.

By the time I came along in the early 1900s, all the bluestem grass which grew under the big trees here was gone. We just never saw any until out on the prairie just west of here. One species of bluestem is short bluestem called prairie hay, and they harvested that for a long time. There was no bluestem grass in the hills where I grew up. It had been overgrazed or burned over.

Of course, now, we're trying to bring it back. What I'm trying to say is that we are trying to make adjustments, and we're going to have to make a lot more of them in order to get enough food and fiber out of what soil we have left to support the population that now exists. That's the reason I'm a tree farmer. I think there is an advantage in double-using the land—grow some tree crop on it and underneath grow grass or some other crop that will produce food like nuts or fiber one, that can be used by people and animals. I'm trying to get my land back to the way it was—big trees with a grass ground cover, something besides poison ivy and saw briars and sting weed that harbor the ticks and chiggers. We're going to have to learn to utilize our soil.

Getting back to early times, what do you think would be the first problem facing a settler that was moving from Kentucky back in 1830 and going to land in this area? What, as the head of the household, would be the first thing that he'd have to do? Build a house, of course. What would he build it out of? Trees. Now that had a double advantage. If the settler was alert, he would cut his trees where he thought the soil would produce some crops, because he'd need the land cleared rapidly to start growing something—some foodstuff and grain for his family and stock.

But, anyway, we've said what he needed first was a shelter, and, of course, he built the first one out of oak logs, probably. Then when he got flush enough, he'd get out and get some pine logs off his neighbors to saw into boards. Another thing they had to provide was a garden. They didn't run to the supermarket and buy garden stuff. They learned to improvise and to do with whatever they had.

So he would clear the land that he could utilize—use the timber off of it in building his house. He'd have some cattle maybe, horses and so on, and he'd need some shelter for them. Second thing he'd have to build a fence around his crops. Now all of the land was open range, they called it. Today, we fence the stock in. We build a pasture fence to keep our stock in the pasture. That day and time they built fences around their crops, fencing the stock out to let them roam around through this lush grassland feed. So the settler'd have to split some rails so he would use some more timber. The point I'm making is that you can't say that he went in there and cut the timber down and burnt it all up, because people utilized a lot.

They could clear only a small patch a year with hand labor, and with the ground covered with stumps, they couldn't get very far with big machinery like the reaper, so they harvested with the grain cradle. Though much mechanization—the Industrial Revolution, the invention of the steam engine and the cotton gin, the sewing machine, and so on—this all happened considerably earlier than the time I'm talking about. But this area couldn't use some of these equipment pieces and some of the inventions and methods of power that they had, because the land wouldn't lend itself to it. Even my wife and I arrived in this area early enough that there was not very much mechanized farming going on. I like to think about it as carried over from the Industrial Revolution in our area when steel and power other than horsepower came into use, they were able to put these to work in industry, but it hadn't gotten over to the farm yet, where everything was hand-labored and horse-powered and get it done any way you could. In this area the starting of the mechanization of farming began in our childhood days.

Now it's true that down in the southwest corner of the state where we grew up, it was slower getting industrialized or mechanized on the farm. There's several factors that caused that. One of them was that the fields that we had were too small, for the most part, for tractors and heavy, wide and bulky farm equipment. Our forefathers first of all had to get the land cleared to grow some crops to feed the stock that they were going to work and to grow food for the family. The farm mechanization moved pretty well up to the binder and just the beginning of the combine. But the thing I'd like for you to think about is that this mechanization, such as it was, was only the forerunner of much greater change, and I'd like you young people to understand the transition—for you might not recognize it—but you're in the beginning of some kind of a revolution and are faced with problems that are more complicated than our forebears had to contend with. They had to contend with the trees, get them out of the way. They also had to contend, of course, with no roads and little or no information.

For instance, all the weather information came out of the almanac. They had no weather forecasts. They had to be their own weather guide. Even in my time I can remember when we lived out in the rural areas, and the daily paper, which was from Joplin, was always a day late, and, of course, the weather forecast in that was just a matter of checking to see if they hit it or not. We had a system though that we particularly depended on in the fall of the year when we were ready to harvest cane to make molasses. You have to strip the leaves off the stalk before the frost hits, otherwise it damages the taste or the quality of the syrup. Well, we lived ten miles south of Granby, which was one of the first mining centers in that area, established in 1850. They smelted and refined the lead there, so the old-timers would go out in the morning and sniff the air. If they could smell the sulphur and fumes coming out of the smelter, then cold spells were coming from the northwest. Then I could get out of school, come home and help strip cane till dark to try to save it.

The settler or the owner of the land always cleared up the bottomland first. It was the best, also the stumpiest. And then he'd move into the floors of the little valleys that came in from the side and eventually cleared the hill if it wasn't too steep, but that took time.

Even after he had cut down his trees, hauled them off to build his house, barns or fences, he still had to contend with the stumps. Nobody ever heard of a bulldozer then. You just had to wait for mother nature to rot the stumps. We could take a plow—the kind of plow we plowed with when we had to plow new ground. They had two or three names—we called them grub plows. They're basically what was called Georgia stock plow or bull tongue plow. The first one that I knew anything about was a wooden one—a four-by-four white oak beam that set about twenty- to thirty-degree angle and then had a tongue mortised into it and braced. It was always a marvel to me how they could do all of that work by hand and get those parts to fit. They didn't have the saws or the tools. They'd chisel a slot out to put the tongue in. On the end of that they would put a wide bit plow—just a piece of steel with no curve to it—pointed like a triangle at the end, and the handles, of course, to hold it, and they could go through the new ground. Now I'm talking about why we had

Settlers used oxen for clearing timber and plowing new land. The wooden yoke lasted many years and through more than one animal generation.

to plow that way on land we cleared up after 1904. There simply was no other way to get stumps, and vines, and so on, out.

We had to have a tongue in the plow because we're plowing along with this beam and a blade on it and we run under a big root. How are we going to get that big plow out? Well, we backed the horses up, and using the neck yolk as an anchor or support for the end of the tongue, lifted the plow up to get out from under the root. That gave a leverage to get the plow out of the ground and over the stump. We weren't straining against ourselves. The Georgia stock was designed for breaking up the ground, to a degree.

Basically, one of the first crops early settlers planted on new ground was corn. New ground means ground that's been recently cleared.

If they were late getting the new ground patch cleared, and it was time to plant corn—when the oak leaves got as big as a squirrel's ear, why you were supposed to plant your corn in that day and time— they went in there with the plow and barred it off. Barred it off meant that they simply cut a straight furrow as far as they could through the ground parallel with the side of the field, moved over three feet or whatever distance they wanted between the rows, plowed another row

*The froe was a shingle maker.
Hitting the blade causes the
chunks of wood to split into
shingles.*

there, and repeated that process until they cut it off in straight rows.
Then they went to the opposite direction, plowed across the other way
with the same process. It made a nice cross there in which to drop the
corn. The boys could do that better than a man, for they were closer
to the ground than a man. They didn't have to go back and pick up
the grain they missed. Someone came along with a hoe and covered
the corn up. We thought we had to plow our corn both ways because nobody ever heard of a herbicide to spray to keep the weeds
and the grass and cockleburs down, so we had to be able to plow both
ways. We went ahead and planted the corn, and then as we had time,
we'd work out the middles as they'd say — break up the rest of the new
ground. Of course that wasn't the ideal way, because later we had all
the roots and all that stuff to burn somewhere to get them out of the way.

The stumps were where the trees had been cut off. You wouldn't
believe the roots that we pulled up with that old grub plow. We
could pull around the stumps. But we tried to keep the row straight,
because there was a certain amount of pride in having straight rows.
Do you know the old cliché, that more corn grows in a crooked row
than in a straight row? Well, the reason is, there's more crooked rows!

We could work our team around the stumps, for generally we cut
them low enough that a team could walk over them, but when we went
around stumps, we would have to swing the plow around. The thing

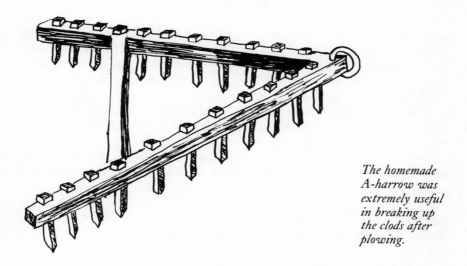

*The homemade
A-harrow was
extremely useful
in breaking up
the clods after
plowing.*

that kept us wide awake on that, especially, was plowing in where
there were post oak trees that have an immense root system and are
just as contrary as they can be. We'd go along and the plow would
catch a root as big as a hoe handle and it would stretch way out
there, maybe a foot before it would slip off of the bull tongue plow
blade. And where do you reckon it stopped? Back against the ankle!
So we stayed wide awake.

I remember that the walking turning plow was still widely used
in our area when I was a boy, because we didn't have another thing
to use in the type of fields we had. We couldn't afford to buy a gang
plow—one that had several blades. Out on the prairie they used it
where they had enough room and the ground was level enough they
could hitch six horses to it and plow a wide swath. We couldn't afford
to buy a gang plow if we only had an acre patch.

Another simple handmade piece of farming equipment was the A-
harrow, the first type of harrow that I remember that we used. As the
name signified, it was simply a long wooden triangle. The legs and the
base were about four-by-four white oak timbers. The teeth that were
available at the time were square teeth, and they bored the right-sized
round holes in each one of two sides of the triangle and drove the
harrow tooth down in it. It was hoped that the tight fit of a square
peg driven into a round hole would make it stay there. But in dry

weather they didn't always stay, and sometimes we'd have to get one out, find an old shoe and cut a piece of leather to stick in the hole, and then drive the tooth back in. We hitched a team then to the apex of the triangle. They'd pull it across the field, and since the teeth were running at an angle, they had a tendency to dig and smooth as they went along. But the problem was, that worked all right in the old fields where there were no stumps or roots to bother with, but you just haven't had fun until you've tried to lift one of those A-harrows over a stump and get the horses to go and to stop when you want them to.

So somebody developed what we called a jumping harrow that was made out of white oak, it we could get it, and used the same principle putting the teeth in, though I remember the one we had, had round teeth. I don't know how that happened, probably because we could get forged steel that was stiff. If we hit the square teeth hard enough, they would break, but the round ones that were tempered steel were stronger.

There was a sort of a double hinge made out of rods between each one of the eight-foot or six-foot bars that fit into a metal bracket that you fastened to the bar. The harrow was flexible. We could adjust the angle of the teeth by a lever. So when we came to a low stump, that tooth was leaned over—or as the old-timers say, it was lent over—it would just ride up over the stump and go on down and then straighten up again, and the next one would do the same thing. That's why we called it a jumping harrow—we could jump the small or the low-cut stumps to work the field without all this business of carrying or lifting the big old A-harrow over. When it wore out, we just got some more oak timbers and made a new harrow.

Getting to the actual mechanized equipment, I think we should start with the invention of the reaper in 1831. The reaper was one of the first machines on the farms, and it was nothing but a sled with a sickle bar on it, to begin with. It was pulled by horses, of course, to harvest grain. The guy ran along with a rake, pulling the cut grain off to make the bundles, for it didn't have the ties or canvasses and all that stuff in the original one. Why, they could grow enough wheat that way to have some to sell from their crop. Of course, when machinery became available, the prairie people didn't have to wait for the stumps to rot out of their fields in order to grow wheat. That was a big change to southwest Missouri. Now the interesting thing about it is, the best that I can find out, the reaper was not used in southwest Missouri till the Civil War or after.

Though I don't know definitely when the reaper came in the Ozarks

In the days of early farming the long rolls of hay were cut by a hay knife.

region on the type of land that most of us are familiar with, I do know that my dad, who was born in 1871, remembered when the first binder came into his neighborhood. This wonderful machine cut the wheat, wrapped it up in bundles, and tied it with a wire. That was really something to see, so the neighborhood turned out to see this machine. Well, as luck would have it, the machine broke down, as farm machinery will do, but they finally got it fixed and went on with the cutting. They asked the operator what was wrong with the machine. He didn't know, but he wanted to appear knowledgeable. He said, "Well, I think the josh pin fell out and fell into the clucking box and broke a spoke out of the siz wheel!" What had really happened was that they had a wheel under there that was not turning.

The problem with the first binder was that the gates weren't big enough for them to get the binder through. They'd have to take the fence down. Later binders improved in design so they could be pulled endwise through the gates.

The hay baler was another machine that changed our farming practices a great deal. Before the time that hay balers came into wide use, we had to stack the hay. Then it stood there till wintertime. When we started feeding it, we had fun when we got up on that stack, trying to tear that loose, and get it off, and haul it out to feed the cattle. You just couldn't throw it off with a pitchfork if it was a legume hay like cowpeas. So that's where the hay knife came in. It was a sword-like knife with two handles on it. It was between three and four feet long, I'd say. So we'd get up there and start on one end of the stack, about four or five feet back, and start sawing with this hay knife as deep as we could. That'd cut it off into flakes four or five feet long, and we'd throw it out. Of course, that was a waste, because we handled the hay two or three times and knocked the leaves off of it. One could drive along the road and see a hay stack that just looked like somebody had sliced a loaf of bread. Well, that's exactly what they had done. They used this hay knife to cut it so we could handle it.

The first baler I saw was [one of] the old horse-powered balers that were in use when I was a boy. The horses go round and round in a sweep. I had the biggest foot of any of the boys, so I usually got the job of feeding the thing. I sat up there and shoved the hay down with my fork. We always used a fork. That kind of held your foot up so you didn't get hung up in that. I never saw anybody actually get their leg cut off, but it could cut it off. Usually we'd get the horse stopped. The plunger came in to press the hay, and it's a little rough on your leg. You'd lose a pitchfork once in a while— break the tines off of it.

Then somebody developed a self-feeder arm, powered also by the horses, which would push the hay down in there, and it would clamp the hay so that the arm always got out of the way before the plunger came in. But anyway, that was an improvement and made it possible to store more hay. Of course today—now they've gone to the huge roller bale, which no one can handle without power equipment.

Soybeans were not developed to the point that they would produce like they do now. We grew more what we called a cowpea, which was in the same family. It's a long vining pea, and that's where we needed that hay knife. Cowpeas would be harvested usually in September, and it was a big chore to put it up in windrows. Because all the vines were hooked together we used to say that if you were stout enough, you could stick your fork in the end of a windrow, and if you pulled hard enough, the other end two hundred yards away would wiggle. The vines were so interlocked it was hard to pitch them in the field. But we managed to get them loaded. To get them off the wagon and stack them in the field, we used a fork and cable stacker, usually stretching the cable between two trees. They used the same kind of a trolley that the farmers used to have in their barns when they put loose hay in the barn instead of baling it.

If we let the peas stand until the pods were practically mature on them, well, then we had an old-fashioned separator that we converted into a pea huller by taking some of the concaves out and some of the teeth. We couldn't run it fast like for wheat, or we would crack the peas. We would thresh the peas out and sell them for seed, and the straw that was left was still good feed because peas are a legume crop. After we threshed it, we would most of the time bale the straw up. It made better hay than Johnson grass.

Again, of course, all of these things have helped to deplete the fertility of our soil and let a lot of it wash away. That's why I keep talking about we're going to have to change our system of farming to try to hold some of this land that we have left, plus build it up organically and through growth of legumes and so on.

I want to talk a little bit about the use of the timber that we took off of the land. Now, unfortunately, a lot of good fuel wood was burned up because they didn't need all that they were tearing down. Sometimes we'd sell a little bit of wood, but there wasn't a big sale for it. So we no doubt wasted some timber that we wish now we had in this energy shortage.

Going back, my great-grandfather built his first log cabin out of white-oak logs which he hewed with a broadax. That's the one that's got the off handle in it—the curve in the handle—so you could stand up on the log to hew, if you were a good hand, or if not, you would cut your toe off. But I never tried to use a broadax, so I've got all of my toes, but I understand some of the people got their toes hacked off in that process.

About the changes, and the things we worked with, and so on, it is interesting that the style of the ax, for example, changed. The pre-Civil War ax was just a straight handle. Then somebody was smart enough to realize that on a single bitted ax, if it had a curved handle, you could use it a lot better. So some of the changes came about by improving the old tools that we were using.

We had a sawmill, which was part of the way of living in this area. Everyone needed the sawmill because most of our buildings were constructed out of oak, even the framing and the siding was made out of oak. You can go off down in the hills here and still see those old oak boxed houses standing there.

The logs were on public land and the people would cut them down. At first people were the power for pit saws. And then later on they developed a crude sawmill, and then finally somebody came out with a big circle saw that they pulled by a belt. It would rotate and they rolled the log on a carriage through the saw, which sawed it into boards.

I don't suppose you ever saw a pit saw? They dug a hole in the ground and they put this guy down in the bottom on the other end of the saw. They sawed on the down stroke to rip off a board. The fellow in the pit had to wear a big hat to keep the sawdust off of him—keep the sawdust from going down his neck, so the history says. Later they developed a kind of a saw where they could saw both sides, and put it up on trestles.

In my time we also worked up the timber we cut. By this time we had a tractor there, which was not suitable to pull a plow, especially

Before power tools, sawing logs into boards was slow, hard work, especially for the one in the pit getting sawdust down his back.

in the small fields, and they rigged up a buzz saw to it. We'd use it to cut stove wood lengths and for other jobs we needed done. We learned to improvise like that and to do the best we could with whatever we had. Have you heard this old saying, "Use it up, wear it out, make it do or do without?" Today we haven't learned to do without. We're going to have to learn to do without some things that are exhausted or are on the point of being exhausted. So, I think we learned that from our ancestors.

Tie Making and Rafting

"Rafting railroad ties down the river was my life from the time I was eighteen for the next fourteen or fifteen years," said Lee Berry, who was born in 1881. His daughter Geraldine Brewer said, "He couldn't hardly wait till he'd get his crops laid by, then he could raft."

"To the best of my knowledge, me and my father Ed Graven, and brother-in-law, Bill Lindsay, rafted out the last ties that ever came down Beaver Creek. I believe there was 108 ties that had been stacked and delivered to the landing up the bluff above Beaver Creek," Vernon Graven said. "We was a-plowing corn in June when Bill Gater, who worked for a tie company, came down, and he offered Dad two cents a tie extra if we would quit and take them down the creek to the Gasconade River and to a point near Richland.

"We nailed the ties there together and picked up all the ties that were down where Beaver Creek empties into the Gasconade, and then we went down to Competition and finished up with 300 ties. I was twelve years old and this was in 1919."

This experience of rafting railroad ties to market is one of Vernon's most treasured memories. "I've lived that trip over in my mind so many years," he said. He got in on the tail end of a fascinating occupation.

Though Tom Price was born too late to get in on the rafting of railroad ties to market, he was just the right age during the Depression to make a living by cutting and hewing hundreds of them by hand. "I had to support a family, and the snow didn't get too deep to go cut those ties," he said.

Improved roads and bridges and the advent of trucks to haul the ties to railroad centers stopped tie rafting on the Ozark rivers that had begun in some places before the Civil War. The nation's expansion to the west and the demand for more railroads created an insatiable demand for ties for the railroad beds, for every one of the 209,000 miles of track laid in the United States required 3,500 ties. Since the oak ties lasted from twenty to sixty years, even after the era of expansion was over, railroads constantly needed many replacement ties.

Millions of these ties came from the Missouri and Arkansas Ozarks. In 1912 alone, 15,000,000 hand-hewed ties were sold in Missouri. The area became a huge supplier of ties not only because the timber was there, but also because the labor to cut the ties was available in the comparatively poor agricultural region. In places where the land was richer, people would not cut ties even if timber was there, for farming paid better. In the Ozark hills, where most people did subsistence farming, cutting, hewing, and rafting ties to market provided needed cash income for many families.

Even though very few tie rafts were floated to market after 1920, many people continued to cut and hew ties by hand as late as 1935. During the early Depression, selling ties kept many families from complete ruin. Then about 1933, when the market for stave bolts opened in the region, people quit making ties. They could make more money with less labor cutting and selling stave bolts.

Also about this time railroads began using ties shaped at the mill. They did not use sawmilled ties earlier because they had thought hand-hewed ties lasted longer.

Tom Price started making ties before he was ten years old by helping his father cut down trees with a crosscut saw. He got his first broadax when he was seventeen.

In the thirties and forties, railroads bought ties of different kinds of wood. "Red oak, post oak, and white oak was among the highest," Tom said. "Years ago they did buy walnut. I've made red elm ties, but not very many of them. I've seen lots made out of pine, but they'd have to ship them in." Pine is a soft wood that does not last as long as hardwood such as oak. Tom never made any out of pine because it didn't grow in his area.

Tie cutters got the timber wherever they could. Some of them cut on their own land; some paid a fee to landowners to cut; and others cut without permission on the property of absentee landowners. Men in the business would sometimes acquire timberland very cheaply by purchasing tax-title land and cutting off the timber before reselling the land.

Making railroad ties was a laborious job. With an ax or a one- or two-man crosscut saw, the first task was to cut down the tree and then to hew out the tie to the exact measurements, using both a broadax and a chopping ax. The sizes of ties varied, but the usual size was eight feet long, eight inches wide, and six inches thick.

The essential tool in making ties was the ax, both the regular four- to five-pound double-bitted chopping ax and the twelve-inch five- to seven-pound broadax. Since the broadax was designed for slicing and

Woodsmen cut tall, straight oaks with crosscut saws. Courtesy D. B. Mabry.

Logs were sometimes loaded onto wagons to be taken to a sawmill or to be hewn on flat ground. Courtesy D. B. Mabry.

trimming, its head was designed differently from that of the chopping ax. Besides being twice as heavy and much broader, it was shaped differently. The side next to the tie as it was trimmed was flat, enabling the worker to cut thin shavings to get a straighter, smoother edge. Tom and others would use the sledgehammer to shape the blade still further to get feather-edge shavings. Because of the flat cutting side, special handles had to be made for left-handed people.

The blades of both axes had to be kept sharp and used with care. Tom hasn't cut himself with one yet, but "I've chopped my shoes," he said. "That was close enough."

Years ago, when he was making ties regularly, Tom could make one in about an hour if he had good timber without any knots. He usually averaged five or six a day. Tom remembered, "I didn't always own a farm and I had to buy timber. I had to pay fifteen cents a tie, and that timber might not be very good. If the timber was too big and too rough, you'd be lucky if you made twenty in a week. But I've seen some guys that could make twenty in a day. Years ago my father-in-law said he might get three or four out of one tree. Timber isn't as good now, but nobody makes ties by hand anymore. They probably wouldn't buy them if you hauled them up to them. They saw them out at a sawmill where they are cut straight."

The broadax is made flat on one side, but the old-timers would shape it with a sledgehammer. The blade is bent in two places — near the handle of the flat side and near the cutting edge — to help in getting a feather-edge on the shavings when hewing.

Most men could cut from ten to twenty ties a day. Cutters naturally preferred bigger trees, because they could make two or more ties from one tree. Earl Riply said, "Getting four ties from a tree they called quarter tie. We had one that was called a bastard tie. That was a tree that made six ties to the cut, and a cut that just made two was a half-moon tie. Then the smaller trees that you just made one out of, was a pole tie." The log to make a tie had to be at least eight inches in diameter, not counting the bark, and at least eight feet long.

It was always easier to have help to cut the timber, but some cutters had to work alone. To cut the tree, the men first cut a notch on the side on which the tree was to fall. Then using a one- or two-man crosscut saw they sawed slightly higher on the opposite side from the notch. While sawing, they drove wedges into the cut, causing the tree to fall toward the notched side.

After the trunk fell, they lopped off all the limbs with an ax, and if it was a long-enough log, they cut it into eight-foot lengths with the crosscut saw.

Some men hewed out the ties in the woods where the tree fell; others, using chains and horses or mules, hauled or dragged the logs to the work lot. There they set the logs up off the ground on wood blocks or split logs to be trimmed. They always worked with the wood while it was still green, because seasoned wood, especially oak, is very hard to work with. Most hewers followed basically the same method.

The first step is to make a guideline with the broadax. Tom said that when he was in practice he could make the line straight just by sighting down the log.

Next, make notches down the length of the log on one side. These notches should be about two feet apart and the depth of the guideline.

Hewing the surface (below) *should eventually leave a smooth finish. The chips ought to have a feather edge. These chips made excellent kindling.*

Though he hadn't cut a tie in years, Tom cut one to show how it was done. To trim, Tom first made a guideline on the log. He measured off the width of the tie and, with the broadax, marked all the way down the log, making sure it was straight.

Next, standing on the log, he cut with the chopping ax about four notches eighteen inches apart down the side of the log he wanted to trim. He cut these notches to a depth of about half an inch from the guideline. They helped in splitting out the wood.

When he had cut the notches, he split out the rest of the bark and wood between these notches, leaving a rough surface. He smoothed all of this side as much as possible with the chopping ax.

To finish that side, he smoothed it with the broadax. Standing at the side of the log, he shaved and trimmed the whole length of the tie. The chips had a feather edge as he hewed them off.

He repeated the process for each of the other three sides, turning the log over when necessary.

Everything about the tie business was done by man power, even carrying ties. Men who worked with ties and rafted them soon mastered the knack of carrying the 200-to-300-pound ties on their shoulders. Vernon remembered a man who worked at his sawmill carrying on his shoulder a sixteen-foot tie, seven by nine inches in diameter, up the gang plank to the boxcar. "I seen the man do it," Vernon said. "That is unbelievable. It'd weigh like 700 pounds. The way the old-timers out in our country figured, when a boy got to be a man was when he could take a tie on his shoulder, carry it, and put it on the landing. It wasn't no easy job. We used to laugh, 'That guy can't even carry a tie.' It wasn't no disgrace, but it made him feel bad at the time."

Those experienced in carrying ties would be able to guess the center of the tie and not miss it more than half a pound from perfect balance. In tie yards, a man who loaded ties would have two men place them on his shoulder, but a man out in the timber cutting ties would have to put them up on his shoulder himself. He would stand the tie up on end and then let it balance back on his shoulder. Earl said, "Oh, we'd always pack them. Wasn't no trouble to flip a tie on my shoulder. I was stout then — pack it up the biggest hill. Maybe we'd throw our cap on our shoulder. It will kind of wear your shoulder out if you don't. Them men that loaded ties at the yards had pads on their shoulders. You can tell it on my right shoulder, for the bone don't stick up as high in it."

Since ties were often cut in steep hollows inaccessible to the wagon and team, the cutters would have to carry them up the hill to load on the wagon. Some wagons would carry twenty to twenty-five ties, but most hauled from eight to sixteen.

If the tie cutter lived close enough to a town with a railroad yard, he would haul the ties there. After it was possible to use trucks, he could haul fifteen to twenty ties at a time. Tom recalled, "When I'd go to the tie yard at the railroad, sometimes I'd sit there for two or three hours waiting to get unloaded, there'd be so many ahead of me."

In many areas too far from railroads to haul ties by teams to market, it was more economical to float them down the rivers to railroad centers. The individual cutters often hauled their own ties to the riverbank.

At the bank, which was usually a bluff or a steep hill right by the river, buyers would purchase the ties. They gave so much for hewing, so much for hauling and stacking. If someone other than the hewer hauled and stacked them, they got a few cents per tie for that. The inspector would cull out any that weren't the correct size, had any bark showing or were in any way inferior, such as showing signs of having lain on the ground. Earl said, "I'm going to tell you the truth. You might have both ends of that tie just as solid as a jug, but if it was holler in the middle, he would know it when he hit it by the sound of the hammer."

Ties were sold at many different bankings along the rivers. In 1910–16, ties brought ten cents in the woods and fourteen cents delivered to the river. Later in the 1930s, they brought up to forty-five cents hauled by truck to tie yards in town. But back in rafting days, the tie buyers were often owners or managers of local stores. Sometimes they paid in script—redeemable only for merchandise at the country store. This amount doesn't sound like a very large sum of money for the labor involved—about $8.00 for a wagon load of ties, but Earl said, "Lord God, you could buy a whole wagon load of groceries with that—eat a meal for fifteen cents and stay all night—two sleep in the bed, twenty-five cents."

The sold ties would be banked up close to the river. Sometimes there would be huge numbers of ties ricked up in stacks of hundreds or thousands in a clearing of maybe an acre, located where they could be pushed off the bluff down the tie chute into the river. These banks were not necessarily high bluffs. A bank might be as close as ten feet from the water's surface or it could be four hundred feet high. The important thing was that there be an eddy, or pool—a big enough body of quiet water below the bank to catch and hold the ties so men could nail them into rafts before they washed on down the river.

The ties brought to the bank had to be stacked in a certain way,

Tie bankings varied from a few stacks to an acre of cleared land on top of a bluff or other bank, where men would push them into the river. Courtesy D. B. Mabry.

high enough that floods or high water couldn't reach them. They were stacked with one layer one way and the next the other way, to allow air to flow through to season them and prevent decay. The ties might have been stacked for some time to be well seasoned. If they were green and heavy, they'd bank them in the winter to float out in the spring or next fall. But even with the seasoning, some ties wouldn't float. Geraldine Brewer said, "Sometimes they'd throw ties in the river and lose them. There's a lot of them old ties in the river yet that got sunk and they couldn't get them out. They used to call them 'old sinkers.'" A few ties that wouldn't float would be put on top of the rafts. The seasoned ties floated high in the water, clearing the shallow riffles.

While the ties were stacked on the riverbank, the buyer would usually brand his ties. These brands were normally a small letter or symbol applied with a device a blacksmith made, similar to animal branding irons, only these were made onto a hammer. The brander would hit the tie on one end to print his brand.

After there had been enough ties brought to the bank to make a good raft, the buyer would hire men to raft them down river. The

Ties by the thousands choked the quiet river eddies, ready to be nailed into rafts and floated to market as far as fifty to seventy miles downstream. Courtesy D. B. Mabry.

rafter's job usually was to do all the work from pushing the ties off the bank to delivery at the railroad, though sometimes different crews would build the rafts and float them. Sometimes men rafted only certain sections of the river, delivering rafts to others who continued the journey to the railroad.

Rafting began each year after danger of freezing was over and continued into the fall. On smaller streams there would be enough water only in the spring after lots of rain. Often during midsummer, because of lack of rain, the water became too low to float the rafts over shoals. Fall was a good time for rafting, for the weather was usually good and the winter-cut ties would be well seasoned by then.

When conditions were ready to raft them, the stacks had to be pushed into the river. Earl said, "They had a chute they run them ties off of, and then they'd hit that bluff and they'd just upend and go everyway. But it would all be eddy water below, to catch them. I've seen them ties piled up and down the bluff. You've got to be careful. Boy, if they'd tear loose, then they'd kill you."

Lee Berry remembered one time they threw fifteen hundred ties over the bluff. "I'll never forget. They lodged about halfway down the bluff. Then we went across the river to eat our dinners. When we started back to tear them loose, well, it come up a rain while we were going up the bluff. We got up there to where them was all piled and scattered around, and we kind of tore them loose. They went right down over that bluff, and most of them went on down the river. They just floated off and we had to catch them and nail them in. We had a lot of things we had to do."

The hundreds of ties sliding down the chutes knocked down all trees and brush. The chutes were completely bare. Though no ties have gone down them for over fifty years, some of the slides are still visible because of the stunted vegetation.

After ties were in the river—or, if there were enough men, while the ties were being pushed into the river—men below, wading bare-footed in the water would pull, push, and work the ties into order and then nail them into sections. The current would be slow enough that they could make a sort of corral of ties to hold them.

The men in the water used poles from split saplings to fasten the ties together. They had gone into shady timber to get tall, straight saplings about four inches in diameter and about fifteen feet long, which they split down the middle. These were called binders. Geraldine Brewer said, "It got to where they had most of the good binders cut out of the woods. Sometimes they'd have to hunt around quite a bit to find them, because with so much rafting going on, they'd cut most of them, and, of course, they couldn't bring them back to use again."

The men positioned the ties side by side about four inches apart. They placed the binders near each edge of the row of ties and nailed them down with one twenty-penny spike nail in each tie. They would make one section, or block, with about ten to thirty ties depending on the length of the binders. Rafts were built sort of like railroad tracks, only the ties were much closer together and the binders were in place of the rails.

The men would then fasten two blocks of ties together with a coupling made of a shorter sapling split in half and nailed to each end. They drove one spike through the sapling into the center of the third or fourth tie back in one block, and the other end to the next block, making a coupling with a foot or a foot and a half space between blocks. With the spike acting as a pivot point, the raft was able to bend around the many curves and crooks of Ozark streams. The men nailing in would continue building blocks and coupling them together until they had built a raft of about fifteen to twenty blocks, contain-ing seven hundred to twelve hundred ties. The rafts were anywhere from two hundred to three hundred yards long and were very stable, hardly moving under the weight of a man as he walked across them. Lee Berry said, "We got to running a thousand in a string. Sometimes you couldn't see the feller that was with you. He'd be somewhere back around the bend. Fourteen hundred was the most ties I ever run."

The river on which the ties rafted was a factor in deciding the style of raft construction. The crookeder the river or stream, the more flexible the rafts had to be. On smaller rivers or creeks, like Beaver Creek in Wright County, Ed Graven used a different means of fastening ties together. Instead of the center coupling, he extended the smaller ends of the two binders over the gap to the next block. The white oak saplings were green and would bend without breaking as the long raft snaked around the turns of the creek. Rafts on smaller streams could not be as long as on larger rivers such as the Gasconade, Niangua, or White.

Those of us who enjoy floating the Ozark rivers today can understand the excitement, the allure and satisfaction these old-time rafters must have felt as they took raft after raft down the river for years, through the sparsely populated and still wild region.

"All ready? Let 'er go," one of them would shout. With long poles the men would push the long, unwieldy-looking craft into the current. It would gradually pick up speed as the front disappeared around the bend in the quickening current. Within minutes the sounds at the tie bank would be gone, as they began their week-long dependence on the river and their own skill to float the fifty to seventy-five twisted miles to the nearest railroad yards.

As we travel those same miles today, we wonder how they floated these eight-foot-wide rafts, when we sometimes have to portage a canoe. Lee explained, "The river ain't anything like it was. There was lots more water and not hardly any gravel and sand bars. It was a bigger river."

It took at least two men to guide the raft, wielding fifteen- to twenty-foot-long poles to push, turn, and stop the raft. The man at the front, the bowman, would guide the raft by keeping it in the current, and he would yell instructions and warnings to the man at the rear, the snubber. The snubber's job was mostly to snub, or brake, the raft by dragging his pole against the bottom.

When building the raft, the men allowed more space than usual between the second and third ties from the stern end. The binders on these ties were double-nailed through the big ends. The snubber stuck a long, strong snub pole of about three inches in diameter between the ties down to the river bed. His was a heavy job. Bracing the pole against the ties, he had to push down against the river bed to control the raft's speed or to stop it altogether. There was usually no need for snubbing in the eddies where the current was slow, but when the front end of the long raft entered a riffle or was going to make a bend, the bowman would call back, "Snub 'er down!"

Vernon Graven explained, "You'd hit some fast water. The end of the raft would be a-pulling too fast and you knowed you were just going to tear up, so you had to brake it down just like when the car's going too fast down hill, you got to use your brakes. And so that's what we did—snubbed it down with that pole. We had to cut a few snub poles in two, for we got snubbing in pretty deep water, and then it'd start getting shallow and that pole would bind between them ties till you wasn't powerful enough to pull it out. So what could you do? You had to cut this pole off right there at the tie and let it drop through."

Occasionally there would be a third or fourth man on the raft, called a poler. They stayed in mid-section to keep the middle away from trees, banks, or rocks and to push around bends. To pass over shallow riffles or to keep moving in eddies, they would pole by pushing on the bottom.

Besides strength and skill, it took a knowledge of river conditions to take a raft downstream. Tie rafters preferred the river when the water was receding or falling. In any stream low water is sluggish, causing floating objects to drag over shallow riffles. Rising water bulges in the center, sending floating material to the side, thus making it harder to keep in the current. Receding water has a slightly sunken middle, a sort of trough, that holds floating material. This condition made rafting easier.

Even in the slow eddies, the bowman had to watch to keep the raft in the center to avoid the back pull of the water in places where it circles and comes back to the bank. But usually, floating the long eddies was a rest period. Vernon said, "When we hit those long eddies, all we had to do was keep it in the current and let it float. In those great long eddies on the Gasconade, we'd even sometimes pole it to boost it along a little bit. It'd pert'near come to a stop, so we'd bunch up and talk. Like take the Dougan Eddy above the bridge on AD, that is about a mile long. I remember we all got together, smoked our pipes, chewed tobacco, or done our thing. All we had to worry about was not to let the raft get to one side where the current backs up. As long as we had it in the stream in the middle of the river, why it took care of itself in those long eddies. We'd have a half-hour rest."

But going over the shoals, or shoots, and around short bends was another story. Earl said, "They were hard to work around, some of them bends. You'd be surprised, that many ties in the water, how much power they have. They won't go fast, but they'll just keep a-pushing. They'll push and double up on you if you don't watch it."

Vernon said, "When we was going around the curve one of us would walk on the raft with that pole and push with our feet to make the raft float around an object. In some places where they'd be an old tree stump or a rock in the edge of the water, we'd have to do that, or where the river would bend pretty sharp. That's the way we kept it from grounding."

Rafters had to be alert for unusual conditions or problems. In low water, they would make temporary brush dams across shoals to deepen the water enough to float them. In some places millers had dams across the river. Though there was a runway through which the rafts could float, an occasional miller was contrary and made rafters pay a toll before he would open the gate.

While floating, Lee Berry often had to do some fast thinking. "We got down to where there was a crook in the river. There was a big sycamore tree had fell across that river and about half of the log was in the water. My brother was snubbing and I hollered, but he couldn't stop it. So I run my push pole under that log and those ties went right down under that log and come right up on the other side. I jumped over that log and hollered back to my brother what he had to do. We went right on out and when he came down, why it drug his push pole off. We had to stop and go out in the timber to hunt some poles. That's the way we'd do a lot of things that happened. A lot of times we wouldn't know anything was even in the river till we got down to them."

Vernon had a similar experience, only his log was not in the water but about twelve inches above, from bank to bank. He was at the end by the grub box. "They begin to holler, 'Tree!' They were both pretty well at the front end. When I seen it, I dropped down right in front of that box. I don't believe it cleared that box four inches. There's nothing I could do about it. I started to lay down behind the box, but thought, boy, I don't want the box on top of me, so I jumped up in front of it. That kind of give me a thrill. You remember things like that. The others probably just put their hands on the log and jumped over it."

At times the raft would get wrecked or torn up on the trip. Then the men would have to make repairs. If the tail section broke away from the main raft, the snubber would have to carry on alone to catch up and tie back on. The bowman might not even have known a back section was in trouble until he reached a long eddy and could see the end of the raft.

During favorable rafting conditions, there might be other rafts on the river. There was the possibility of running into one around a bend or being rammed from behind. But that wasn't very likely. If the raft was very close, the man could usually hear the rafters' instructions shouted to one another. A trick to hear one farther away was to put an ear in the water. The water transmitted the sound of the snubbing pole gouging the bottom from quite long distances.

The rafters took with them only the essential equipment — ax, hammers, nails, and ropes for repairing the raft, and necessary food and supplies for themselves for the length of the trip, for they'd have to carry everything home on their backs. Vernon's father built a discardable oak box on the end of the raft for their food and camping outfit. They covered it with a wagon sheet, which doubled as a ground cover to sleep on and as protection from rain. Some rafters built cross pieces on the raft to keep their belongings up out of the water.

The men would raft all day until near darkness, when they would tie up in an eddy to stay for the night. Earl said, "One old rafter, Fred Johnson, had a cabin that he placed on the raft that he stayed in." Some would take along all their food and camping materials needed to cook and camp right on the river. Vernon talked of making biscuits by first letting the fire burn down to coals. Then they put the biscuits on an oak board greased with bacon drippings and placed the board beside the hot coals. "We'd stir them coals to keep them bright. You'd be surprised how good the biscuits tasted. We had worked in that water all day and we were wore out and very hungry."

Many who rafted frequently had regular stops where they would stay overnight at nearby farmhouses. They'd pay something like fifteen cents for a meal and usually nothing for bed.

In the sparsely populated areas where visitors were rare, the rafters were welcomed by people in most farmhouses. Geraldine Brewer, who lived as a child on the Niangua River, remembered her excitement when rafters would come. She could hear them shouting instructions to one another on the raft long before they reached her house. "I've seen three or four rafts come down in a row. We used to hear them yell about two miles up the river. My brother and I would take off to the river to see the rafts go by. Then, when they was going to stay all night or have dinner with us, why we just thought that was a big treat. We'd run to the house and tell Mama, 'The rafters are coming and they're going to be here for dinner,' or 'They're going to be here for the night.' Then Mom and Dad and the rafters, they'd sit and play pitch at night. They used to talk rafting—that's all they talked. They knew every sandbar, every snag, every shoal, every eddy by name. If Dad wasn't running just then and the rafters came by, he'd ask them, 'Now how did you run such-and-such a place?" or 'How did you run Iron Holes?' They'd tell him. Maybe it had changed. "Well, there's a bar at such-and-such place you have to bear to the left!"

The men who rafted had the whole river nearly memorized, so they could know what to expect. But on each trip the river might be different. After high water they expected some changes. The rafters on the Niangua usually spent from three to six days on each trip, depending on the starting point and the water level of the river. Most of the rafters on the Niangua River would stop at Old Linn Creek on the Osage River. This, of course, was long before there was a dam at Bagnell, forming the Lake of the Ozarks. There the Osage River was wide enough that the rafts would be nailed together four abreast, and usually another crew would float them on down to Bagnell, where they were dismantled and the ties loaded on railroad cars and taken to tie yards. At tie yards, ties were loaded on trams—circular-topped rail cars—and taken through the processing plant, where they were heated in creosote so that pressure forced the solution into the wood. Eight hundred ties composed a charge, which was treated at one time. One of the biggest yards was in East St. Louis.

The hardest part of the rafters' trip must have been the long walk back home. The only transportation at that time, of course, was horseback, and it was obvious they couldn't take a horse with them on the raft. They had to carry their equipment and walk home. The walk was straight across country, not as many miles as the crooked river trip. Lee Berry used to put in at several different landings on the Niangua River. The trip from Corkery, for example, where he often started, to Old Linn Creek would have been over fifty river miles, but the walk back was about twenty miles to his home at Celt, which was about eighteen miles downstream from his starting point.

Some walked as much as fifty or sixty miles. Vernon said, "We walked the forty miles back home through the woods." His river mileage would have been close to seventy miles. "We'd go up to farmhouses, for we'd run out of food, and we would buy eggs or something to eat. Sometimes a farm lady would bake us a pie. We'd give her a dime or fifteen cents for a pie. We'd never have nothing for nothing. Of course, we could have went up and eat, for they'd asked you to come up. People in them days was so scarce and far between, they was glad to see you come and talk with you."

The men were usually paid for their work on delivering the ties

On the trip down the river, rafters would pick up lost ties, or sinkers, from earlier rafts. Courtesy D. B. Mabry.

or after they returned to the place where they had nailed in. Most often they were paid cash. The money that they received was good wages for that time, better than cutting ties. Lee was paid a dollar and a quarter a day. Some rafters contracted the trip; some were paid so much a tie. Vernon remembered that they got twelve cents apiece for delivering the ties they began with. For the ties that were on previous rafts that had broken up, they got ten cents each for picking them up. "We were well satisfied with the trip," Vernon said.

The big virgin timber has long been gone from the woods. Even second and third growths have been cut and the tie hewers have long since disposed of their broadaxes. The tie chutes have grown up, while the lost ties still in the river have almost all rotted away. The rivers are silting up, and the many people who now live along the banks are busy with farming activities or vacationing and resort businesses. The old rafters left, like ninety-nine-year-old Lee Berry, have only their memories to remind them of the days when, with pole in hand, scanning the approaching shoot that rumbled and sent spray in all directions, they used to stand on the bow of a raft made of a thousand ties.

"Snub 'er down!" they'd shout as the current pushed the raft to the left toward the root-entangled bank. "Bear to the right. Snub 'er down!"

Take a Drink of the Best Water There Is

A Spring for All Seasons

Seventy years ago a small girl on her way to school loved to pause by the Charley Wood Spring, which was in a rock formation under the crest of a tiny wood-covered hill. She would get a cold drink and savor the beauty all around before the long day at school. The small basin where the water came up was a round hole just big enough to dip in a bucket. Though it wasn't too deep, the water was always cold and bubbly. Little ferns grew among the rocks. Occasionally she would meet the Wood children getting water for the house or the mother bringing their basket of wash to boil in the black iron kettle that stayed in a little cleared place just by the spring. The spring branch disappeared in the lush watercress below, but the girl knew that it flowed through both the Charley and Eli Wood barnyards, supplying water for all the animals at both farms.

In an abandoned area nearby there was another spring that emptied into Cobbs Creek near Oakland called the Willie Owens Spring, where, a generation earlier, the girl's grandmother had done her washing. Since this spring was in a wooded area half a mile from any house or barn, stock seldom used it, and it was too far away to carry water from to do the laundry. The husband would hitch up the team, the wife and daughters would load the wagon with soiled clothes, kettle, tubs, washboard, and soap, and he would drive them to the spring. While the husband returned home to work, the women at the spring spent the morning building a fire under the kettle to heat the water, scrubbing the clothes clean on the board with lye soap, and afterward rinsing them off with the spring water.

These springs and hundreds of others like them were a valuable natural resource to the pioneer families. Fortunate were those who had one on their farm, and doubly fortunate were those with several springs—a quite common occurrence in the Ozark plateau region.

The spring is a natural source of water that comes out of the ground

239

Small springs like this one are common in the Ozarks.

Once the source of pure, tasty water, many of the springs are now endangered by pollution.

Springs vary in strength. This is a medium-sized, all-weather spring with lots of flow.

to flow on the surface. As water filters through the underground rocks, it finally reaches a resistant layer that it cannot pass through. It is caught in pools, the excess flowing horizontally. This groundwater, which can be tapped for wells or which surfaces as springs, is what makes up the underground streams.

Natural erosion often exposes these underground streams. Wind or erosion from surface water that forms rivers, creeks or hollows sometimes creates bluffs, hills, and valleys cutting across underground waterways and causing the water flow to continue on the surface. Many springs flow directly into streams or come out of hillsides and bluffs, but they also occur on level places. Underground forces may cause the water to flow through the rock strata uphill, rising until it finds a crack or a place soft enough to allow the water to emerge from the ground, forming a natural freshwater spring.

In many instances the water in these springs accumulates to great quantities and flows underground in cave-like canals. Where such canals reach the surface, as at Big Spring, Round Spring, Bennett Spring and Greer Spring, large quantities of water may erupt from the ground, creating gushing spring branches that tumble and rush to the nearest rivers.

However, the springs most useful to the early Ozark settlers for home water and cooling were the less spectacular ones, which in early days were plentiful. Then, almost every farm would have one or two in varying sizes. This abundance of water was one of the reasons people settled in the hills, even though the soil was not suited for agriculture.

Since the presence of the spring determined the original home site, obviously the spring was near the house. Any spring with enough flow to form a natural or rocked-in pool and keep it always full with some runoff was adequate for family use. Even drip springs—which did just what the name says, release one drop at a time—by dripping constantly formed pools of water big enough for a family supply.

Usually the spring was downhill from the house. Before every meal it was a chore for the women or children to make a trip to the springhouse. Nora West remembered, "They used to carry water up from our spring. And time you would get up that steep hill with two buckets of water, you'd know you'd been somewhere."

In some cases settlers did nothing to change the spring, going to it several times a day with buckets for household water. Sometimes they improved the natural pool by deepening it and bordering it with flat sandstone rocks so that they could sink a three-gallon bucket and not stir up the water. To keep the water good, everyone would clean out leaves and trash continually. But many people who had springs took

The flow of water from springs ranges from a steady stream, as pictured here, to one drop at a time. Channeled into holding tanks, even drip springs will furnish water for several head of stock all summer.

further advantage of them by building a house either directly over the spring or down from the actual spring a way, where the building could be built. The house protected the water supply from contamination from domestic or wild animals and provided a safe place to store food.

The natural freshwater springs were ideal for keeping foods and milk, for they kept an almost constant temperature year around of about 58°F. This was cool enough to keep foods fresh in hot weather and warm enough that the constant flow from the spring kept foods and water from freezing in the winter. Though it was not impossible, spring water would hardly ever freeze over. When it did, it was not the spring that froze, but the top water that ran out into the trough or on the ground. Break the ice, and the warmer water was flowing underneath. The presence of the spring even affected the air inside the house, making it cooler than outside temperature in summer and warmer in winter.

Though the surface temperature did not affect the spring, other weather conditions did. Obviously, during dry seasons, especially prolonged ones such as in the mid-thirties and fifties, some springs went dry, and all springs suffered less water flow, because groundwater is dependent on rainfall.

Conversely, great quantities of rain affect springs. Surface run-off gets into the spring and muddies up the water. Since water flows through the porous underground waterways of the Ozarks so rapidly, even the underground water becomes dingy for a few days after prolonged or heavy rains. The flow from the springs at these times is greater, sometimes flooding the house temporarily.

Warren Cook said, "We carried water from the spring and kept the milk there. If a thunder shower came in the middle of the night, somebody had to get up and go to the spring and take the milk out. Otherwise, you had chocolate milk the next morning because of the muddy water."

This was a minor inconvenience, however. In hours, or a day or two at most, the water would clear again and be back to normal levels. Food could be replaced in the springhouse and water used for drinking once again.

Since the main purpose of the springhouse was to keep food, mostly milk and butter, cool and safe for family use, the houses were built with shelves and troughs for holding containers of food. Earliest houses were built of logs on sandstone foundations, but they soon rotted out. Later, more permanent ones were built of thick rock walls for better insulation. Some were constructed simply of rough oak, with no attempt at insulation, but only as a protection against animals and wind. Most houses were small, from six by eight feet to eight by ten feet. Some were as large as fourteen feet square, but the larger the building, the harder it was to keep cool.

The simpler ones had dirt or gravel floors, with rocked-in troughs to set crocks of milk around which the spring water could flow, or deeper places where sealed jars or fruit like melons could be immersed in the water. Still later some houses had troughs built deep enough to hold milk cans. When cement was available, houses were built with poured concrete floors having spillways or troughs for the water to flow through. The spring water might be piped in or flow directly into the troughs, which were often lined with gravel that acted as a filter. In some houses the troughs had wider places or deeper places designed for storing different foods that needed to be in direct contact with the cool water. At the other end of the house would be an outlet, a hole or pipe or trough, for water to continue on its way. Often it would flow outside into a trough or pool for watering the stock.

Inside there were usually shelves to set food on and nails on which to hang meat and other foods.

Before farmers had cream separators, they had to let their milk stand in open crocks for the cream to rise to make the butter they sold. The Fern Dale Creamery of the Creed Summers family used the springhouse for its dairy business. After milking the cows, they put the milk in large crocks until the cream rose to the top and could be skimmed off and sold or made into butter. Since this process took several hours, the milk had to be kept sweet. The springhouse was also a holding place for the cream and butter until it was taken to Springfield, Missouri, to the closest dairy distributor at that time. Milk would keep in the water for three or four days.

The Summers family also made cheese and butter at the springhouse, putting them into crocks and lowering them into the trough to store. The water flowed around the crocks and over sealed containers, keeping things fresh.

Some people kept stone jars of pickles in the springhouses. Cucumbers were put into crocks with brine, and were kept there while making pickles. After the brine had finished its work of turning cucumbers into pickles, Adley Fulford remembers they would pour the pickles and brine out on the concrete slab and let the spring water run over them to wash out the salty brine.

Some meats were also kept in the springhouse. If the house was cool enough, fresh meats like chickens and beef would be placed on shelves to cool out a few feet above the water trough and would keep good for overnight or a day or two. If the air was not cool enough, the meat would be put in containers and placed in the water. Cured pork not consumed during the winter might be moved from the smokehouse and hung on nails on the wall during hot weather, to keep it from getting so strong.

The family laundry was often done beside the springhouse in the shade of a big tree. Since most of the springhouses were a distance from the main house, it was easier to take the wash down to the spring than it was to carry the water to the house, even in the wintertime. The women dipped the water into large black kettles and heated it with a wood fire underneath. With scrub board and lye soap in hand, they washed their clothes.

Bathing was not done there because the water was too cold, even in the summer. People carried the water to the house to heat for bathing.

Creed Summers summed it all up, "We always done our washing down there . . . and everything down there. It was just as cool and nice. Oh, it was a fine place, there ain't no question about that."

Lois Beard agreed, "Our springhouse on my old home place was a beautiful place and clean as a pin. We did a lot of our work down there—our laundry in summertime, our food in the summertime, and carrying water for the house anytime of the year. We just really enjoyed the spring and springhouse."

People were not the only ones to enjoy the moist coolness. Adley Fulford said, "You might find a snake or a frog or something in there. We always kept some little perch fish in the spring. We just kept them 'cause we liked them. We fed them butter. They liked it. They'd get very tame after while. We could put in a little flake of butter and they would come up and almost eat it out of our hands. 'Course, we liked to watch them play in there. We generally had, oh, a half a dozen little ones in there."

"There was sometimes excitement when we opened the old milk crate," Warren Cook said. "It was just a slatted crate about six or eight feet long with a lid on top of it that discouraged the dogs and hogs that might get into the milk. We got shook when we started to reach down to get the bucket of milk, and there was a big old water moccasin lying down in there."

All the uses discussed so far have to do with work. But after a hard day of work in the hot fields for the men and a hot day in the kitchen for the women, the springhouse was a good place to go in late afternoon. The adults would pull up a seat, open the door to the springhouse, sip on a cool drink of good-tasting water or lemonade made of cold spring water, and relax, while the children played school or house. The springhouse made a dandy air-conditioner, too.

None of the water going through the springhouse was wasted. After the water cooled the food and washed the clothes, it ran out on to the ground or into troughs for the cattle and other stock to drink from. What the livestock didn't use evaporated, sank back into the ground or, if the flow from the spring was great enough, flowed down to a creek or river to begin the cycle again.

Though rarely used anymore, there are springhouses still standing, some in excellent shape, some quite dilapidated. Following are descriptions, photographs, drawings, and floor plans of four different, yet typical houses.

Creed Summers's springhouse in a hollow between two hills was built directly over a spring that used to run a four-inch stream of water. The walls were constructed of native sandstone about one foot thick. It had a concrete floor and trough that the spring ran through. A shelf was built over the trough on one side of the room against the wall, to set things on. It had one small door and six small windows, three

The Fern Dale Creamer springhouse, according to owner Creed Summers, used to be the finest place there ever was. Since the installation of electricity, the Summers no longer use the springhouse in their dairy operations. No longer needed, it has deteriorated.

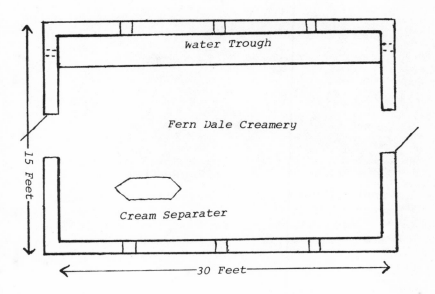

In the Summer's dairy, the spring ran through this water trough, which was large enough to hold several cans of milk. The large quantity of spring water held in the trough, as well as the insulated construction of the building, kept the inside temperature many degrees cooler than outside.

Most springhouses were some distance from the house. Though this one is not too far away, the family had to carry the water up a steep hill to the house.

The second springhouse on Nora West's farm is one of the oldest, possibly built by slaves. It was built into the side of the hill that forms the back wall.

on a side high on the wall. The wooden framed ceiling was roofed with metal.

This springhouse once used in their dairy business is well over a hundred years old and would still be standing intact if a tree hadn't ·fallen on one corner of the roof. But since the house was no longer used, the damage was not repaired.

Nora West's springhouse was constructed of sandstone like the Summers building except for one outstanding thing. There is no back wall. The back wall is a bluff, for this springhouse was built up against a spring that came out of the bluff. The sills are crossed at the corners and held together with wooden pins driven in. This springhouse is very small, about nine feet square, with only one door and no windows.

The spring that came out of the hill flowed through the concrete trough, which was about three feet off the ground and about eighteen inches deep. The water then ran out a hole in the front wall into an oval-shaped trough used for watering livestock. The excess water then ran out into a branch that emptied into Goodwin Hollow.

This spring used to have a strong flow and a big pool of water. Mrs. West said she stopped using it in 1955 because the water was disappearing and what was left was getting bad. There is very little water there now. She believes that the five wells drilled near there and the dry years have weakened the stream.

The third springhouse is the best preserved of them all and is still being used. This house has a totally different appearance from the other two. It is about six by eleven feet, with an overhanging roof or porch extending about three feet over the spring area. The walls are about six feet high, with the first two and a half feet concrete and the remainder oak frame. It has one door leading into the side, and no windows.

The spring in this house comes out right under the porch roof, runs through the house and flows out the back into a creek. On the back wall opposite the porch are shelves to keep things in storage.

This springhouse is near the old Dalton School. Since the one-room country school had no water supply, the children would carry their buckets to the spring, fill them, and carry them back to school.

The house that was on the place when the springhouse was built, burned. When the Floyd Smiths rebuilt, they installed an electrical pump in the springhouse to pump the spring water to their new home.

The water from the third springhouse still furnished all household needs of the owners. But instead of carrying water in buckets to the house, the Floyd Smiths pump it by electricity.

The fourth springhouse was built in two stages, first the part around the well, and then the part over the gutters and troughs where the food was stored.

This deep spring was rocked up. Though dry now, it used to be always full and overflowing. Family members could fill buckets for household use easily by simply dipping in a bucket. The well overflowed constantly, channeled by a pipe into the next room where it cooled milk, eggs, and other perishables.

Some natural springs have been dammed by a modern bulldozer to make large, fresh spring ponds. The springhouse, no longer needed, quickly rots away. Courtesy Bob Wright.

The fourth springhouse is probably the oldest, since it still has some logs used in its construction. All the studdings are logs that have been hand-hewn to a rectangular shape. The sidings are oak, the roof, wooden shingles. The house now sits in a picturesque spot under sycamore trees in a meadow beside a pond.

This springhouse is of fairly good size (thirteen by twenty feet), with two rooms. The outside door opens into a room that was the original house where the spring was. Years ago someone had dug a hole or open cistern about eight feet deep and lined it with rocks. Down in the hole about a foot is where the spring came out. The water accumulated in the well until it overflowed and ran out a channel.

To the right is a door leading into the second room of the house, which was built in 1925. It has a concrete floor divided by a runway constructed to channel the water. There are concrete shelves for cooling. The water spilled through a hole in the well, through the floor of the first room, into an open channel in the cement floor of the second room. The floor of this room is lower than the top of the well. Water from the spring was channeled in two-inch troughs to a larger and slightly deeper holding area, then to one much deeper (about eighteen inches), and then out the far end of the house.

Like so many springs, this one is now dry, with only a few inches of water in the bottom of the deep hole.

The coming of electricity to rural areas in the early 1940s to power refrigerators made the springhouses obsolete. People drilled wells closer to the house and pumped water directly to the kitchen for all household uses. No longer did the women have to carry loads of clothes to the springhouse to wash, then lug the wet ones back to hang on the line. Modern dairy farmers installed electric milk coolers to hold their whole milk to await the refrigerated milk trucks coming to the farm to pick it up.

Even stock does not use the spring water much now. Farmers have ponds in every pasture and automatic waterers in the barnyards. With air-conditioning in most homes, no one needs the springhouse to cool off.

The deserted springhouses are falling down on top of the springs, some of which are dry anyway, because of the lowered water tables. Fewer forested acres means more surface run-off and less seepage into the ground, and greater use of underground water from the thousands and thousands of drilled wells in every county have slowed down or stopped the flow in many springs.

The importance and use of springs and springhouses in the earlier way of life in the Ozarks lives now only in the memories of our older people.

Ice, A Winter Harvest

One would think that the last thing on anyone's mind on a below-zero day in early 1900 would be how to keep cool during the next summer. But just as we today are planning how we can store summer sunlight for winter warmth, so did some energetic people figure out how to harvest the winter cold for next summer's comfort. Simply harvest the ice and store it for summer.

The process really was simple. All it required was an ax, a crosscut saw, a team and wagon (which everyone had), ice tongs (which the blacksmith could make), a pond or river close by, a shed or temporary building, sawdust from one of the many saw mills and—here's the catch—lots of heavy labor during the coldest weather of the year.

Most people stayed close to their fires, but a few braved the weather to cut, haul, and store ice. Some people, like Dick Luthy's family, cut ice as a business and sold it during the summers to townspeople and businesses. Some people, like Ernie Hough's family, cut ice for their own use. Some, like the people in the McBride community in the 1920s, cut and stored ice for the use of the entire community. And most others did without ice during the hot summers.

In the early 1900s Dick Luthy's family was the first to cut and sell ice in their area, although some people in other places sold ice earlier. Their ice house looked like an old barn, large, but completely open inside, with no partitions. The house was made of oak lumber, with the sidings cut thicker than boards in ordinary buildings. Since the ice was stacked with all the weight on the dirt floor of the building, there was no side pressure, but the walls had to be thick to help insulate the ice.

The Luthy family cut ice off an acre pond near their ice house. "That pond was dug when clay was taken from there to make bricks for a house being built," Dick said. "That old pond water wouldn't be fit to put in drinks to cool. But, you could use it for ice boxes and other things." They used the pond because it was convenient. The river was too far away to haul ice from, nor would the moving river water freeze as quickly as the pond.

Dick and his six brothers cut the ice when it was around zero-degree weather and ice had built up to about eight or ten inches thick. They would work until the house was filled, usually about a week. "Sometimes we had a little hurrying to do if it would warm up before we got the ice house filled," Dick chuckled.

To start cutting they chopped a hole in the ice with an ax and then used a coarse-toothed crosscut saw to saw the blocks. Each block was about three by five feet and weighed about a hundred pounds. They started cutting in the middle of the pond and worked their way back to the banks, sawing as far back to the banks as the saw would cut without hitting the ground and getting as much ice as they could without getting wet.

"When that ice was cut in a cake, it was just a-floating in there. You would have to throw a spear and hit one side and you'd tip it up so you could grab the cake with a hook. The end of the spear had a hook on the one side of it and a sharp point on the other side. When my brother'd tip the ice up, he'd catch it and jerk it up on top of the uncut ice on the pond, see? You had to be careful doing that, though. I remember my brother once hit a cake of ice with his gig just to tip the ice up so that he could jerk it up on top. But the gig slipped and he went into the pond. It was down below zero and I thought he would freeze."

Once cut, the ice was carried with ice tongs to a horse-drawn wagon equipped with an end gate and sixteen-inch side racks where it was stacked like bales of hay are stacked today. It took two men with ice tongs—one on each end—to load a hundred pounds in the wagon. Each wagon load of ice weighed about two tons. The ice was then hauled to the ice house, where about twelve inches of sawdust was already spread on the floor.

At the ice house, the ice was stacked one cake on top of another, eighteen inches from the wall. "We'd build it up just like you was

Cross section of a shed turned community ice house. Sawdust serves as insulation.

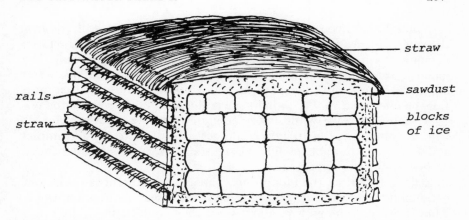

straw

sawdust

rails

blocks
of ice

straw

Cross section of a temporary rail pen ice house. Temporary ice houses were made of rails and straw. As blocks of ice were stacked, the pen was built around them. Sawdust filled all the spaces to keep out the air. Straw on top shed the rain.

building up brick or stone," Dick said. Then they filled all the space between the walls and the ice with sawdust and covered the top with sawdust to keep the air from getting to the ice. They got their sawdust from local sawmills they had paid to hold the sawdust for them.

To get the ice ready to sell, they swept the sawdust off with a broom and used a little water to clean it. Then they sold it to businesses in town and to many residents. Their customers would buy twenty-five to fifty pounds at a time. The price of the ice ran about five cents a pound, or a big chunk for a quarter. Dick made rounds twice a week in summer in a wagon without insulation. "We just had to let it melt. It didn't melt so fast, because we wouldn't take enough out at a time to be gone long enough for it to melt too much. We just had to do the best we could those days." Dick added, "You couldn't make a living off of ice alone, though. We also had a farm and ran a dairy."

Ernie Hough's family cut ice for their own use in the early 1900s. "We never sold ice," Ernie said. "We'd give it to people sometimes." Ernie didn't have an ice house, but used what he called a "rail pen." It was a temporary building built of rails much like a log building, with straw stuffed in the spaces between the rails to keep the sawdust from falling out. They built up the pen around the ice as it was stacked. The rail pen had no door or roof. They simply crawled in from the top to get the ice. The size of the pen depended on the amount of ice cut. The pen might be eight to ten feet square and "as high as you wanted it."

Since Ernie lived on the river, he cut ice off a big, still eddy on the river. "Ice from a pond wasn't fit to use. But the ice from the river, it would wash off so nice and clear we put it in our lemonade. We made ice cream with it, too. I can remember when we drank water out of the creeks and rivers. I guess you wouldn't want to do that now. But then it was clean. We didn't have polluted rivers like we do today."

Usually the river would freeze enough to cut ice at least once each winter. Sometimes the Houghs could get enough ice to last all summer and sometimes they got enough to last just half the summer. It depended on how much the river froze.

Like the Luthys, the Houghs used an ax and crosscut saw with one handle off to cut the ice. They cut ice when it was about a foot thick. They'd saw off a long strip, about what they could handle, then they cut it into blocks. They handled the blocks with ice tongs to load on the wagon. They would cut what ice they could before it got dangerous. Where they cut, the water wasn't very deep.

Ernie also used sawdust to insulate the ice, since his family also had a sawmill and sawdust was handy. They put sawdust on the ground and then stacked the ice, leaving a space between the wall of the pen and the ice to be filled with sawdust. It took about a foot of sawdust to prevent air from getting to the ice. As long as the air doesn't get to the ice, it won't melt. To complete the temporary ice house, they covered the top of the ice with sawdust and then spread layers of straw to shed the rain.

When the ice had all been used, they took down the rail pen and cleaned up the spot until the next ice harvest.

Sometimes the men in a rural area like the McBride community would work together to cut ice for the whole community. One year the ice would be stored in someone's granary, and another year in someone else's shed. The whole community was welcome to use the ice as long as it lasted. Myrtle Hough remembered, "We used it mostly to cool water and for ice cream. Usually the neighborhood would make ice cream out of it. If someone was sick, why, we'd always take ice cream to them."

A few women had ice boxes in their kitchens. "That icebox was the first convenience we had," Annie Fike said. "And that wasn't very convenient, because we couldn't put a very big pan under the ice to catch the water when it melted. We had to empty that pan about twice a day. The box'd hold a hundred pounds of ice, and by putting paper over the cake of ice and not opening the door any more than we had to, we could have cream pies and cold milk. That ice would last most all week. Almost every Saturday we'd put a new cake of ice in."

This sandstone ice house has a drive for easy loading.

Cutting ice, whether done as a community, a family, or a business was hard work. Ernie said, "Not too many people cut ice too much anytime. They could have, but they didn't. They just did without ice." As soon as plants began manufacturing ice, people like Dick Luthy quit cutting ice. "People could get clean ice then, not like that ice cut off the pond. Besides, cutting ice was quite a bit of work," Dick remembered. "But, that's all us people did in them days was work."

Water Witching

"Hey, it's moving, it really is!"
"It's pulling down. I can't hold it still!"
"I don't believe in this. There has to be a trick!"

These were our various reactions as we first became acquainted with the art of water witching.

As we watched Bill York work, I had my doubts. Finding underground water with a freshly cut forked twig from a peach tree sounded a little farfetched. But grasping the stick in his hands in front of him, Bill walked slowly over the open meadow intently watching the tip. "When it moves it will point to water," he explained. After a few steps he smiled. The stick began to turn. All of his knuckles on both hands were white because he held it so tightly. "Watch my hands to see if I'm turning it. See, I can't stop it turning." When the tip pointed straight down, he stopped. "There it is. The water is down there."

Disbelief showed on all our faces. "It's not unreasonable for people not to believe it," he said, "but if they don't believe it, that's their own prerogative. I have no idea how it works. Here, you try it."

He handed me the stick. Feeling very foolish, I backed up and walked the same ground. "It doesn't work with everyone," he warned. Nothing happened to the twig I held in front of me. "Here," he said, "try again." This time he put his hands on my wrists, and the twig actually turned in my hands and pointed straight down at the same spot it had for him! I couldn't stop its turning, and all he did was to lay his hands on my wrists.

One by one the others tried, positive that there wasn't anything to it. Some of us had the "talent," others didn't. Some became convinced that there was something to water witching, though we couldn't explain it, but others remained certain that it was some kind of trick.

"He's moving it himself. The pressure of his hands in that awkward position forces the stick to turn," they reasoned.

Regardless of whether there really is a "gift" or "power," the belief in water witching is still widespread in the rural areas of the Ozarks today, with almost every community having one man who can water witch. Some well drillers continue to use their services to decide where to drill, to look for the strongest point of the stream, and to find underground caves and caverns to avoid. Some people use water witching to find buried water pipes.

The art of water witching has been recorded far back in history. In the fifteenth century, Germans used divining rods to find metals in the ground. Later this practice was adapted to find water. The skill goes by several different names, such as dousing, water wiggling, and divining.

According to Bill, the best time to water witch is in the spring when the sap is in the limbs, making them limber. The stick has to be limber because it is held tightly, and when it turns to point to water, it twists in the hand. If it wasn't limber, it would break. Some men can find water with one kind of wood and not with others.

Water witchers can often determine the strength and width of a stream. They can tell the strength by the pressure of the stick as it goes down and the width by approaching the stream from opposite directions.

There are many different ways to witch, depending on the person. We've talked to three people about their ways of doing it.

BILL YORK—"I suppose I learned through my dad when I was a kid. I was fourteen years old." Bill started by watching and eventually caught on. "I forgot all about it until two or three years ago. My son and daughter-in-law were out here, and the first thing I knew we were outside showing them." He hasn't checked for the accuracy of his witching yet. "I've never water witched for wells, but my dad used to."

Bill can witch with cedar, dogwood, and his favorite, peach. "I like to use peach limbs in the spring and summer because they're limber. I've tried oak. It doesn't work at all.

"I cut a limb that has a fork. I try to get the forks about the same size so they will bend equally. The limb where the fork meets should be a foot long and the limbs from the fork about eighteen inches long."

He holds the stick pointing up with the two protruding forks in his fists with his palms up while he walks along. "The branch moves forward or backward depending on you. It'll go down or straight back to you. It seems like this morning this one is trying to come back to me. The main thing is to hold it tight. When it finds water, there isn't any way to stop it turning. It would twist out of your hands. I've seen it in the spring, I was holding the branch so tightly that the bark would twist around where I held it."

When Lyn Marble reached a spot where he suspected there was water, the metal rods crossed. In history most of the water witchers have been men, though some women have this talent.

Bill York (left) uses various kinds of forked sticks. This one is peachwood. Sometimes the stick will turn toward him and other times it will turn away from him. But either way, it points down when he reaches the greatest amount of underground water.

Lyn Marble, holding a bent bough in his hands, slowly walked along, waiting for it to start pulling. When he came over water, the bough pulled down. Snow or water on the surface doesn't affect it; it has to be an underground flowing stream.

LYN MARBLE—"I've been water witching since I was twenty-four. There was a man up in Michigan who witched a well for me, and I just took it up from there."

He has two methods, bronze welding rods and a straight limb bent in a circle.

"The two bronze rods are about one-eighth of an inch in diameter and thirty-three inches long including the handles, the bent part. One end of each rod is bent over about four inches. Hold them by the handles with the rods parallel. Keep them level and don't put your thumbs on the top. As you come over water in the ground, they'll cross. Bronze is more sensitive than wood."

To show us how to witch with a limb he selected a limber stick about two feet long and the thickness of a pencil. He got a good grip on the underside of each end of the stick with his palms turned under and face out. Then he brought his hands inward to make a circle. "I hold it against my body. When you come to the water, it will pull down. Now watch it. It's starting to pull." Sure enough as he walked along it turned downward.

"I like to use elm best. It works for me better than the rest. But last year we used peach. This year I saw this nice cherry, and since I knew I could do it with peach, I wanted to see if I could do it with cherry instead. It worked."

Lyn can tell the width of the stream by walking various directions around the spot where the rods cross or the stick goes down. He walks along until the rods cross, and then goes farther down, turns around and walks back to where they cross again. If they cross immediately, he has to go back up farther and try again. The distance between where they cross the first time and the last time he tries is the width of the stream. "But you have to witch across the stream instead of the direction it flows," he explained.

As we were witching at Lyn's house the rods and bough all kept pointing to a particularly strong stream near his shed. "I'm going to drill a well there soon," he said.

And so he did. The 224-foot-deep well yields fifteen gallons of water a minute. Grinning in triumph he showed us the photos he had taken. "Here is the proof that water witching works."

LILLIAN HUMPHREYS—"I started to water witch by watching my father when he took me along when he witched wells for people." She can first remember knowing she could water witch when she was eight years old.

She has picked wells for several people, including, very recently,

Lillian Humphreys begins holding the stick in this position.

At the strongest point the stick points downward.

Lilliam Humphreys holds a straight elm stock. She has determined water is there with the forked stick. Now she finds out how deep it is. The straight stick bobs once for each foot down to water.

four different wells in her neighborhood. She witches with a green forked stick, using elm, peach, cherry, or oak. Getting a good grip with her fists palms up on the two protruding branches she walks along slowly. The stick pulls down to point to the underground water. Her husband, Harold, said, "We've used smaller sticks than this, and she'd hold them so tight it would break the stick."

Lillian has told the people not only where to dig but also how far down to drill by using a different method with a straight green stick. This stick should be the width of a pencil and three and one-half feet long. "Hold the small end of the stick with your fist against your hip to steady it, and in a few seconds the end of the stick will start bobbing." We stood watching and in a few seconds the end actually started bouncing about four inches up and down, once every second. "One, two, three . . ." Silently counting the bobs, we waited for the stick to stop bouncing. "One hundred ninety-seven, one hundred ninety-eight." The stick stopped. "One bob is equal to one foot down. When it stops it will start again after a few seconds and go the same number of times. When the stream is stronger the stick generally goes up and down farther. The number of bobs measures the depth where the stream is the strongest. The drillers usually hit water right before I say but go on a few feet farther. Then the wells fill up with water."

When Lillian moved back to the Ozarks, she found the place to put their home by witching the spot to find the best water supply. The long stick then, as now, bobbed 198 times. When the well drillers set over the spot they drilled two hundred feet and got an average of forty gallons a minute.

When asked what she thought made it work, Lillian replied, "I don't know what makes it work. I can't explain it."

Hand Dug Wells

"When we had to depend on springs for water," Lois Beard said, "we didn't use near the water we do now. I'd say we'd use thirty gallons a day and that's a lot of buckets when a bucket was two and a half gallons. Our dishwater and bathwater was always saved and used for scrubbing the floors or slopping the hogs. The last thing we usually did of a night was to go get a couple buckets of water."

Water for stock was also a problem for many farmers without springs. There were no large ponds gouged out of the earth in a few hours with a bulldozer. Instead, there were small ponds painstakingly dug with a team and a slip, but they would go dry. Then farmers would either have to take the stock to a river or find some other solution. The best solution for household and stock needs was a well.

The early wells, from 1850 to 1900, were hand dug, usually round, though there were some large wells that were dug in a square shape. They varied from three to four feet in diameter up to as large as ten feet or more. They had to be at least big enough for a man to swing a pick. The depth of the wells varied from home to home. Sometimes the settler could go twelve feet and have a good water supply, and other times he might have to go down a hundred feet. He would dig until he hit a seep or a stream of underground water that would supply his need. Then the hole was rocked up to hold and protect the water.

The early wells tapped small underground streams near the surface, but today, with need of greater quantities of water and lowering of water tables, drilled wells going as deep as three hundred feet use only the water tables.

Cliff Wallace started drilling wells in 1933. "We drilled a lot of wells only a hundred and some odd feet deep and some less than a hundred. I quit drilling about a year and half ago and it averaged about 300 feet. I think a lot of that was caused by the amount of wells being drilled. One time in the fifties we had drilled a lot of wells and they were good wells, we thought. In that drought, they went dry. We would go back and drill them deeper. Some of them didn't have a drop of water in them."

A straight, rocked-in well.

Earlier, people were satisfied if they had enough water to fill a bucket when needed, therefore, they could use seeps. Cliff continued, "Most of the shallow dug wells were just a seep well. Oh, sometimes they'd hit a stream when they dug them. They dug in a dry time and when they'd get down deep enough, they would catch some water. Maybe when they'd leave it all night, the ground would be a little moist the next morning. In the rainy time the water is closer to the surface, then it gets lower and lower. This is the water that would seep into the well. That was the source of water. This well of mine out here in front of the house, at times you can see the water running in. The surface water goes down so many feet and then there is a layer of sandrock and this seepage is coming in between the sandrock and the dirt formation above. It gets to the rock, then runs over to the well and drips in.

"I don't know why, but water out of a shallow well or cistern like that is much colder than out of a deep well. I don't know how many degrees, but it is colder. On a summer day I can go and pump a drink of water and tell whether it's a shallow or deep well by how cold the water is."

Other people were lucky enough to hit a strong stream close to the surface. Lois said, "It's amazing on certain veins, water is so much closer to the surface than others. Where my dad lived, that well isn't more than thirty or forty feet to the bottom, but I've seen it when you could dip the water out with a long-handled dipper."

After deciding to dig a well, the first thing was to pick the location. Lois said, "They'd go out and take a crowbar or something and keep punching around till they found a spot they thought there was more dampness than in another spot. In the summertime if you find a damp spot four or five feet down, you know water is pretty easy to get at." Sometimes, people would have a water witcher come and decide where would be a good place to dig.

The actual digging process was really quite simple. They would mark off as big a well as needed and start in with a pick and shovel, like digging a grave, dynamiting if they hit solid rock. A lot of the dug wells have a big mound of dirt around them that has never been moved away. Sand and gravel pockets in the walls sometimes made it difficult to keep the wall true.

Digging in the rocky, cherty Ozark soil is not easy. In many places there is only a thin layer of topsoil, then the hardpan, a heavy, extremely hard-packed clay formation, to break through. Ozarkians have taken a lot of ribbing about their poor soil where the hardpan is on top of the ground. "No, it ain't," is the common quick retort. "It's under a layer of rock." Cliff betters that answer. "Sometimes the hardpan is up on top of the fence posts!" But once through the one and a half to fifteen feet of hardpan, the digging is easier in the clay and flint rock where most water is found.

Many times, if people ran into trouble or didn't want to dig their own well, there would be someone in the community who could help. From their experience, they would know how to dig the well and how to help in trouble spots.

In the Ozarks, sometimes diggers didn't go very far down before they hit solid rock. In that case they either took a bar and pounded through or used dynamite to break up the rock. They had to be careful, though, to avoid blowing up the walls.

"It is very dangerous to dig a well," Cliff said, "because they work without anything above them to keep that rock and stuff from falling in on them until they get through and wall it up. Some of them might have put in boards or timber to hold the dirt back. But in time they would have had to take out the supports and wall it up with rock, then fill in behind with dirt and gravel or sand."

In the process of digging there were other dangers. One of these was the constant danger of a poison gas. Cliff said, "In those days they called it foul air, bad air, the damps. Air without oxygen is what I

This jug well was dug in the late 1800s. The opening in the center of the big rock was cemented in when the well was no longer used.

think it is. In digging those wells they had what they called a sail which was about five or six feet in diameter at the top and had a wire or wooden band to hold it apart. It was made of canvas and flared out at the top more like a sail and then it tapered down to a tube ten to twelve inches in diameter that went down in the well. They would turn the sail to the wind and let it catch the wind and blow it down in there. It would drive the bad air out and put the oxygen in. They claimed you could tell when the bad air was there, because when you went down in the well, you would have a hard time getting your breath.

"I've heard that years ago they used canaries to put down in the well. If a canary could live, so could a person. That bad air was usually in a well that had been dug a long time ago and hadn't been worked in for a long time. I've heard about people getting in that bad air while they were cleaning out the well or cistern."

There are now many different contaminants other than foul air in the environment, and quite often they find their way to these shallow dug wells. Cliff said, "A person probably wouldn't even drink the water now. I'd say most of the problem is from the septic tanks and lagoons,

Housewives made many trips to the well each day with bucket and rope. They soon learned the trick of flipping the rope to sink the bucket.

because there are more wells, more buildings and septic tanks all the time. We drilled wells in places where they never heard of bad water, but later on they got to building houses and they got bad water in their water supplies. I'd say where most of it comes from is where a well caved in and was left standing there, and someone put a septic tank near, which flowed into it."

A top to the well kept children, dogs, cats, and other animals out of the well. This was sometimes a platform of boards, with a box about knee-high to drop a bucket through. Sometimes the box would be large enough for two buckets to be in the well at the same time. They would be rigged for one to go down while the other came up.

Another kind of top was a small cement pad built around the well with perhaps a cement top built on that. One unusual top is made from the bed of a child's wagon.

There were usually only three ways to get water out of a dug well: a windlass, a bucket on a rope, and, if you had the means, a pump.

The windlass was a round beam set in the cradle of two Y-shaped posts. This beam had a rope fastened on, with a bucket on the end. The beam had a crank on the end to let the bucket down into the water and then crank until it wound the rope enough to reach the bucket.

An old hand pitcher pump.

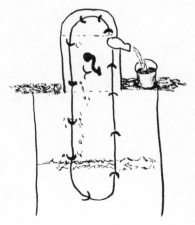

As you cranked the handle of this pump, the chain would rotate and the cup would scoop up water and pour it through the spout. This is called a chain and cup pump.

Mary samples hand-pumped well water.

If only a rope and a bucket were available, the rope was tied to the bucket bail and let down to the water to fill, and then pulled up "by main strength and awkwardness."

A sucker-rod pump had a cylinder at the bottom of the pipe that would pull up a slug of water each time the handle pumped. Some of the more modern kitchens would have had a pitcher pump. This pump had a cylinder near the top that would have to be primed from the top by pouring some water down the pump.

While visiting with Lois we learned of some stories about hand dug wells. "One woman was getting water in one day when the rope on her bucket broke. She thought she could climb down—there were some rocks that stuck out. She climbed down and got the bucket, but she couldn't get back out. She had to stay there on a little rock ledge till her husband got in at noon to get her out."

To a little boy, a well can be a very interesting place. "A very inquisitive boy I knew was always sticking his nose into everything. He and another little boy were playing in the yard. This kid got to wanting to know what was in that well, and fell in. It was almost empty, and since they hadn't cleaned it out, it was just gooey mud. When they brought him out covered with that old gooey mud all over him and his little eyes just a-shining, his mother fainted!"

With the coming of the drilled well, hand dug wells became another relic of a by-gone era. Though some wells are still used today for watering cattle or even for household use, most of them have gone dry because of the lowering of the water tables.

Even so, these old wells still hold an attraction for people. Often the remains of an old well that has been filled in will be the last reminder of an old homestead. Other homesteads, long deserted, still have lonely pumps standing guard over a well full of memories.

Rainy Day Savings

An improvement over the rainbarrel at the corner of the house to hold soft water for convenient household use was the cistern. Usually dug near the kitchen, these containers of rainy day savings supplied families with water during long periods of dry weather.

Cisterns, manmade underground reservoirs that store water for household use, could be built round, square, or any other shape desired. Sizes vary greatly, from as small as four feet in diameter to as big as fifteen, ranging in depth from nine feet to as deep as twenty feet, depending on individual water needs of the family. The walls, six to eight inches thick, had many different kinds of linings — clay, brick, cement, or smooth rock — although cement is the most common material for modern cisterns. All were watertight, insuring that no impurities would seep through and that water would not seep out.

Unlike a dug well, a cistern had no natural seep or stream flowing into it, so water had to be put in some way. In early times water was hauled from a nearby spring. This was a long, taxing process, using a bucket, barrel, team and wagon. Men hauled the empty barrel to the spring in the wagon. Men filled the barrel by hand, hauled the barrel to the cistern, and, again by hand, dumped the water into the cistern — trip after trip.

Many people expanded the idea of having a rain barrel to supply their water needs and eliminated hauling water to the cistern. They installed eave troughs on their house and nearby barns and other buildings close to the cistern to catch the rainwater. Rain would run down the roof, into the eave trough, into the downspout, and into the cistern.

The size of these cisterns would depend on how often rain fell. In regions of little rainfall, the cistern would be big, to store large amounts of water for long periods of time. Where there was abundant rainfall to refill the cistern often, it did not need to be as large.

Cisterns were popular in the thirties, but after 1940 were rarely built. At one time people depended on a cistern because no other source of water was available. In some places water was miles away, and underground water streams were too far to reach by digging until modern

People installed eave troughs on their house and nearby barns and other buildings close to the cistern to catch the rainwater. The cistern is located in the center barn. This cistern, still in use, was built in 1910. It is 12 x 30 x 8 feet in size and holds seven feet, five inches of water.

well-drilling machinery. People today are less likely to use a cistern because it is easier to use water from a county waterline or drill a well, and it requires less care and upkeep.

But some people even today prefer a cistern to a well or water from a waterline. The soft, pure water of a cistern is a major advantage. The water stays cool year-round and doesn't freeze in the winter. Since the rain goes into the cistern, mud puddles around the house don't exist.

But cisterns have disadvantages to match the advantages. Eave troughs and filters have to be cleaned, as do the cisterns. Trees will drop leaves, blossoms and other pollutants in. Roots can crack the walls. The water supply depends on rainfall and in drought years can be an ever present worry. A cistern is especially undesirable in big industrial cities, because air pollution there would contaminate the water.

Clay Gum is one of those people for whom the advantages of a cistern outweigh the disadvantages. He dug cisterns all over this country, including the one by his house that furnishes his water needs. He hasn't dug many since 1940, but Clay, at eighty-two years old, still has an occasional call to dig one.

Clay dug cisterns year-round, though most were dug in the spring or summer months. "It didn't matter what time you dug them. It was just any time you wanted or just when you needed to." Clay dug a

These are the inside pipes leading to the concrete cistern. The two top pipes come from two different buildings. The bottom left pipe leads to the cistern and the right one goes back outside. The handle in the center closes the pipe not being used.

Even in recent times, Clay Gum used his cistern for drinking water.

cistern in about two or three weeks, working eight to twelve hours a day. The time required depended on the hardness of the dirt, the weather, and the depth.

After selection of a convenient site near the house, the next step was digging. "I would always dig mine round. Most were round, not square. Most measured six feet across, but some are five and some four feet. The size and depth was determined by how large the family was and what they used the water for. It's just any size you wanted. If you wanted to, you could make them sloped down on each side, but I always made mine straight up and down."

The cisterns were dug with a pick and shovel. The men dug down and shoveled the dirt out to one side until they were so deep they couldn't throw out any more dirt. Then they used a simple device, a windlass, usually a round wooden beam held by two forked supports driven in the ground. One end of a long rope was fastened to the beam and the other end to a bucket. The beam, when turned, raised or lowered the bucket. The man in the hole filled the bucket with dirt, the man on top wound the bucket up, then dumped it. Frequently, hitting solid rock would slow up the construction, necessitating dynamiting the rock. The workers lowered someone down to drill a hole. He slipped the dynamite in the hole and lit it. His co-worker pulled him out as quickly as possible. The dynamite usually blew away the rock, so they could continue digging.

After the cistern was the desired depth and shape, the next step was to wall up the sides, making them strong enough to hold water and keep out tree roots. Several different materials were used. Early cisterns used a clay and dirt plaster to seal the walls. Rocks or bricks morticed together made a much more durable lining. Cement was the latest material used. "They'd mix cement and make a plaster out of it and plaster it on the wall."

Sometimes after the cistern was rocked to within six feet of the surface, they would shape the opening like the top of a jug, gradually sloping the sides in until the opening was only eighteen to twenty-four inches across. Dirt filled in the cavity around the top, giving the cistern, or jug well, the appearance of a giant jug buried in the ground.

People sometimes intended to dig a well but would not reach a water seep. Instead, they walled up the well and converted it into a cistern.

The next step would be to make a platform for the top. Unlike the jug well with the opening flush with the ground, the tops of most cisterns were one and one-half feet tall and about two feet square, making it unlikely that anyone would fall in. There was a hole in the middle of the platform for a bucket to go through. The hole was covered when not being used.

After the cistern was dug and finished, the last step was installing the filter to clean water that was piped off the roof. Filters varied greatly and were not always used. The first filters were layers of different-sized gravel and charcoal. Later, better ones were built with different layers of gravel, sand, and charcoal. The first tray held gravel, the next sand, the next a finer sand, and the last tray held charcoal.

The filter wasn't really necessary, because the rainwater was pure, and if the roof was not very dirty, it was safe not to use one. If the filter wasn't cleaned very often, it would carry bacteria and make the water unsafe to drink. If the roof was dirty, letting the roof rinse off before letting the rain flow into the cistern allowed only clean water to enter.

Cisterns were usually cleaned out once a year, in the spring and summer months. When the cistern was almost dry was the best time to clean. The windlass bucket was used in shoveling out the debris on the bottom of the cistern as it was used when the cistern was dug. The walls were then washed down with vinegar water or Purex and scrubbed with a broom or brush. Then clean water was used to rinse the cistern out. Cleaning the cistern also gave an opportunity to examine the walls for any cracks or leaks and to repair them.

Cisterns have been used for years to store the family water supply. But now, with the proliferation of drilled wells and county water systems, the use of cisterns has decreased almost to extinction. People like Clay Gum who are willing to go out in the snow for a bucket of water are few.

The Wells of My Father Were Victims of a Revolution

By Ralph Gray

Often in my thoughts there comes back to me the memory of the wells on the farm in southwest Missouri where I grew up. Yes, wells. Those indispensable sources of water made a deep imprint on me as a child.

I remember my first encounter with a well very clearly. I was with Miriam and Harold in the Big Pasture. Gathering blackberries, we had crossed a dry branch and were working our way up through the underbrush toward a higher grassy area. Suddenly my older sister and brother yelled a warning. "Look out! There's an open well there!"

A dread note in their voices stopped me stock still. "How come there's a well here so far from the house?" I wondered.

"There used to be a house here, right up there where the grass is growing," said Harold.

He carefully felt his way through the vines and weeds and said, "Here's the well. Come on and look." And while he gripped one of my legs and Miriam the other, I stretched out my full five-year length, with my head over the water, and looked down for the first time into another world, the netherworld of wells.

A mystical feeling came over me. My skin tingled. First of all I saw my reflection, as though a watery counterpart of myself lived in the well and was staring up in surprise at me. Then I was able to look through the reflection into the inner mysteries of the well itself.

This well was about three feet in diameter, lined neatly with small rocks as far down as the eyes could reach. Indeed, a trick mirroring of light made the circular rock wall seem to go down forever. The well suddenly became a passageway from the everyday sunlit world above to unknown, fearsome realms below. A slip, and I would break that shiny looking-glass of water and sink down. Down I would slide—past the place where frog, newt, and salamander live, beyond the haunts of giant snakes blindly moving through the ooze, into the kingdom of the dead, where octopus-like spiders with eyes on stalks keep watch to see that you never return to daylight.

280

   And yet, as I shifted my body for a different angle (accompanied by renewed viselike grips on my legs), I suddenly saw the sky reflected beneath me. Clouds of intense white floated through the bluest of blues. Now I was looking into the eye of heaven. The stygian nightmare of the moment before was gone.
   Thus the vision of life's impossible mix of horror and beauty, good and evil, came to me early while looking down a well. But something of harder reality was born there, too—a sense of archeology. Harold's comment that there was once a homesite just up the little hill from the well was almost as intriguing as the well itself. Who were the people who built a home here, who farmed "our" farm, who lived and died and left no trace but the well? We never knew, but this spot always seemed slightly haunted.
   Strangely enough, in a region that had only begun to be settled about eighty years before Papa bought "The Wayside" in 1903, there was still another abandoned homesite on our 160 acres. It was closer to our own house, in a small field. Its only traces were a straggly cottonwood that finally gave up the ghost, a few shards turned up as Harold and Papa plowed the field, and—a well.

Actually, it was probably a cistern. It went down only about twelve or fifteen feet, was about ten feet in diameter, and was absolutely dry. In fact, the bottom was filled with junk deposited by our predecessors. Before my sense of archeology had developed enough to burrow among these artifacts, Papa announced one day, "I'm tired of plowing around that hole, and I'm afraid you kids might fall in it. Let's fill it up."

With a crowbar he attacked the sandstone slabs that formed the circular wall of the cistern and tumbled the top two or three courses into the pit. Poor dirt, then good top soil finished the job—and Papa had established a precedent that would be followed several times later when he bought two other farms with abandoned homesites and useless (and dangerous) wells staring at the sky.

But this homesite, the one where the lonely cottonwood stood vigil so long, did leave one other trace. Part of the house had been moved to our barnyard, where it served as a granary. It finally sagged to the ground and was dismantled for its lumber when Harold was in high school. He retrieved some of its walnut timbers for his carpenter shop assignments and made bookends, vases, and other objects still in use.

Near the granary was the third well I will speak of. It is still there, its waters still covered by a slight film of oil. We did not know it then, but underlying our farm is Mississippian sandstone impregnated with slight amounts of oil. Above this well, Papa built a rather fancy concrete well curb enclosing a longhandled steel pump. In my memory, that pump never worked, and Papa left it that way because of the oily water.

Instead, Papa, who was a mover and doer all his life, embarked on a grandiose water supply scheme that still serves the barnyard and household needs sixty years later. He built a big new barn and beneath its floor installed a huge concrete cistern. The roof caught enough rainwater to keep the cistern from going dry, except for one scare during the droughts of '34 or '36. A gasoline-powered pump and an air pressure tank drove the water through underground pipes to the house and other outlets.

A couple of times when the cistern got low, Harold and I, with our younger brother Vernon, laboriously dipped it dry and cleaned it. Bucket after bucket, the final inches of water came up. Then one of us would enter the great caisson by ladder and, with a scoop shovel, fill more buckets to be raised. Finally the inevitable layer of silt at the bottom would be scraped up and the cistern readied for another decade of service.

When it came my turn to work inside the tomblike tank, the old creepy feelings would come back. Though I knew better, I looked warily around for the underworld monsters of my childhood. I glanced as often as possible toward the reassuring eye of daylight offered by the one porthole entrance.

The old superstitions lived again when my brothers and I cleaned the well at the corner of the house. This was the original well for this homesite. It was a half-cistern, since runoff from the house could be shunted into it. A giant slab of sandstone safely covered it.

Mama didn't like the bland taste of the cistern water, so it was my little sister's chore to keep the family supplied with drinking water. Lowering the gallon bucket to the water, she would give the rope an experienced flip so that the bucket hit the water upside down and filled. One day Papa said, "Why don't you boys empty and clean out the old well at the corner of the house?"

When we lowered ourselves through the small circular opening, we could see that this well was shaped like a jug. As the water level fell lower and lower, bucket by bucket, we discovered that elm roots, as fine as the hair of sacrificed virgins, had burst through the rock walls and were waving with each movement of water as if alive. We were glad finally to have all the water out and the roots hanging limp and dead and free of myth.

We scraped the roots off the walls, and cleaned all the crevices in the masonry and in the solid rock at the bottom, twenty-five feet down. This well was alive and well, for two or three seeps on the floor accumulated water almost as fast as we could fill a bucket with a dipper. Vernon and I, who finished this three-day job, looked up often at the eye of heaven above. Bending again to our work, we cherished the golden circle of light that moved backwards, from west to east, across the floor of our world as the sun went its accustomed way in the upper world.

As time went on, Vernon and I became inseparable buddies and discovered a lot about the world, and ourselves, together. We explored the limits of courage, and occasionally found the beginnings of fear. One such time involved an abandoned well on the Horn eighty just north of our farm. Papa had stopped keeping dairy cows of our own, so Vernon and I walked the mile round-trip each day to buy milk from old Mrs. Horn.

About two-thirds of the way through the fields stood a rusty pump on sagging boards that covered a rectangular cistern, about twelve by eighteen feet in size. In the past there must have been a barn or shed here that directed rainwater into the underground compartment. On our errands we often, on impulses or dares, clattered across the cistern on the loose boards.

One time we decided to lift one of the boards and look in. A slab of sudden sunlight shot ten feet down to the bottom where, in a foot or two of water and banked earth, a writhing mosaic of snakes big and small slithered and twisted. We were transfixed. The snakes covered the entire bottom, seemingly several layers deep. Some were fighting and eating each other. Some were trying the corners, and two were twisting their way up the pipe leading to the pump.

Dante's vision of hell could not have outdone what we saw that day. What if the boards had broken as we gaily tripped over them? What if we now lost our balance and fell in? From that moment on, we never again presumed that we were immortal. Struck with fear, we carefully edged our way off the boards and put the lifted plank back in its place. We never said a word about this living hell so close to our world. We avoided the place like the plague.

As things turned out, Papa eventually bought the Horn property. In our absence at school he hired local men to make one large wheatfield of it by taking down all fences and outbuildings, transforming the house into a granary, and—filling up wells and cisterns! These included

a well practically inside the Horn cottage where Mrs. Horn often refreshed me with a brimming dipperful on my frequent visits and a
pasture well where Mr. Horn watered his dwindling livestock, and—
the snake-pit cistern. When I returned to the farm from school, I
criss-crossed the area where the evil crypt had descended and could
find not the slightest trace of it.

"Why did you fill up the two good wells?" I asked Papa.

"A well is like anything else," he said. "It's only useful as long as
it is used. You don't need a well in a field of wheat. It's just in the
way."

All the same, putting out those two eyes of heaven saddened me almost as much as the nearly concurrent deaths of the elderly couple
they had served so long. The well-springs of life lay buried in marked
and unmarked graves.

Mama accused Papa of being land hungry when he bought the
Truskett eighty, the last of his land acquisitions. "I'm not land hungry.
I just want what joins mine," he said in a time-tested retort. Vernon
and I, who were in college now, were given the job one summer of
clearing this one large field preparatory to sowing it to wheat. It had
lain fallow for years and was blanketed with weeds shoulder high in
places and spotted with occasional volunteer thickets of pawpaws and
persimmons.

But the biggest part of the job was clearing the old homesite on a hilltop. The house on this site had stood vacant in all my memory and had in recent years burned down. Neighborhood lore had it that the Truskett house had been a station on the underground railroad before and during the Civil War. Now only sandstone foundations remained, outlining a shallow basement where runaway slaves may once have hidden.

Nearby was a well and a barn's foundations, all overgrown with locust saplings up to six inches in diameter. Papa's idea was to obliterate everything so that our tractor-pulled five-bottom disc plow would go right over the hilltop without a snag or a hitch.

Vernon and I did the job, all right. The final step, one blistering August day, was prying the foundation stones loose and dumping them down the well. The top four feet we filled with good soil. Shades of yesteryear! It was sad when the plow later went over the site of the well without the slightest dip of acknowledgement.

More time passes. I am married and I return to visit the old home place with my wife and children. The kids and I go down to the Big Pasture to see the well where it all started. I would hold their city-bred legs while they peered one by one into the netherworld of wells.

With high expectancy we made our way to the never-to-be-forgotten site. I looked and looked. The well was gone! The original eye of heaven had been put out!

Papa had struck again, and I was irritated. Why couldn't he have left this one relic of the past? But the feeling didn't last long. I was grown up now. I could again hear Papa saying, "A well is only useful as long as it is used. You don't need a well in a field of wheat."

When he first said that, Papa knew what I only now understood. We had lived through a revolution—the revolution of the American farm. Now one farmer produced more food than twenty used to. Tractors and machines had taken the place of livestock. Farms had increased in size from around eighty acres to five hundred or more acres. The former small farmsteads with their outmoded sources of water had become "just in the way."

The wells of my father were victims of the revolution.

We Eat Like This Every Day

Wild Greens

Just as the land furnished good water, it also provided good food. Some food was there for the picking, while much of it had to be painstakingly cultivated. But the essentials were furnished. All it took to produce good food was industrious people.

During the first warm days of very early spring, before canning became widespread, people anxiously combed the fields and streams looking for the first signs of wild greens. After a long winter of their monotonous diet of salt pork, stored potatoes, and corn bread, they were very hungry for something fresh. Long before garden lettuce and onions were ready, cow parsley and poke gave a delicious and nutritious change to their menu, as well as serving as a sort of internal spring cleaning agent, whether used cooked or in fresh salads.

Wild greens have always been plentiful even in the most remote places. This wild food, besides being nourishing and good tasting, is a food that is completely wasted unless picked for use as food. Harvesting it does not diminish anything, because proper picking insures that the greens will come right back.

This excellent way to get an extra dish for the table has been almost forgotten in recent years as the knowledge of what to pick and where to pick it has been put on the back shelf. Since it has been easier to run to the store, open a can, or take something out of the freezer, not many people take the time anymore to tramp the byways to discover the pleasure of finding little bits of shawnee peeking out of the earth or even recognize the value of the dandelion right in their front lawns.

Yet a few people like Ellen Gibson and Imo Honssinger still enjoy the old-time goodness of a mess of greens. They faithfully roam the countryside in the heart of the greens season from early spring until mid-summer, looking for a treasured bunch of black leaf lady thumb or a gurgling spring brimming with water cress.

They take their finds home and fix a mess to eat and, if there's enough left over, maybe can or freeze some for use during winter months when the plants die down.

The early pioneers turned to the Indians, who taught them about greens. This knowledge, added to and handed down, is preserved in order for today's amateur to learn how to distinguish the good greens from the bad. For instance, the experienced greens pickers know that poke is best picked when it is young and tender, for when it gets good-sized and forms a berry, some parts are poisonous. And they know that if it is not picked early, wintercress soon becomes bitter. Many of the plants seen every day could be eaten, but this does not mean one should go out and sample something just because it looks good. One must first learn which greens can be picked and which to leave alone, learn when to pick and what parts of the plant are edible.

Though we are writing mostly about the green or leafy portion of the plant, other parts are edible, such as the seeds of shepherd's purse and lamb's quarter, the stalks of poke and purslave, the roots of clover and chicory, and even the flowers of plants like violets and bluebells.

There are two main classes of greens, those that grow near rivers and streams or on marshy land, and others that grow in fields, pastures, gardens, and roadsides. However, some of these greens can be found in both types of environments.

The first section below contains the river greens and those that grow near the river.

Watercress

Watercress, a member of the mustard family, is one of the most familiar river greens. Many a weary hiker, coming upon a clear, running spring filled with tangy watercress, has plucked a handful of the tender leaves to make a tasty sandwich. The growing season for watercress usually lasts from May to October, but if warm weather prevails, it may begin to come in as early as February. Watercress ranges from four to eight inches in height, and grows in mats on the top of the water, its roots reaching down through the water. Besides its snappy flavor, which

Watercress: Nasturtium officinale.

tastes somewhat like a radish, the watercress also contains many important vitamins. In picking this plant take only the leaf and tender stems. Never pull up the whole plant, lest you destroy the root system. Mid-spring is the best time to pick this green, when its flavor is at its peak. Caution should be taken to pick only the watercress that is growing in a continuously-running stream where there is no danger of pollution. Watercress is identified by its smooth, shiny leaves, long slender stems, and small white flowers. If carefully transplanted in dirt and watered frequently, watercress can be grown as a winter crop, assuring crispness for salads all year long.

Wintercress

Another member of the cress family is wintercress. It can be found from April to June, and, unlike watercress, wintercress grows in fields or in moist places near streams. This is probably the first of the yellow mustards to bloom. The stem is smooth and the leaves are toothed and deeply incised at their bases. The lower leaves are stalked and larger than the small ones that grow up and down the stem. Those along the upper stem are stalkless and have clasping bases. The bright yellow flowers are dense and cylindrical. Most wintercress blooms from April to June and possibly later. Wintercress is full

Wintercress:
Barbarea vulgais.

of vitamins, and although it is kin to mustard, it lacks the pungent mustard taste. Wintercress is best after the last frost of spring. Pick the small leaves just after the plant has come up, because the cress becomes bitter as it matures. After cooking this green for a meal, some people like to drink the juice that cooks out of the plant leaves. This is sometimes called pot liquor.

Black Leaf Lady Thumb

If you are a novice at picking greens, there is one green you could be certain to identify with no trouble at all—black leaf lady thumb.

This riverbank green is not only unmistakable but also plentiful and delicious. Its unusual leaf is about one and a half inches wide and comes to a point at the end. A shadow of an arrow is found in the center of the leaf. When cooked, both the stem and the leaves can be used.

Cow Parsley

Cow parsley is found in early February if the weather is warm. It is a long-lobed plant, looking like a close relative of the watercress. It can be picked until the first of May or until the stalk becomes milky looking. The stems and leaves are good greens and can be picked until they begin to become coarse. Cow parsley is usually found near the river in marshy locations.

Dock

The dock family is one of the most popular families of greens in the Ozarks. Narrow leaf dock (curly dock) and broadleaf dock (sour dock) are two favorites. Dock can be found on riverbanks, but some of the best bunches are found in ash piles, along roadsides, and in other waste places. To be at their tenderest the young leaves should be used when they are a foot or less in length. Tender dock tips are tasty boiled and served like spinach. In fact, many Ozarkers prefer dock to spinach because of its superior taste and greater vitamin

Curly dock: Rumex crispus.

content. Sour dock adds much flavor to a mess of mixed greens. Curly dock can be found blooming from June to August. The plant grows almost anywhere and ranges from one to four feet tall. The leaves have curly, crinkly edges. Dock was one of the many native plants used for medicinal purposes. Cleaning the liver was thought to be its main value.

Wild Lettuce

A member of the daisy family, wild lettuce is known for its unusual height, which can range from one to eight feet. Wild lettuce can be found growing in meadows, open woods, and moist thickets along rivers. Its leaves are blue-green and lobed. The stems are tall—four to nine inches. The smooth leaves may grow from six inches to a foot in length. The top of the leaf is dark green and the underside is a pale green. The flowers are pale yellow and grow in clusters but are quite insignificant. The unusual height of

Wild Lettuce: Lactuea canadensis.

the plant is the most obvious factor. Wild lettuce forms feathery seed clusters during the fruiting season. The leaves are good as a cooked green and in salads.

Chickweed

Chickweed is a common pest that has probably at one time or another taken over your yard. There are two types of chickweed. Mouse-eared chickweed reached a height of between one and thirteen inches. Giant chickweed reaches heights from two to twenty-four inches. Both varieties grow from May to October in sun or shade and in lawns, pastures, woods, and wet to damp disturbed ground. The small

Chickweed: Stellaria media.

variety of chickweed has small, weak, fine hairy stems. On each side of the stem are pairs of eliptic or oblong leaves that are from one-half to two inches long and are pointed on both ends. The small white flowers have deeply notched petals that make a ray-like formation. The leaves and stems can be boiled to make a tasty dish. Chickweed is good mixed with a mess of different greens.

Violets

Sure to be found growing in small beds near springs or rivers is the vitamin-rich plant the violet. Violet blossoms range in color, but the blue is the richest in needed vitamins. These small, fragile flowers can be found all summer long. Although the flowers are good to eat, most people do not use them in

Violet: Viola sororia.

their greens because of their appearance when cooked. The tender leaves and roots, however, can be used as a green. As with all plants, the new tender leaves are the best to use. The root tastes surprisingly like hickory nuts.

Bluebell

Another flower used in greens is the bluebell, which grows in moist, rich bottomlands. It has a smooth erect stem one to two feet tall and large floppy leaves. The flowers are pink when opening and later blue or lavender. Like the violet, the flower can be cooked, but is not pretty in the greens. The tender leaves and stems can be used in greens. The leaves and flowers of both the bluebell and the violet are among the richest sources of vitamins.

Bluebell: Mertensia virginica.

Wild Onion

The pungent smell of the wild onion seems to fill meadows, thickets, and moist wooded slopes near the river during the summer months. Wild onion is easily recognized not only by its smell but by its sharp slender leaves and pale yellow flowers. Its soft, grasslike leaves are

Wild onion: Allium species.

usually shorter than the stem. The bulbs, perhaps the most important parts of the plant, are small and in short supply. Sweet and palatable, they are an excellent seasoning for a mess of greens. The bulb for cooking is found in the late autumn or early spring.

The next section of greens are those that are located in pastures, fields, and along roadsides.

Dandelion

Though many people regard the dandelion as just another pesky weed that takes over yards and gardens, the dandelion is a useful plant. Besides being used to make dandelion wine, it is also a tender green that can be used almost year-round. The dandelion can range from one to twelve inches in height. It grows from April to November on a short stem with large basal leaves that are deeply lobed or sawtoothed. The bright yellow heads of the flowers are about one and a half inches across. The early spring dandelion

Dandelion: Taraxacum officinale.

is the best to pick for a mess of greens, although some of the fall dandelions can be just as tender and good in salads. The leaves of the dandelions that grow in lawns have a stronger flavor than those growing wild. This can be remedied by cooking in several successive waters. Besides being used as a green, the young sprouts can be used as a potherb, and its dried roots are used as a substitute for coffee. The flowers can be cooked just as the violet and bluebell, but are not pretty in a dish of greens. The buds make a dish of their own. Ellen Gibson describes the taste as being quite similar to brussel sprouts. Dandelions grown in the basement during the winter will produce fresh crisp, leaves for salads until spring.

Chicory

Chicory, a pretty roadside weed, is not often thought of as a useful plant, but the fried roots of the chicory are used in coffee, and greens can be prepared from the tenderest succulent growth. It is commonly found in fields and along roadsides. It is an erect plant, often reaching more than three feet in height, and on its upright rigid branches are bright blue flowers. The flowering season lasts from May to October. The lower leaves of this plant are three to six inches long and vary from toothed to lobed, tapering to the long stalks. Those upward along the stem have clasping bases. Some varieties are cultivated, either as a leafy green or for the valuable roots.

Chickory: Chicorium intybus

Poke

When it comes to trying to pick the most widely known and picked green, it seems pokeweed—commonly called poke—is the unanimous winner. Otherwise known as pigeonberry, pokeberry or inkberry, poke is a tall, branching perennial herb with greenish white flowers and juicy deep purple berries. The plant flourishes in wastelands, roadsides, and along fence rows. The stem, growing from four to twenty feet high, is reddish purple and sturdy. The roots are poisonous to man, as are the berries, a favorite of birds. The broad leaves reaching

Poke: Phytolacca americana.

from five to ten inches are scattered along the stem and branches. The leaves may become mottled by a virus carried by insects. In this case the plant must then be cut off below ground level to kill the disease. The young shoots and tender leaves may be used as greens and can be prepared like asparagus. When picking, choose only the freshest, tenderest leaves of the new growth. Be careful when picking after a frost to be sure the leaves haven't been ruined by the cold. Usually after a frost new pink stems and light green leaves will appear. Feel safe to pick these, for they will be undamaged. The freshly growing roots can be dug up, covered with dirt, watered and kept in a warm cellar as a source of new young sprouts throughout the winter. This green can be frozen successfully.

Shepherd's Purse

One of the most common wayside weeds is shepherd's purse, which
grows almost everywhere and with
such persistency that it has earned
the nickname pickpocket. Its title
arose from its small seed pods that
were said to resemble small change
purses. Shepherd's purse is found
in fields, along roadsides and near
rivers, blooms from about April to
August, and grows from four to
twenty-four inches tall. The leaves

Shepherd's purse:
Capsella Bursa-
pastoris.

on the stem are arrowshaped, while those near the root are clustered,
incised and toothed. The tender leaves may be used in a mess of
greens and the seeds may be used to season soup and other dishes.

Wild Mustard

Another quite popular and boun-
tiful green is the wild mustard. The
large, thick and toothed leaves are
a deep green in shade. The greens
may be harvested when tender. If
the leaves are not harvested, the
plant stalk becomes strong and un-
fit to eat. The flowers are bright
yellow and grow in clusters. This
plant springs up anywhere and grows
from spring to late summer.

Wild Mustard:
Brassica species.

Red Clover

Red clover grows from eight
inches high, and is found in open
fields, meadows, and lawns. The
tender, tooth-edged leaflets are good
food used in greens. If you wish,
you can also eat the roots and the
globular flower heads made up of
many flowerets.

Red clover:
Trifolium
pratense.

Lamb's Quarter

One of the most frequently found greens in the garden is lamb's quarter, which appears about when your garden does, but has more food value than garden lettuce. All of the tender plant is used for greens. Nicknames for this plant include pigweed and goosefoot. The seeds may become a nuisance to the farmer if they become mixed with grain seeds, but the seeds are also put to practical use in pancakes.

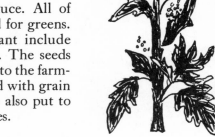

Lamb's Quarter: Chenopodium album.

Purslane

Purslane is another often-ignored plant. Its reddish purple stem and small, fat leaves are familiar to anyone with a garden. The young leaves and stems when cooked make a far better dish than garden spinach. Sometimes called pigweed parsley, this green cooks down rapidly and requires a good mess of other greens to mix with it. After a summer rain, purslane can be found popping up everywhere. The thick fleshy leaves and stems are easy to find. The leaves can also be used raw in a salad, and the succulent stems make a good dill pickle. Purslane is a truly versatile plant.

Purslane: Portulaca oleracea.

Garden Sorrel

As the garden begins to grow, garden sorrel begins to appear. The leaves have an arrow-shaped leaf within themselves and are good used with other greens.

Garden sorrel: Oxalis stricta.

Shawnee

Shawnee is a very nourishing plant. It cannot be picked when you first begin to pick greens, but comes in later. It cannot be used after the stem becomes milky. It makes an excellent green to mix with others.

Although these are by no means all of the greens that can be found, these are some widely used regional favorites. Sometime when you're driving home along a country road, hiking in the woods, or walking along the riverbank, see if you can spot any of these greens. If you are lucky enough to find some, gather yourself a mess and have a delicious, vitamin-filled supper.

Henbit: Lamium amplexicaule.

There Should Be Sticky Thistle Growing in the Fence Rows
By Loma L. Paulson

Greens-gathering was almost a ritual for my grandparents at the turn of the century. Standing in the log cabin door, Grandfather used to say, "Hear that old bullfrog? There should be sticky thistle growing in the fence rows."

It was then that the winter sun rays were lengthening, and the lingering snow was melting on the Ozark hills to join the spring stream, where, all winter long, brown oak leaves were huddled. Now the over-flowing spring sent them gliding away like gondolas. Clusters of watercress, bleached by the covering leaves, quickly started greening up.

Sticky thistle was the first cooking green of spring, and the gathering belonged to Grandfather. Although the season for this particular green was short, he never missed the timing. With a homemade basket and a sharp knife Grandfather followed the rail fence rows in quest of the favorite green.

Grandmother, knowing there would be greens for supper, put a piece of hog jowl to boil, and waited Grandfather's return. When the basket of greens arrived, she picked them over, and washed them many times in cold water before cooking. She lifted the pork, juicy and tender by this time, out of the broth and put it aside "to set."

Into the boiling liquid, Grandmother dropped the crisp greens by the handful. The "stickers," as the tiny white briars were called, disappeared as the greens simmered and stewed on the shiny, black wood stove. And, in the red-hot oven, cornpone baked—each little pone bearing the imprint of Grandmother's fingers.

When all was ready, Grandmother drained the greens, mixed in little cubes of the white, fat pork, and heaped them into a large bowl.

As everyone enjoyed the greens Grandfather told of what he had seen, "Oaks budding pink, the creek brim full, red cedars turning green and squirrels hopping like popcorn in a hot skillet."

Grandfather had met spring in the Ozark hills. Most small girls learned to gather greens, and since Mother was busy with little brother and baby sister, it fell to Grandmother to teach me to discern the good, the "just no good," and the poison greens.

As the days were growing longer and warmer, Grandmother and I set out to find more of the "green sass." First, we brought home snappy wild lettuce and juicy wild onions. The lettuce was best when wilted with hot bacon fat and vinegar, and "just a mite of sugar," as Grandmother said. Cleaned and placed in cold water to crispen, the onions looked like small knitting needles. But no one complained of the task of cleaning them, so hungry were we all for something fresh and green.

Spring brought many responsibilities, but none concerned Grandmother more than the well-being of her little yellow-headed granddaughter, always tagging at her heels. Looking at my sun flushed face she'd say, "Not becoming for a lady to be sunburnt and freckled. Fetch me that scrap basket and I'll make a calico bonnet."

Starched and airy, this little bonnet, with a long tail to cover my neck and wide strings to tie under my chin, certainly defied the Ozark sun. Grandmother also fashioned little mitts from the tops of my worn out, black ribbed stockings. While protecting my hands from sunburn and bramble scratches, the mitts were also hot.

"A little sweating will not hurt anybody," Grandmother often said. So I consoled myself with the thought that sweating would whiten my hands, and I was that much nearer to becoming a lady.

As spring progressed, Grandmother mixed and cooked the young plantain, dandelion, poke, slick thistle, square stem, and three kinds of dock. Mixing the greens was most important. She added the curley leaf and the sour narrow-leaf docks in good amounts. However, because of its laxative properties, she added the broad-leaf dock with caution.

Wild flowers grew everywhere and were much more to my fancy than assorted greens. Grandmother didn't hold to picking wild flowers. Nor did she ever gather the marigolds, touch-me-nots, and poppies that marched in long rows across her garden. With gentle admonition for my fervor in gathering wild flowers, she finally gave me permission—providing I didn't disturb the roots.

Late spring gave us lamb's quarters, wild mustard, sharp tongue grass, wild sage and shepherd's spray. And, along the creek bank, crow's foot and colt's foot grew in abundance.

The month of May brought an abundance of sheep sorrel. These little sour, clover-like leaves mixed with wild strawberries made excellent tarts of jam, thus putting greens in the dessert class.

Another delightful part of greens-gathering was the awareness of wakening life. The hills and valleys came alive with a moving population—flying bugs and butterflies, hopping frogs, nesting birds, creeping lizards, and terrapins.

Each year, from the sun-lit valleys and over the hills, spring comes, bringing new life to the Ozark hills in the same way as in Grandfather's day. Flowers bloom in profusion of color. And, the same tender, edible greens are there for the taking.

As Grandfather said, "There's a lot to learn about Almighty God when it's a-coming spring."

Greens Recipes

Fresh greens can be served in almost any way you want to prepare them, whether it be with hard-boiled eggs, bacon, beans, and cornbread, or other foods. Experience is the best teacher when it comes to mixing greens. Depending on your taste, almost any greens are good mixed together. River and upland greens can be mixed together, or those that are growing at the same time are good together. Garden sorrel and sour dock, lamb's quarter and chard, poke and cow parsley are examples of greens that can be mixed.

Preparing Greens

Most cooks prepare their greens by this simple method. Rinse freshly picked greens in several different waters, lifting them out carefully each time to avoid bruising them. Then select the tenderest undamaged leaves and drop them into boiling water. To remove the bitter taste you can boil greens in three different waters, lifting them out each time before adding fresh water. Or you can cook the greens until tender in one pan of salted water in order to retain more vitamins A and C. Stir once in awhile to keep them from packing together.

Wilted Dandelion Salad

Gather a quantity of dandelion leaves, wash, and let drain on a paper towel. Then soak for a few hours in salt water to remove bitter taste. Put in a skillet containing hot ham or bacon fat. Stir the leaves briskly. When they are barely wilted, season with salt and pepper. Serve when leaves are completely wilted.

Also, to remove the bitter flavor of the dandelion, cover the leaves with boiling water instead of bringing to a boil in cold water.

Dandelion with Bacon Dressing

Wash the tender new leaves of the dandelion and then cut the leaves across into several bite-sized pieces. Place in a bowl and add a pinch of sugar, salt, and a little chopped onion. Cut some bacon into small pieces and brown in a frying pan. When crisp you may, if you wish, add vinegar to the fat (twice as much as there is fat.) When this boils up then pour over the leaves and stir. Garnish with bacon. A combination of greens can be used in this dish.

Dandelion buds

Gather a mess of dandelion buds. Rinse thoroughly and cook in a small amount of water until tender. Butter, then serve.

Purslane

Prepare diced strips of cold pork, partially fry, then add a mess of purslane and cook. Serve with butter, salt, and pepper.

Poke Shoots

Gather the tender young shoots of pokeweed when they reach from four to six inches in length. Pick the leaves from the stalk, wash, and boil in two waters. On the second boiling cook until tender and serve with butter and seasoning in the manner you would fix asparagus.

Although greens can be eaten during their growing season, many people also enjoy greens later in the year, whether for use as a laxative or just for good eating. Canning and freezing are two ways to keep greens fresh for use all year.

Canning Greens

Wash tender, freshly picked greens through three or four waters, adding salt to the last one. Steam or parboil about ten minutes, until wilted, then dip out of the water and put hot into jars, covering with boiling water to half an inch from the top. Put one level teaspoon of salt in each quart jar. Wipe off the top of the jar and adjust lids. Tighten canning lids, then turn back one turn, just enough to loosen it a little. Then boil three hours in a water bath or in a pressure cooker at ten pounds pressure, quarts for seventy minutes and pints for sixty minutes. Remove from canning bath, tighten the lid, and let cool. Tame and wild greens are good canned together, such as mustard, swiss chard, lamb's quarter, narrow dock, and poke.

Freezing Greens

Rinse the freshly picked greens thoroughly in several waters to remove all dirt, checking carefully for any damage to the leaves. Select only the best. Blanch greens in boiling water for two minutes. Drain and cool quickly in cold water before packing in plastic bags and sealing. Freeze immediately. Frozen greens can be kept several months. To prepare, put the frozen greens into a small amount of boiling salted water and cook until tender.

Early spring is the best time to dig the roots of most herbs.

Good for What Ails You—Wild Herbs

Today when people get sick, they go to a doctor who prescribes a medicine bought at a drugstore. The medicine usually has some long Latin name that is meaningless to anyone except a doctor or pharmacist. But in the past when someone was sick, they went to the woods for medicinal herbs with names everyone could understand—goldenseal, mullein, mayapple, and snakeroot.

Ella Dunn and Earl Stiles both used their knowledge of herbs, passed down through generations, to doctor their own families and neighbors for fevers, aches, arthritis, skin diseases, and other ailments. Using the roots, bark, or leaves of plants found growing wild in the woods or cultivated along the yard fence, both of these persons helped to ease the pain and misery of many people. "I never charged a dime," said Earl. "Once we spent sixty dollars for doctor medicine and I went and got thirteen cents for my own remedy and done the same thing."

Ella learned about medicinal herbs from her father. However, some of the herbs she prepared and used, such as digitalis, known as foxglove, Ella did not use because these herbs became readily available already prepared in the drugstore. "Even though my husband had heart trouble," she said, "I never used digitalis. I don't even know how my father prepared it, because we could buy it already prepared." But many other herbs became fever and cold remedies, spring tonics, and salves and ointment.

The roots of most herbs have to be dug when the plant is dormant, before the sap begins to rise in February or March, for the roots lose their value after the sap rises. From her long experience with them, Ella can identify plants she uses any time of the year by their barks or shapes, but looking at the leaves is usually the easiest way for beginners to identify a plant. She suggests identifying the plant in the summer or fall, marking it, and then digging the root during the winter.

Following is a partial list of herbs either Ella or Earl has used. Some plants have more then one name or have different names in different parts of the country. Even living no farther apart than a

Ella Dunn holds a bunch of herbs she has collected to make her special spring tonic.

The root should be dug before the sap rises in the spring, because the medicinal properties are lost after the sap rises.

hundred miles, Ella and Earl sometimes used different names for the same plant. We have been unable to find a scientific name for some plants described here, indicating the name is used only in a localized area. But all the plants, native or naturalized, survive readily in the Ozarks.

Asafetida (genus *Ferula*) is a bitter, foul-smelling, yellowish-brown material prepared from roots. Asafetida was bought and worn around the neck in little bags to ward off colds and diseases. It was also taken daily with one teaspoon of Jerusalem oak *(Chenopodium botrys)* to prevent illness. Jerusalem oak, found in waste ground and along railroads, is also odoriferous, smelling like turpentine. Children were not es-

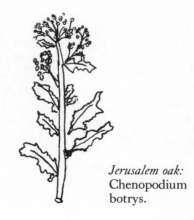

Jerusalem oak: Chenopodium botrys.

pecially fond of this preventive medicine. The name asafetida is particularly appropriate, coming from the medieval Latin meaning smelly or fetid gum.

August flower grows along roadsides to a height of about twelve inches. It has a hard gray stem and small yellow flowers the size of a common nailhead. August flower was used as a tea for fevers, to induce sweating.

Balm of Gilead:
Populus balsamifera.

Balm of Gilead *(Populus balsamifera)* is also called balsam poplar. Almost all old home places in the Ozarks used to have a balm of Gilead tree, but the trees are uncommon now. The purple flower was used to make a salve or poultice that was used to treat sores on feet and legs. To make the salve put the buds of the flower and mutton tallow in a pan. Cook until the oil comes out, then strain into a jar and store.

Black cohosh—see poke

Butterfly root *(Asclepias tuberosa)* grows in pastures or near fence rows to thirty inches high. It has four or five stems. The long bloom that looks like a rooster's comb stays on the plant for months. A tea was made from the root to purify the spleen and blood.

Catnip *(Nepeta cataria)* was raised around the yard fence or house. It grows sixteen to eighteen inches high, with a light green leafy stem and dull-white purple dotted flowers. Its leaves were steeped in boiling water to make a tea to put fretting babies to sleep.

Comfrey (genus *Symphytun*) grows wild with large, rough hairy leaves and small blue, purple, or yellow flowers. The leaf was bound on cuts to stop bleeding.

Dogwood—see spring tonic.

Elm (genus *Ulmus*). Many medicines were very bitter tasting, es-

Catnip: Nepeta cataria.

Comfrey: genus Symphytum.

Ginseng: Panax quinquefolium.

American elm: genus Ulmus.

pecially quinine, which was used for headaches, colds, conjested lungs, fever, and rheumatism. There were no capsules to put quinine in to take, so people used elm bark. To prepare the bark they split up the inner bark into pieces about the size of a thumb and soaked them in water overnight. The sap, a jelly-like substance which rose on the water, was used like a capsule when taking quinine. The sap coated the powder and concealed the taste of the medicine.

Ginseng *(Panax quinquefolium)* grows wild. It has small greenish flowers and a forked root that resembles a sweet potato. Every year a nut and ring grow on top of the root, making it easy to determine the age of the plant. The oldest ginseng Earl has found in Missouri is ten years old. Ginseng is enjoying a modern-day popularity, but was not used as a medicine in the Ozarks. It used to be and still is gathered and sold. Earl said the price has never been below eighteen dollars a pound, with modern-day prices as high as forty dollars.

Goldenseal *(Hydrastis canadensis)* is also called yellow root. It is found in rich ground or leaf mulch in 85 percent shade, usually on a north hillside. It grows to about ten or twelve inches high. Until it is two or three years old, goldenseal has just one leaf, that looks like a grape leaf. When the plant is three, the stem forks, so it has two

Golden seal: Hydrastis canadensis.

leaves. In the fork is a button with six to eight seeds inside. The roots are very knotty and stumpy. Half the weight will be in the little roots right on top of the ground. The roots, yellow on the inside, are the part of the plant used.

Goldenseal root was put in maple syrup and given to babies for sores in the mouth (thrash). It was also good for sore gums or sinus, and was used as an eyewash for red, sore, or itchy eyes. Put in mineral oil or made as a tea, it was good for stomach ulcers. To make the tea, steep the root in hot water for twenty-four to forty-eight hours. Never boil goldenseal roots, for boiling kills their healing properties.

Ground ivy *(Glechoma hederacea)* is also called gill-over-the-ground. It is found in sunny places in the yard or along creeks in moist, rich soil. It grows close to the ground in vines five or six feet long. Ground ivy has a small rounded, scalloped leaf similar to red clover, gray-green in color. The tiny flowers are blue. The leaves were used for

Ground ivy: Glechoma hederacea.

relief from poison ivy or poison oak and to cure most skin diseases. Put the leaves in a cloth and mash them to extract the juice. Rub the juice on the affected part of the skin.

Hickory (genus *Carya*). The inside white bark next to the wood of this tree was used to make a sweet-tasting tea to relieve a cough. The root was also sweet and was chewed like candy for its sweetness.

Horehound *(Marrubium vulgare)* is an aromatic plant that has leaves covered with a whitish fuzz. It was cultivated alongside buildings or in yard fences. The leaves were made into a candy or syrup by first

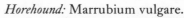

Hickory: genus Carya.

Horehound: Marrubium vulgare.

boiling them to extract the flavor and then adding sugar and cooking to desired consistency. Horehound candy was kept in the winter for colds.

Horseradish: Armoracia rusticana.

Horseradish *(Armoracia rusticana).* The thick, whitish, and strong-tasting root of this garden plant had many uses as a medicine as well as a food. Put one part grated horseradish in four parts fresh milk and let set for one hour. Then put the mixture on the skin to cure itch and other skin problems.

A skin freshener used 2 cups distilled witch-hazel water added to one-half cup grated horseradish root. Allow the two to stand overnight before straining and discarding the horseradish. Then add one-half cup rubbing alcohol and one-fourth cup white vinegar. Some cologne added to the formula improved the smell.

To treat influenza a wine glass full of warm horseradish wine was given to the patient four times a day. To make the wine heat a pint of claret to 160° in a double boiler. Stir into the heated wine two tablespoons of prepared horseradish root, two tablespoons honey, a dash of nutmeg, and a twist of orange peel.

Horseradish root was also good for hoarseness. Infuse one table-spoon of vinegar, two tablespoons of grated horseradish, and one-third cup water for one hour. Pour off the settled horseradish. Add two-thirds cup of honey to the liquid and take one tablespoonful every hour until hoarseness is gone. Since this remedy contained no dangerous drugs, it was safe and good for children.

The leaf of the horseradish had medicinal uses, too. A bruised leaf laid across the back of the neck was a cure for headaches. Also, a bruised leaf laid on a part of the body grieved with sciatica, gout, joint ache, or hard swellings of the spleen or liver eased the pain. If

Jack in the pulpit or Indian turnip: Arisaema triphyllum.

Lady's slipper: genus Cypripedium.

one had facial neuralgia, some horseradish held in the hand on the affected side gave relief.

Indian turnip *(Arisaema triphyllum)* is also called Jack-in-the-pulpit. It grows along fence rows to twenty-four inches high. It has two stalks to a plant and a pale blue bloom. The root was used to heat up the stomach. Dried and put in horse's feed, it was a remedy for heaves. Indian turnip didn't cure heaves, but eased them so the horse could work.

Jerusalem oak—see asafetida.

Lady's Slipper (genus *Cypripedium*) grows at the break of a hill, usually near nerve root. It is light in color. The stem looks like it grew through the leaf but there are really two leaves. The larger leaf is about 3 inches long and the smaller one-eighth to one-fourth inch. A tea was made from the root to cause abortion.

Lily of the valley: Convallaria majalis.

Lily of the Valley *(Convallaria majalis)* was cultivated near houses. It has a wide blade-shaped leaf and a cluster of fragrant white bell-shaped flowers. The roots and blossoms were made into a tea and used for epilepsy.

Mayapple *(Podophyllum peltatum)* is also called mandrake. It grows along fence rows or in the woods in rich soil. It has a five- or six-inch umbrella-like leaf. A small yellow apple grows in a fork. The roots were used alone as a purgative and in mixtures with other herbs in spring tonics. The roots, seeds, and leaves are poisonous if too much is taken, but the fruit is edible.

Mullein (genus *Verbascum*) grows wild in pastures, yards, and along the roadside. It has several velvety leaves that can be as wide as a hand and up to ten inches long. The yellow, lavender, or pink flowers bloom on a single tall stalk. A tea made of the leaves was good for fevers, hives, and measles and for bathing swollen areas. Binding a leaf

Mayapple: Podophyllum peltatum.

Mullein: genus Verbascum.

on a swollen area was also used to reduce the swelling. Bathing a cow's udder in mullein tea was used to open the tits if they were swollen shut.

Mullein was also used for piles. To ease piles, sit on a jar filled with boiling water and mullein leaves.

Nerve Root (genus *Cypripedum*) is also called moccasin flower and is similar to lady's slipper. It grows at a break of a hill in the shade. The plant has several sprouts and several roots that grow out from it. The roots are wrinkled about every one-fourth inch. The leaf is six to eight inches long. A tea was made from the roots to calm the nerves.

Pennyroyal *(Hedeoma pulegioides)* grows wild in the woods. It has hairy leaves and small lilac-blue flowers. It has a six-inch stem. The top leaves were picked and rubbed on the body to keep off ticks and chiggers.

Poke *(Phytolacca americana)* grows around barns and in fence rows and banks of dirt where the sun hits it. It reaches five feet in height.

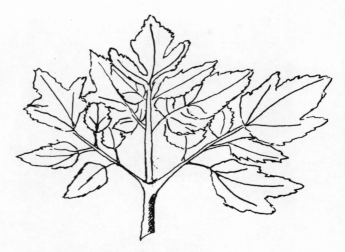

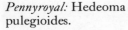

Pennyroyal: Hedeoma
pulegioides.

Black Cohosh: Cimicifuga racemosa.

Its seed is in a grape-like cluster of purplish berries. The leaves when tender make good greens. The raw root is poisonous and will cause temporary blindness, but the root boiled in water was used as a cure for any kind of skin poisoning.

A mixture of equal parts of poke and black cohosh *(Cimicifuga racemosa)* was used to treat arthritis. Take all the poke root a man's hand will hold and cut the ends off even with the hand. Add an equal amount of black cohosh root. Chop fine. Put in a quart jar and fill with good grain alcohol or whiskey. Let set for twenty-four hours. Before taking the first dose, take something to work the bowels out well. Then take one tablespoon of the poke mixture once a day for two days. On the third day take one tablespoon morning and night. Repeat for four days. On the eighth day take one tablespoon morning, noon, and night. Be sure to keep the bowels open while using poke, since the root is poisonous.

Red root *(Geum canadense)* is similar to, but larger than, ginger. It is found in rich or rocky woods on hillsides, in valleys along streams, in ravines and sandy thickets. It takes its name from its red root, which is about the size of a lead

Red Root: Geum canadense.

Sassafras: family Lauraceae.

Seneca Weed: Polygala senega.

pencil. It is used in nearly all animal blood conditioners.

Sarsaparilla—see spring tonic.

Sassafras (family *Lauraceae*) is a large shrub or tree found in the woods, old fields, and fence rows. It has three kinds of leaves on the same plant, unlobed, mitten-shaped, and three-lobed. In the fall the leaves turn brilliant orange. The root was dug before the sap rose and was used in tea in the spring to thin the blood. Earl said, "It thins your blood for the spring change—change over from winter and heavy blood to lighter blood. An old doctor dug sassafras root and put it up as his medication. He'd say if you would drink that a certain month, either February or March, three times a day, he'd doctor you the rest of the year for five dollars. That was what the old doctor thought of it. If your blood is in proper shape you're not liable to take disease."

Bathing cows and dogs in sassafras tea kept off lice and flies. One bath lasted about two weeks.

The root put in dried apples also kept bugs away.

Seneca Weed *(Polygala senega)* is also called senega root. It grows in the sun on top of a flat hill in damp places where water seeps out of the ground. It reaches twelve to eighteen inches high and has no branches. Its leaves are half an inch wide and three-fourths inch long. Seneca weed grows in bunches eight to ten feet around. The leaves were used for a purgative. It is still available in drugstores.

Sheep sorrel *(Oxalis stricta)* is found in grassy fields or yards. It is a very small plant with oily-looking leaves somewhat like white clover. Part of the leaf is green-colored and part mahogany-colored. To use, hang the leaves and stems in the sun until the sun brings the oil to the surface. The oil, applied to the sore, was used to delay skin cancer.

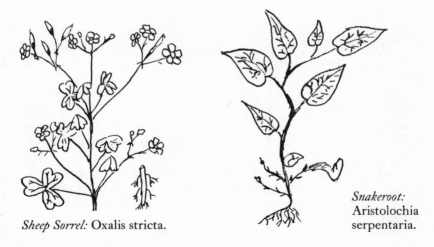

Sheep Sorrel: Oxalis stricta.

Snakeroot: Aristolochia serpentaria.

Snakeroot *(Aristolochia serpentaria)* is known as Virginia, Kansas, and Missouri snakeroot. This strong-smelling plant has vines two to four feet long and grows around the roots of post oak or white oak timber. Its root grows up to six inches long. A tea made from the roots was used to break out measles and to treat malaria cases.

Watermelon seeds steeped in a cup of water and sweetened made the kidneys act.

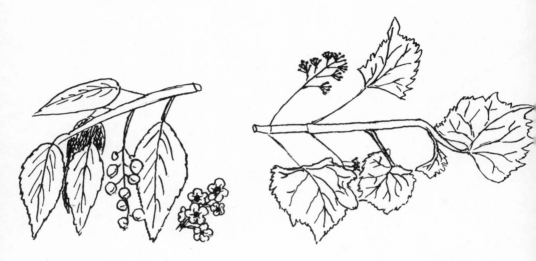

Wild Cherry: Prunus serotina.   *Wild Grape: genus* Vitis.

Wild Cherry *(Prunus serotina).* Make a tea of the bark and strain. Take two or three teaspoons as needed for a cough.

Wild Grape (genus *Vitis*). Juice made from wild grapes drunk twice a day over a period of three months was used as a cure for cancer.

Earl said, "That's a miracle that doctors really hate. They might turn me over to the CIA for telling you. Now for six years I've used wild grape juice. I take it three times a year whether I need it or not. Drink it morning and night. The blood's got to take care of disease. That's a long time to get medicine in blood or change the blood to flow to some other part of the body that needs it. It'll take sixty days if grape juice is taken two times a day. It'll cure any cancer that's ever been on any human. It takes about three to four gallons to kill the average cancer. It's old stuff. It's been proven hundreds of years."

Wild Ginger *(Asarum canadense)* grows in patches in shady places under bluffs or along a creek. It has one round leaf that is about three inches long. The root, dark brown and big as the little finger, is very hot. It was used to heat up the stomach and for colds.

Wild ginger: Asarum canadense.

Witch Hazel: genus
Hamamelis.

Witch hazel (genus *Hamamelis*). To make your own distilled witch hazel extract, cut two pounds of dormant witch hazel twigs into half-inch lengths. Put the chopped twigs in a blender with eight cups of water. Blend until the witch hazel is cut into very fine pieces. Let twigs soak overnight. The next day pour the twigs and water into a drip still with very high heat. Collect two cups of distillate. Discard the spent material in the still. To the two cups of distillate add half a cup rubbing alcohol and bottle the extract.

Flowering Dogwood: Cornus florida.

Sarsaparilla: Aralia nudicaulis.

Distilled witch hazel had many uses. It was used in first aid treatment of minor burns and scalds and to soothe insect stings, mosquito bites, and broken varicose veins. It was used to strengthen the muscular fiber of veins. It was also used on internal and external hemorrhage, for bruises, inflammations, hemorrhoids, diarrhea, dysentery, and for reducing bags under the eyes.

Spring tonic. Many herbs were used in combinations to make tonics to tune up the body for spring. One such tonic is the spring tonic Ella Dunn's family made every year. It built up the body's system, purified the blood, and cleared up the complexion. The tonic was made in March or April, when the herbs were up enough to identify. To make the tonic, use equal amounts of sassafras roots, burdock roots, sarsaparilla roots, blue burvene, wild cherry bark, and dogwood bark. Add one-third as much mayapple root. If mayapple is not available, yellow dock, also a purgative, can be used in place of it. Wash all roots and barks well. Cut all ingredients into fine pieces and add water. Boil down until it makes a good heavy liquid. Strain and either put in whiskey to preserve it or add sugar before cooking it down to a syrup and bottling. Every morning and night for two weeks to a month adults would take one tablespoonful. Small children would take a teaspoonful three times a day.

Ella's family has used this tonic for years. She knows just where to get the various plants and used to gather them herself each year. Dependent now on her son to get them, she will still occasionally make a batch. "I think if I had some now, I'd feel better," she said last spring.

Black Gold—Blackberrying

The gold that Ozark women treasured was not yellow or recognized on the world market, but was nevertheless a valuable part of their lifestyle. The "black gold" of the Ozarks was the wild blackberry that grew nearly everywhere and gave Ozarkians a plentiful and sweet treat just for the picking. Blackberrying became as much a part of their lives as the spring planting or the fall harvest. It is a tradition that has survived the years and is still carried on today.

The blackberry as we know it today got its start about one million years ago when two widely varied species of blackberries were brought together by the shifting of glaciers during the ice age. This union caused literally thousands of species to develop. Often the varieties of berries differ from county to county, with some species identified in only one location in Missouri. One extremely interesting, and extremely rare, mutation that has been identified is a strange albino "blackberry," *Rubus speciosa alba*, with berries of a whitish color. Although there are thousands of species, all are edible and only an expert can distinguish between the many different ones.

The blackberry plant is a member of the rose family. It can be recognized by small pink or white blooms that appear from April to June. The flowers are followed by tiny, hard green berries that ripen in July and August. When the berry first sets on, it is a pale green color. Then it turns white, then brilliant red. As the berry ripens, the red eventually deepens into a purplish-black, thus giving the plant its name. Because the berries are not properly ripened until they are black, one can hear people talking about the red and white blackberries, which are green, meaning the berries aren't quite ripe yet. When the berry reaches maturity it consists of many small, round drupelets adhering to a juicy core. Blackberry patches are often started by birds dropping the seed from the berry. Once started, the patch grows by sending out runners or shoots. The blackberry plant may grow as dark green bushes close to the ground or as running vines. Species growing on the ground as vines are commonly called dewberries. The leaves of the plant are coarsely toothed and often have a fine fuzz on the under-

side. Because it is a member of the rose family, small but sticky briars are present on the stems of nearly every species.

Blackberry patches can overtake a farm, and for this reason many farmers, like Della Snyder's father, would cut the plants back, saving only a small patch for the family to pick berries in. They would usually try to save a patch that was not only in the shade but also conveniently close to the house or orchard.

Since the berries usually ripen in July and August, in order to pick, protection is needed from both the sun and insect bites. The best way to provide both is a long sleeved shirt and a heavy denim pair of jeans. The long-sleeved shirt and jeans also protect against briar cuts on arms and legs while reaching and walking into the bush to pick the berries. A sun hat is also helpful. Another vital part of modern-day picking is a strong insect repellent. Choose one with a large percentage of N.N-diethyl-meta-toluamide, the active ingredient in most insect repellents. As a final precaution against chiggers and other insects, do what people did before prepared insect repellents were available, bathe in soda water immediately upon your return.

It is best to take both large and small buckets for picking. The small buckets are easier to manipulate while picking and can be emptied into the larger buckets when they become full. One- to two-pound lard buckets and children's sand pails make good small picking buckets. It is usually better to leave the large buckets stationary until ready to go. This avoids chances of dropping or spilling the berries.

Della Snyder picks blackberries every summer for canning and freezing.

It is advisable to go picking early in the morning before the dew is off, or late in the evening. Picking at these times avoids some of the heat, insects, and snakes that always seem to inhabit a blackberry patch.

The actual picking of the berry is a simple process. Select one branch of the bush and pick all the ripe berries. Remember to leave the red and green ones for picking later on. To pick the berry, take it between finger and thumb and give it a gentle tug.

Our "picking party" included Della Snyder, Vickie Massey, and myself. As we set out to pick eight gallons of blackberries one early July morning, we all agreed the weather couldn't be more perfect. It was bright and breezy. The pale yellow sunlight that filtered down through the trees was just warm enough to be pleasant. While we drove along the country roads and got acquainted with each other, I could tell it was going to be an enjoyable day.

The patch was located on a steep hillside. There certainly was an abundance of berries, but the difficulty came in obtaining them. However, we quickly solved that problem by crawling down the hill. Once on the scene we started to work. Our first step was a thorough spraying of an insect repellent which had, to say the least, a rather strong odor, but it did the job. As we began to pick the berries, our first topic of conversation was a discussion of whose insect repellent smelled the worst. But it wasn't too long until we got into the swing of things and Vickie and I began to deposit almost as many berries in our buckets as in our mouths.

For the most part our blackberry picking went smoothly. Of course, we had those typical accidents and mishaps which always seem to occur, such as carefully picking a whole bucket of plump, juicy berries and dropping them just seconds before pouring them into the larger bucket. Although that was certainly annoying, it was even more aggravating to trip over a rock and smash some big berries in your hand. It seemed like the largest, most delicious looking berries were always deep inside the bush, just out of reach. Often while pushing into the bush for these berries, we'd find ourselves standing in the middle of a painfully familiar vine and quickly counting its leaves.

We met one box turtle, but fortunately we didn't see any snakes, although I was thoroughly convinced I heard several rustling through the grass, and from the sound of things, they were pretty fierce.

As the time passed and the heat increased, I began to wonder how those poor berries stood it day after day, because halfway through our job we had to take time out for a break. Occasionally blackberry picking can be a dull and monotonous chore, but with Della Snyder it's

more like a long awaited and pleasant outing. Her smile and enthusiasm reflect her outlook on life. As we lounged in the shade of a tall oak tree, drinking the icy cold water she thoughtfully brought, we forgot the heat and insects and became thoroughly caught up in what she had to say.

"I was picking blackberries over on this place near our home. That's not been too long ago. I was just picking away by myself. I took my dog, but he didn't turn out to be much help. I felt something under my feet and I was standing right on this big snake. He was under the grass trying to get out. I just ran like I don't know what! Lands! It liked to scared me to death.

"Another time I had a young bull chase me. We had this little Guernsey bull. He was just a calf, but he always hated me. He'd try to butt me and he'd just paw the ground. Dutch [her husband] told me to open the gate so he could drive that bull through. I just got it open and here came that bull. I ran behind the chicken house just as hard as I could go and that bull was right after me. I ran in an old toilet in back of the chicken house, and that bull just about butted it down. It was just a-rocking with me in it! I was sacred to death until Dutch ran the bull off with a stick."

One story led to another as we postponed returning to the patch.

"My two sisters and I were going squirrel hunting once a long time ago. It was up in January and real cold. My big sister was the best shot, so she was going to shoot the squirrels. I was supposed to climb up in the trees and get them because I could climb the best, and my little sister was to carry the squirrels. Well, we got sixteen squirrels and my little sister couldn't carry them all. So we all had to help her. It was getting late and we knew we'd better start back. We were a long ways from home and somehow we got turned around and we just kept walking in circles. We finally came to a house we knew and we asked which way was home. The lady was real nice and she told us how to get back to the main road. Once we got there we knew where we were at. I never was so glad to see our house," Della laughed.

Della told us that generally only the girls of the family would go picking. They'd depart about six o'clock, after an early breakfast. Their clothing would consist of overalls, a cotton long-sleeved shirt, and boots.

"Do you know when I was a little girl they didn't make jeans? It was overalls. Mother would buy us overalls just to have something to work in," Della said.

For protection against insect bites they would take rags soaked in kerosene and wipe their socks, the cuffs of the overalls, their ankles and shirt with it, and of course, bathe in soda water upon their return.

The girls would return around eleven to help prepare the noon meal and wash the berries. They did this by placing the berries in a pan of cold water, being careful not to bruise them, then picking out the particles, stems, and green berries.

Today, people usually pick only enough berries for fresh pies or dessert, but it hasn't always been that way. In Della's childhood days the berries were picked by the gallons for jams and jellies and for canning to use in pies or cobblers later in the year. Because there were no refrigerators and few ice boxes, which had only a limited amount of space, the only way to preserve the berries was to can them. Women would can many quarts each year.

Many times the cook simply opened a can, sweetened it, and set it on the table. Perhaps the most common dish using blackberries was cobblers. But there were other ways to prepare and serve the berries. Following are a few recipes using the black gold of the Ozarks.

BLACKBERRY DUMPLINGS

1 cup flour	3 Tbs. fat
½ tsp. salt	¼ cup water
1½ tsp. baking powder	½ cup sugar
½ cup milk	2 qts. berries

Cut fat into the sifted dry ingredients and add milk to form a soft dough. Bring water, sugar, and berries to a boil. Slowly drop spoonfulls of the dumpling dough into the hot berry mixture. Let dumplings cook in the boiling berries for about ten minutes. Serve while warm with ice cream or whipped cream.

BLACKBERRY ROLL

Make a rich biscuit dough and roll it out one-fourth inch thick. Sprinkle sugar on the dough and dot with butter. Spread well-drained canned or fresh berries over the dough and roll up like a jelly roll. Bake at 350° for 35 minutes. Serve while still warm.

JAM PUDDING

4 eggs	1 cup milk
1 cup flour	1 tsp. cinnamon
1 cup white sugar	pinch of nutmeg
1 cup blackberry jam	1 tsp. baking soda

Sift dry ingredients. Beat eggs and add milk. Slowly add milk and egg mixture to dry ingredients and mix to get a smooth batter. Mix in the jam. Pour into buttered pan. Bake at 350° for 35 minutes. Serve with whipped cream.

BLACKBERRY KUCHEN

1½ cups flour	1 or 2 eggs
½ tsp. salt	¼ cup melted butter
2½ tsp. baking powder	¼ cup milk
½ cup sugar	3 cups drained blackberries

Sift dry ingredients and slowly add beaten eggs, milk, and melted butter and beat until the batter is smooth. Pour it in a well-greased shallow baking pan. Over top of the batter, spread the berries. Sprinkle the top thickly with powdered sugar. Bake at 350° for 35 minutes.

BLACKBERRY JAM

4 cups fresh blackberries (use some red-ripe berries)
4 cups sugar

Sort and wash the berries. Remove any particles. Crush well. Put the crushed berries into a kettle, add sugar, and stir well. Boil rapidly, stirring constantly until mixture thickens in twenty to thirty minutes. Skim off any scum that forms on top. When thick, pour into hot, sterilized jars and seal with melted paraffin. Makes 1½ pints.

BLACKBERRY JUICE

2½ qts. of fresh blackberries
¾ cup water

Sort and wash berries. Crush and add water. Cover and bring to a boil on high heat. Lower heat and simmer for five minutes. Pour the mixture into a muslin cloth and gently twist it to squeeze the juice through. This removes the seeds and pulp. Catch the juice in a large bowl and can. Serve cold, or use in making jelly.

BLACKBERRY JELLY

4 cups blackberry juice (use berries ¾ ripe and ¼ red-ripe)
3 cups sugar

Measure juice into kettle. Add sugar and stir well. Boil over a high heat, removing the scum that accumulates. Boil until jelly sheets from a spoon. Pour into hot, sterilized jelly jars and seal with melted paraffin.

BLACKBERRY PIE

Line the pan with pie crust. Spread sugar and a bit of flour in the bottom. Add one quart of canned berries, juice and all, or fresh berries, adding about ¼ cup of water. Dot with butter and sprinkle liberally with more sugar. Cover with a top crust or a lattice-work crust. Bake at 350° for 30 minutes.

CANNING BLACKBERRIES

Wash and drain berries. Use ½ cup sugar to 1 quart of blackberries. Put sugar and berries in a large enough pan to hold and bring to a boil. Pack in hot sterilized jars. (Long ago many women canned berries without sugar, sweetening the berries later when used.)

FREEZING BLACKBERRIES

Wash and drain the berries well. Place in tightly sealed container, leaving an inch head space, and freeze.

Sorghum Molasses, Bittersweet Style

A hundred years ago if you did not have a few jugs of molasses you were in for a sweetless winter. Sorghum molasses, sometimes called long sweetening, brought the main sweet, sugary taste to cooking. When the crop did not turn out well, the Ozark people were in for bitter gooseberry pie or had to be content with just butter on biscuits and cornbread. Sugar was an expensive and difficult-to-get luxury, and finding a bee tree was too unreliable. Farmers could be more self-sufficient with something they grew and made themselves, like the nearly always dependable sorghum cane crop.

However, not everyone that endeavored to make molasses was satisfied. The molasses might be green from not enough cooking, or it might be cooked too fast. It could be murky from dirty stalks or from improperly strained juice, or black from being scorched. It might be bitter because the cane had been frostbitten or from improper handling of the harvesting. A poor growing season could produce an inferior crop, or the seed might be inferior. So it was very important to know what to do while growing, harvesting, and cooking the sorghum cane. The making of good molasses was a skill not every one had. Those who made it well were sought after.

Very few people had their own sorghum mills even years ago, usually there was one in a neighborhood. As sugar became more available, the number of mills became scarcer as time went on, until now there are very few in production.

The decline in the use of molasses was partly because sugar became more readily available and cheaper. Sugar allowed women to make finer cakes, jellies, and other foods. But on Ozark tables, sugar did not completely take the place of molasses, which continued to be in demand as long as it was available. The Charles Hough family and the staff of *Bittersweet,* under the watchful eyes of Elva and Myrtle Hough, raised a cane crop and went through all the processes of making molasses for three consecutive years. From our experience, and from talking with people who used to make molasses, we believe the main reason for its scarcity today is the tremendous amount of hand labor involved. Most

It takes a lot of people to work both mill and pan together. Notice stripped cane stalks at left and pummy pile on the right.

people are not willing to work as hard as is required to make molasses, and those who are willing cannot get the necessary labor to help them. For molasses making requires a fairly big crew.

Back when people depended on molasses, they could obtain it in several ways even if they did not have a mill themselves. If they had the money, they could buy their year's supply in the fall from mill owners or the general stores that always carried it. They could raise their own cane, cut, strip, and top it and haul it to the mill. The mill operator would custom grind the juice and make the molasses for a share of the product, or for pay. Sometimes the owner of the mill would move it to the cane patch to custom make the molasses right on the farm.

Power to operate the mills was furnished by either mules or horses in the early days. Even after gas engines or tractors were common, it was cheaper and just as efficient for many to use their horsepower as before. The animals were harnessed to a pole that turned the mill to extract the juice from cane. When tractors came into general use, pulleys could be attached to engines to turn the belt, giving the same results. The difference in sources of power, however, did not change the taste of molasses.

The size of the patches of cane would depend on how much molasses was needed. Men usually planted enough for just their family, a small patch that would produce ten to twelve gallons, enough for one year.

For the children, harvest time in late September and early October was indeed a time of mouth watering, getting to suck on the cane stalks, and eating all the good things that could be cooked from molasses. For the parents, it meant lots of labor before the job was over.

The finished product of molasses was often stored in stone crock jugs. These would keep the molasses well through the winter months. By spring the liquid might turn to sugar, but all that needed be done was to get the jug out of the cellar and put it on the back of the wood stove to heat up. The molasses would pour as well as before.

Besides being a table spread, molasses was used in gingerbread, cookies and cakes, to sweeten pumpkin pie and spicewood tea, to make popcorn balls and taffy, and in many other foods. As some older Ozarkians would say, "Them molasses make baked foods taste better. Just put a gullup in to flavor." This humorous term for a measurement is somewhat hard to explain because it is a word to describe the sound that the thick molasses makes when being poured out of a jug. What comes out between two sounds is a gullup.

When molasses mills were common, you could buy molasses for seventy-five cents to a dollar a gallon. Nowadays, even in the Ozarks, you rarely are able to buy homemade molasses for any amount of money. Only with the hard work of families and neighbors gathering to help one another was the joy of having sorghum molasses for the winter made possible.

Planting

Work for making molasses begins in May when the sorghum molasses cane seeds are planted in rows to begin the process.

Warren Cook remembered how he used to plant it. "We would get to where we could take a long necked bottle, regulate our thumb over the mouth of the bottle and just walk along to sow the seed in the row. We'd lift our thumb up and the cane seed would fall out. We got to where we were fairly deft to it.

"We had to cover it lightly. We tied a rope around our waist, then found a chunk about four inches around or a little bigger, tied the rope to it and as we walked along and sowed the cane, the chunk would drag through and cover the cane deep enough for it to come up. I've dropped a lot of cane that way."

Cultivation of the ground begins a few weeks later to remove weeds growing between the rows and to loosen up the ground around the plants. In the early days a man used a horse and single stock plows to break the ground, lay off the rows, and cultivate (plow). Now the planting and plowing are done with power machinery, but even today, with all the machines available, a man must do almost all the rest of the work himself as the hard work of making molasses begins.

Thinning

Cane seed is too small to be planted spaced apart like corn. Even with careful hand planting or with drills stopped down as much as possible, more seed is planted than needed. Therefore, when they reach knee height the rows of young plants must be thinned to one

When cane reaches knee height, it must be thinned by hand. Robert uses a broad hoe.

plant every foot or so. Thinning is done with a broad hoe. Sometimes it is necessary to pull out by hand the excess plants around the one to be left.

It is important to dig or pull up the plants by the roots so they will not sucker out, causing four or five new weak plants to grow where one was cut off. Thinning gives the remaining plants room to grow tall and develop thick stalks. If improperly thinned, the resulting cane will be a thick row of underdeveloped stalks. Small stalks cut down on the juice production besides making the harvesting much harder.

Water is the most important factor in the growth of cane. Cane stalks can and will stand through a hot, dry summer, for they simply curl their leaves and wait for rain. If necessary, they can wait until the late summer rains of September to continue growing, but the cane stalk must mature before it can be cut and used for molasses. This makes a race for time in October, because the first frost on the leaves will drive the juice down into the roots. Since the juice in the stalk is the product, the stalks should be cut before this happens or most of the juice is lost.

To enable us to grow a crop during a dry summer, we watered the cane patch all summer from a spring-fed creek, using a small, one-cylinder gasoline pump. This innovation may not have been very authentic, but we were making molasses rather than making history.

Harvesting

You can tell when the cane plants reach maturity in late September or early October by looking at the seed tassels, which change in color from green to medium brown.

Harvesting begins with stripping, or removing the leaves. Debris from the leaves, if run through the mill, would make the molasses bitter. The leaves must be stripped before the first big frost to prevent damaging the juice in the stalk. If there is danger of frost, plants can be stripped and left in the field until ready for cutting since without the extra surface of the leaves the frost damage is not as great.

To strip, you can use two sticks about thirty inches long, bringing them down on each side of the stalk to knock the leaves off. Some people use a thin board about eighteen inches long with looped notches in it. The teeth would catch and pull off the leaves. By this time the leaves are dry and break off easily. Some molasses makers especially skilled in stripping can give the heads one blow and knock off all the leaves. Leaves are sometimes stripped by hand after the cane is cut and hauled to the mill. Either way is tedious work.

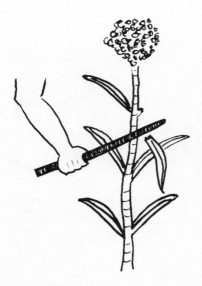

The dried leaves can be easily knocked off with a stick.

Cutting off the head in the field.

The stalks are cut close to the ground.

Cutting, topping, stripping, and loading. There is much hand labor involved in harvesting cane.

Topping the plants is next. The seed tassels must be cut off to keep the seeds out of the juice. Cutting off the heads is done with either a corn knife, a sharp hand sickle, or a butcher knife. The heads that are cut off and left in the field make excellent feed for wildlife or for stock that may later be turned in to the field. If the cane is cut in the field before topping, the heads can be cut off several at a time and saved for seed or stock feed.

The last step in harvesting is cutting the cane stalk itself to be hauled to the mill. The stalks should be cut as close to the ground as possible without getting into the dirt. This step is important, because dirt on the stalk will get into the juice. Since the larger, lower end of the stalk contains much of the juice, one should get as much of the stalk as possible. After cutting, with no loss of quality the stalks can be stored for up to two weeks before extracting the juice.

Extracting the Juice

The mill is the first place to get a look at what will soon be molasses. Before tractors, horses were used to turn the rollers in the mill. A horse or mule harnessed to a pole walked in circles. The pole was attached to gears that turned the rollers of the mill. The animal was usually

*Near Bennett Spring, Missouri, four generations of Smiths made molasses in 1905
—a family tradition carried on by Charley Smith* (right) *until a few years ago.
Courtesy Janelle Smith.*

trained to start and stop on verbal commands, keeping a slow, steady
walk around and around. If it was not well trained, someone had to
lead it around to keep it from tearing up the mill or possibly hurting
someone.

In more recent years, tractors replaced horsepower. The tractor
power take-off throttled down to a slow rpm is hooked up by belt to
a wheel, which turns the rollers. This method is more dangerous, since
it would be impossible to reach the motor in time to stop the rollers
if someone caught a hand or an arm in the mill, whereas a verbal
"whoa," would stop the horse.

The cane stalks are inserted into one side of the mill. The rollers
crush the stalks, squeezing out the juice very much like a wringer on
a washing machine. The juice flows off the rollers into a metal trough
leading to the collection bucket or barrel. Over the bucket are several
thicknesses of cheesecloth to filter out any pieces of stalk or seeds that
may have dropped down with the juice. The stalks, flattened by the
three rollers, go on through the mill and come out on the other side
as plummies. These plummies can then be used as feed or compost.

Old-timers used horse or mule power to turn the mill to extract the cane juice.

Caution must be used while feeding cane into the mill, since it cannot be stopped quickly.

After going through the mill, the cane juice is filtered through cheesecloth before being taken to the pan for cooking.

Cooking the Juice

The raw, greenish looking juice is still a long way from finished molasses. Even before beginning the hours of cooking in the big open vat, you need to do considerable preparation getting the vat ready for this next operation.

A foundation of rocks is built about three feet high, or at a comfortable working height, and as long and wide as the vat. Concrete blocks or bricks can be substituted for rock. A flue is built at one end. The other end has an opening for adding wood to the fire and for a draft. Permanently built foundations have doors and regular stove drafts built in, but a temporary structure can be devised with asbestos or other non-flammable material to control the air intake on the open end. The foundation should be built with the end section where the molasses comes out a few inches lower than the first section.

The fire can now be laid. Most Ozark sorghum molasses makers used wood for fuel because of its availability. The fire is the most

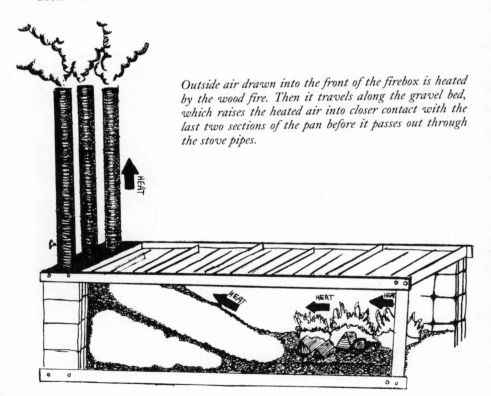

Outside air drawn into the front of the firebox is heated by the wood fire. Then it travels along the gravel bed, which raises the heated air into closer contact with the last two sections of the pan before it passes out through the stove pipes.

critical factor and the easiest to err on, for it must be set up just right to ensure proper cooking.

First, the fire must be very hot in the front, or first, three sections of the pan, in order to heat the green juice and start it boiling. Also, the fire must be hot enough to keep the heat consistent. Since new wood is continually added, there must be enough heat to set this wood on fire without cooling off the pan. Second, the fire should not extend to the sides of the pan, because the juice should boil in the middle, rolling the scum to the edges to be skimmed off. If the fire covers the whole width of the pan, the juice will boil all the way across, preventing the scum from separating.

The fire itself should extend only halfway back from the front of the pan. From here we laid in gravel, sloping upward to the back, leaving about a one-foot clearance from the bottom of the pan. Air drawn in from the front and heated by the fire is hot enough to cook the nearly finished molasses in the last two sections. A hot air draft is used instead of direct fire, because the cooking molasses should simmer rather than boil. A fire would be too hot. There should be enough stove pipes to create enough suction for the air flow, which gives more even cooking.

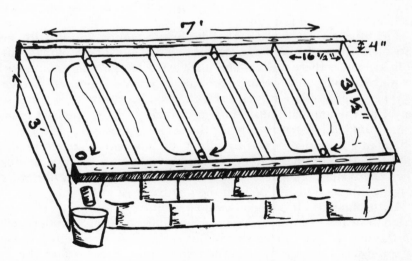

Diagrams of the cooking pan showing five sections. Raw juice is put in the section on the right and comes out finished on the left.

On some pans each section is divided into thirds for better control and adequate stirring during cooking.

The pans or vats are made of copper or steel and usually are divided into five sections with holes or other opening for the juice to be transferred from section to section during the cooking process. In some vats the sections are further divided off into three more segments. This aids in skimming, for the skimmers fit exactly into the smaller sections. As we ran the skimmer down each section, the scum could not get out of the skimmer.

The divisions are to ensure that the cooking of the molasses can be a continual process. As the molasses cooks, it is moved down the pan, with fresh juice continually being added in the first section. Some vats are not divided at all. This type of equipment means cooking just one batch at a time until it is done.

The juice can be stored a few days before boiling, but usually molasses making for a family was a one- or two-day job. The cooking would begin as soon as there was enough juice extracted for one section, with the mill running and molasses cooking in several stages all at once.

When the foundation is laid and the wood is ready for the fire, set the vat on the foundation, stop up any cracks or holes the heat might escape from, and you are ready for the cooking process.

Cooking the juice begins by filling the pan with water to protect it until the fire reaches a temperature hot enough to keep it boiling. When the water comes to a boil, you are ready to remove the water from the first section and pour in the first batch of juice.

As the first batch of molasses boils well, it is moved to the next section. The first section is replenished with fresh juice. Section by section the batches are moved slowly down the pan, each being cooked more and more until it reaches the last section. There before you, in the five sections, you can see the color change from a sickening opaque green to a rich medium golden brown, just slightly darker than honey. The consistency changes from thin watery juice to thick, syrupy molasses.

Elva and Myrtle Hough supervise the molasses making.

The juice in each of the sections boils, reaching a desired stage before being moved on. You can even see a difference in the way the liquid boils in the five different sections, changing from a rapid foamy boil to the slow blurp of the thickened molasses.

To move the juice from one section to another, use a long-handled wooden pusher built just the width of one section of the vat. Put a clean doubled cloth under the pusher at the end opposite from the hole. Lay the pusher on the cloth. Slowly push the juice up the section toward the hole.

The holes are stopped with clean rags. Remove the rags to allow the juice to flow into the next section. When all the juice has been transferred and before you remove the pusher, stop up the hole with the rag to keep the juice from returning.

In a like manner the juice in each section is moved forward, new fresh juice being added to the beginning to keep a continual cooking process. Finished molasses comes out of the last section and raw juice is added to the first all day long and sometimes into the night and next day, until all the juice is cooked.

When cooking the juice, keep it stirred and remove the skimmings. The pusher makes a good stirring tool. Stirring is especially needed in the last two sections to prevent scorching. The skimmings, or impurities, boil to the top like the scum in jelly making. These must be removed from the first three sections in order to have a clear product. Remove the scum with a long-handled skimmer, a flat-bottomed scoop-shaped metal strainer with holes in the bottom. Just sweep the bubbling surface of the juice, collecting the skimmings. The good juice will escape through the holes back to the vat. The skimmer, dunked in a bucket of water after each skimming, is ready to use again.

When the molasses in the last section reaches the desired consistency, it is drained out through an opening in the bottom of the pan. Collected in clean buckets or stone crocks, it is stored in jugs, barrels, crocks, metal buckets, or other containers until it is used.

There are several different ways to test the molasses in the last pan to see if it is done. One indication is seeing the size of the boiling bubbles appear almost as big as a dime. Another is when the molasses runs off a stirrer and forms a long hair. Neither test is perfect. If you run it out too soon, the molasses will be runny, and if it cooks too long, the molasses will harden into candy. A guess is almost all there is.

When the molasses is ready, several things need to be done all at once. The plug is pulled out of the pan to let the boiling hot molasses run out a trough through a cheesecloth strainer into a bucket. The cheesecloth filters out bugs and debris, for molasses is too thick to be

The molasses in the last section is ready. Be careful to keep fingers out of the way while pushing the molasses through the plug spout, or risk a bad burn.

filtered any other way. As the finished molasses runs and is pushed out of the cooking pan, more must follow behind from other sections. But the new batch should not run in so fast as to mingle with the cooked molasses in the bucket. This is a very frenzied time, requiring people to hold the strainer, push the molasses through the opening into the bucket, and push the juice from each section into the next. When the last section containing finished molasses is emptied, the juice in each section must move up one section and raw juice from the mill must be poured into the first section all at once, because the fire continues heating the pan from below. Without juice in any section, the pan will scorch. While all this is going on, everyone should see that the sections do not mix and be careful to keep fingers out of the way. Hot molasses sticking to the skin burns badly.

After the molasses is done and the fire is put out, the pan is cleaned thoroughly and coated with vegetable oil to prevent it from rusting. Note the five major pan sections, each divided into three smaller ones.

Cooking molasses requires constant attention to keep the fire regulated so that it is not too hot or too low; and it takes constant attention to tend to the cooking so that the molasses does not scorch or cook too long or not long enough. It takes experience to move all the sections quickly before the pan gets too hot. It takes endurance to tolerate the wood smoke and pungent steam rising from the vat into the crisp autumn air. There is plenty of action going on when the mill is operating and the juice is being cooked.

After our molasses cooled off, the actual yield turned out to be twenty-two gallons of finished molasses to two hundred gallons of raw juice, or approximately one to nine.

Few people can understand or appreciate the effort going into the making of even a single gallon of sorghum molasses—several hot summer months just waiting for the cane to grow, then a week of swinging a cornknife, cutting the stalks, stripping, heading, then several more days of grinding and cooking. Molasses making like this could hardly be considered a profitable business today. Man-hours alone, at even minimum wage, would cost hundreds of dollars, and few people would pay that much for molasses. Also, the equipment used for making molasses is almost impossible to find now, and is difficult to set up. And even with all of these problems solved, to produce an acceptable product you still need the know-how or skill, which can come only with the experience of making molasses, as we have discovered.

But through the making of molasses we have obtained just an inkling of what earlier generations had to work at. The heritage that we at *Bittersweet* are trying to preserve can be fully understood only through learning first-hand the difficulties experienced and the work necessary to survival in our grandparents' youth. It was indeed the bitter with the sweet of life.

Cooking with Molasses

Whether you are a hardy soul with ambitions of homemade molasses or a timider person who buys it in the supermarket, these following recipes are worth making.

MOLASSES COFFEE LAYER CAKE

½ cup butter or margarine
1 cup brown sugar
2 eggs
½ cup molasses
½ cup made (perked) coffee

2 cups flour
*½ tsp. mixed spices
½ tsp. salt
2 tsp. baking powder

*If you don't keep mixed spices use cinnamon, a little nutmeg, and about ¼ tsp. ginger.

Beat butter and sugar until creamy. Add eggs, then molasses and coffee; lastly the flour, salt, spices and baking powder. Bake in layers until done (at 350°) and put together with frosting.

Many Ozarkians of the past and present have enjoyed combining molasses with other ingredients to make spreads to eat with pancakes, cornbread, biscuits, or homemade bread. Perhaps the most familiar of these is Sorghum Butter.

SORGHUM BUTTER

Mix together molasses and soft butter. Some people like to melt it, but be sure not to cook it. Just let it get warm enough to mix the two together easily.

Another delicious topping to liven up an ordinary breakfast or an evening snack is egg butter.

EGG BUTTER

1 cup molasses   2 eggs, beaten

Put the molasses on and let it come to a boil. Slowly stir in the two eggs which have been beaten until frothy. Cook the mixture slowly until as thick as desired. Let personal preference dictate here. Remove from heat and add ¼ tsp. nutmeg if desired.

Eula York shared a Molasses Taffy recipe, as well as her childhood experience making it with her mother who, born in 1894, never owned a cookbook until the 1930s.

Molasses Taffy

If you have never experienced a molasses taffy candy pull you have missed an Ozark treat and should be introduced to this fun-time occasion.

The date was 1920 and winter was beginning. There was little to do for fun — especially for little girls. Maudie Ellen, (born Maudie Ellen Bailey, 1894) knew what it was like to be the only girl in a big family of boys, and understood her one daughter's desire to have fun with other girls.

Now that the fall crops had been harvested and stored in the cellar, the butchering was done, molasses making was completed, and things generally readied for winter, it seemed a favorable time to allow her daughter to ask a cousin and two other girls to spend the night.

After supper was over, everyone assisted in clearing the big kitchen table. Usually the table was not completely cleared—some things were left on and covered with a cloth until the next meal. In this instance everything was cleared and clean plates were placed around the table for each girl.

Maudie Ellen began the preparation for making molasses taffy, and to keep four girls busy and out of the way she insisted that each get a pencil and paper and write her recipe to save for their hope chests. Since this was something big girls did, it was accomplished with some difficulty, since spelling words like molasses and vinegar was not easy.

The basic recipe was as follows:

MOLASSES CANDY

2 teacups molasses   1 Tbsp. cider vinegar
chunk butter, size of an egg

Maudie Ellen melted the butter in a big iron skillet placed near the back of the old wood cook stove. Then with a teacup she dipped molasses from an earthenware jar. As she stirred the mixture she moved it toward the front where the stove was hot. After the mixture began to boil, she stirred it constantly. Soon she began to test the boiling mixture by dropping a little from the spoon into a cup of cold water. When the testing showed that the candy was brittle enough, she moved the skillet to the back of the stove and added the vinegar.

Now other preparations must be made. Hands were washed and greased with butter. Maudie Ellen then placed some of the hot candy on each plate with instructions not to touch it until she gave permission. (This meant that it must be tested to make sure it was cool enough to handle.)

Everyone watched as Maudie Ellen picked up her candy from the plate, doubled it over and pulled it out several inches and doubled it back. It did look easy. She pulled it out a few more times and handed it to one of the girls with instructions to keep pulling it and doubling it back. She made the rounds of the table and soon each one was pulling candy.

Most of the girls had trouble keeping the candy from coming apart as they pulled it out, but Maudie Ellen was always helping, and the girls soon discovered that it could just be put back together and pulled some more. As it was pulled it became a lighter color and became harder and harder to pull.

At Maudie Ellen's instructions, when the candy had been pulled enough, each one stretched the candy out on the oilcloth that covered the kitchen table. With the back of a case knife she quickly marked each strip of candy into lengths of about one inch. Then picking up the long piece of candy she lightly tapped it with the handle of the knife, and the candy broke into bite size pieces. Now it was ready to eat.

Certainly, the giggles of girls with sticky fingers and the squeals of near disaster were thanks enough, and the girls were excused from any clean-up duties. Maudie Ellen hummed a hymn as she stacked the plates. The girls were sharing their candy with father and the brothers, and there was no doubt that everyone was having fun.

Jump Right In — Cider Making

"Well, just jump right in," a cheery voice invited me when *Bittersweet* visited the Stanley Beard farm to witness the making of apple cider. I had been standing around not knowing what to do in all the bustle of activity, feeling somewhat out of place among all the strange faces. Charlotte Davis reinforced her friendly invitation by handing me a bucket of apples and pointing me to the apple press. Esther Jones paused in his work of poking the apples into the press to grin at me.

"Dump them in," he said pleasantly. "Ever see an operation like this before?"

"Never did," I admitted.

It was October as we drove deep into the hills. As the crooked road wound its way through the steep little hills, I noticed what a beautiful day it really was. The sun was bright and the sky was deep blue. The Virginia creeper, which spread through the treetops like the Spanish moss of the South, and the sumac had both turned a brilliant scarlet. The sassafras trees were turning bright orange and butterflies danced over the goldenrod that was as bright as the sun. The oak-covered hillsides were just beginning to be painted with the bright fall colors. There was a slight fall chill in the air, but at the same time the sun had a comfortable warmth to it.

After the pleasant drive, we arrived at the farm. There was a house, several small farm buildings, and a large metal barn where all the activities were taking place. The air was filled with the scent of sweet apples as we were greeted with warm smiles and friendly talk by Myrtle and Elvie Hough. They were both huddled over buckets of red apples, cutting out the bad spots.

Myrtle put a large bucket of apples in each of my hands and told me to take them into the barn. Inside the barn there was even more activity. I set the buckets beside some others, amazed and bewildered by what I saw. Girls were laughing as they poured cider into jugs, a little boy ran past me, and men were working and joking together. I stood there, an outsider, and though everyone smiled my way, I still felt out of place before Charlotte invited me to join in the work.

Making apple cider on this scale takes several families working together.

"This here is a cider press," Esther and Stanley explained to me as we fed it apples and tasted the cider flowing out the bottom. The men were poking apples with a big stick into the mouth of a contraption such as I had never seen. The wooden machine was very old, but still sturdy. It stood on four wooden legs and at the top had a square funnel-shaped box called a hopper, into which the men were constantly pouring and poking apples. At the spout of the "funnel" was a large rotating cylinder with sharp prongs on it that grabbed the apples, tore them up and spat them into a container that looked to me like a small bottomless barrel with spaces between the staves. This was called a slat. After the chewed up apples (now called pomace) filled this, the men slid it under a round piece of wood the same size as the mouth of the barrel. Attached to this round press was a long, threaded shaft that, when turned, caused the press to come down and smash the apples. When this happened, juice from the apples would pour out between the slats of the small barrel into a chute. This chute had a small hole in the end of it, where the cider ran out into a large bucket.

Whenever they would run off a batch, everyone would grab a cup and catch some as it poured from the press. They would taste it to give their opinions as to whether it was too sweet or too sour, a good or bad batch.

In the corner of the barn behind the press was a table where a group of women and girls were straining the large buckets of cider through cheesecloth into smaller one-gallon jugs. They labeled each jug with the name of the owner of the apples before taking it to a large table in the middle of the barn, where they had over a hundred gallons of cider already stored.

All the while I was working I got to sample each batch of cider. Some of the cider was smooth and sweet and some of it was so strong it would make your eyes cross, but it was all good. It wasn't a beverage that you would just drink down. You would take the time to savor it, letting it linger in your mouth in order to appreciate the natural smooth flavor of the sweet apples.

The antique press was a remarkable machine, and the cider was really great, but what was truly remarkable were the people. They were old and young, big and small, all friends working alongside one another to harvest their crops of apples, enjoying Stanley and Helen Beard's neighborly sharing of their press with others. It was an atmosphere of friendship and sharing few people ever experience in this busy modern world, where people seldom take the time to enjoy the simple pleasures that working with others can bring. It was a place of friendship and warmth, kindness and smiles, laughter, and a rare feeling of togetherness. I found myself dreading the time that I would have to leave.

But of course, we had to leave and say goodbye. Although I carried home a gift of a gallon jug of cider under each arm, I left with much more than that. I left with a feeling that I had never had before—a feeling of knowing what people are really all about. And although only a few hours earlier I had thought of the event as going to be "slightly more exciting than a chess tournament," it changed my outlook on people and turned out to be a day that I will not soon forget.

The most commonly used apples for cider are Jonathan or Winesap, but for a sweeter cider try red and yellow Delicious apples. The quality of the apples need not be that of table fruit as long as they contain no insects, have not been sprayed, and are not rotten, so most of the apples you have on hand that are not good enough for other purposes may be used for cider. Notice should also be taken that the apples are not in brown decay, or the cider will ferment too rapidly. It usually takes a bushel of apples to yield two or three gallons of cider.

Esther Griffin places the slat under the hopper where apples are first ground into pomace. Then the hopper is moved under the press to squeeze out the juice.

One man pokes the apples into the hopper while another turns the press to squeeze the juice from the pomace.

Above right: *A close-up of the pomace.*

The crushed apples, called pomace, fall into the slat, which is then moved down the trough under the press.

Right: *The press has squeezed the juice from the slats into the trough. It then flows down the trough and out the spout, where it is caught in pans or, occasionally, in a thirsty worker's cup.*

It takes two people to operate the cider press effectively. While one person pours the apples, which are whole, unpeeled, and washed, into the hopper a few at a time, the other turns the crank, thereby turning the gears inside the hopper that grind the apples into pomace. This pomace is thrown downward, out of the hopper into the slat located directly below the hopper. A slat somewhat resembles a bottomless bucket; the sides of the slat are made of vertical strips of wood which do not quite touch, thereby letting juice seep out when the pomace is pressed.

When the slat is full you are ready to press the juice out of it, although some cider lovers prefer to let the pomace be exposed to air for about a day and then ground again.

The squeezing of the pulp is done by a metal, threaded shaft with a metal disc attached to the bottom of it so that when the wheel on top of the shaft is turned clockwise, it lowers the disc. The slat, which is filled with pomace, is moved down the trough so that it is now under the metal disc. A wooden disc the same circumference as the slat is placed on top of the pomace in the slat. This wooden disc is pushed through the slat by the metal disc as the wheel on top of the shaft is turned clockwise, thereby forcing almost all of the juice contained in the pomace to seep out and run down to the floor or trough of the press. This trough is slanted in such a way that all of the juice will run off into a container on the ground beneath the press. This container cannot be aluminum or any other unglazed metal, or the taste of the cider will be bitter. This entire process takes about fifteen to twenty minutes.

Most cider presses have two slats, so it is possible to squeeze and grind at the same time.

When you have squeezed all the juice that you want, you are ready to strain it. This is done by fitting a clean cloth such as a dish towel or cheesecloth over another container and pouring the cider into it, then removing the cloth.

After straining the cider you are ready to store it for aging. Cider does not have to be aged; it can be served right away, but as you will probably want to store part of it, you must know the process.

Cider can be stored in jugs, bottles or jars, but be sure you use sound glass or the container will burst with the increasing fermentation. Cover these containers with cotton-wool plugs and store the cider at room temperature. Do not put the plug in too tightly or it will not ferment properly.

In about four days you will begin to see sediment settling on the bottom and you should notice fermentation bubbles forming on the top. For a mild sweet cider, siphon the liquid away from the sediment and store in a cold place for immediate use. Do not disturb the sediment on the bottom of the container.

Now that you know basically how to make apple cider you may want to keep your eye out for a cider press. It would be a profitable investment in addition to providing some good drinking.

Copper Kettle Magic—Apple Butter

"Smoke follows beauty," teased John Playter when we tried to avoid the smothering gray smoke while helping stir the big copper kettle full of bubbling apple butter. His adding more wood to the fire only increased the smoke, so that no matter where we stood, it found its way from under the kettle into our eyes and lungs.

We had been cooking and stirring for eight straight hours that chilly October day when Charlene asked her husband for the second time, "John, don't you think it's done now?"

Rising from beside the kettle after carefully distributing the wood to keep the fire burning evenly, he peered over the edge and for a minute or two watched the bubbles breaking into soft craters on the surface of the apple butter. Everyone gathered around eager for a confirmation. "No, it's not quite firm enough," he said. "We'll let it cook just a little longer."

But from his expression the entire Playter family, along with a few friends and us, knew it would not be long. We had all worked together since the evening before, visiting, eating, and anticipating this moment. The daughters and their husbands carried out the cans and jars, getting everything ready for the final canning. With clean cloths, protective gloves, and sauce pans for dipping, they stood assembly-line fashion, ready to finish the job.

This gathering of people to help one another used to be a common occurrence. On many farms during apple harvest, neighbors gathered to make the work go faster while enjoying one another's company. The Playters are still carrying on this tradition.

John and Charlene began making apple butter on their own after helping a friend for several years. They've made it every year since 1956 and have encouraged many other people to start making it, too. Even while they were cooking apple butter, across the hedge the next-door neighbors were also busily stirring their own apple butter in a thirty-gallon copper kettle.

For one batch of apple butter the Playters use five bushels of the

362

Uncle John Playter makes apple butter in a copper kettle every fall.

Kent.

Mother

The first job is to cut the apples into small slices.

best quality Jonathan apples available. They prefer Jonathans because of their tart flavor, firmness, and red color.

From experience, the Playters have decided that in order to make apple butter of optimum quality, they must allow an entire day for the cooking and canning processes alone. Therefore, they completed all other preparations the previous evening. The following directions explain how the Playters make apple butter in an outside kettle.

Washing the apples is the first step in making apple butter. Then cut out any bad places, quarter, and core the apples. Remove only the seeds when coring, because the natural sweetness of the apple lies next to the core. Some people also peel their apples, but the Playters believe that the peeling adds flavor, color, and pectin to the apple butter.

Slice the apples as thin as possible to reduce cooking time. Use a very sharp knife and frequently alternate slicing methods to relax your fingers. Use a wooden cutting board when slicing by hand becomes uncomfortable.

Store the sliced apples in clean, air-tight, plastic trash bags. Tie the top of each bag securely to prevent discoloration and preserve freshness. Place the bags outdoors in the cool night air or in a cool place until morning, or when ready to cook.

The copper kettle measures twenty-eight inches in diameter, is eighteen inches deep, and has a forty-gallon capacity. The base of the kettle is fifteen inches above the ground in an iron stand. Each leg is two and a half inches wide and is angled slightly outward from the rim of the stand.

Early the next day the Playters begin preparing the kettle and equipment to be used throughout the day's events. Equipment needed:

kettle	two saucepans
stand	several rectangular flat pans
two apple butter paddles	several stone crocks
jars, lids, rings	protective gloves
several colanders	long-handled spatula

The kettle is the most important piece of equipment needed for making apple butter. It is advisable to cook apples and other fruit in a brass or copper kettle. Apples cooked in iron will have a poor flavor and will be discolored because the acid will react with the metal. The contents of a copper kettle will heat evenly, advantageous in making apple butter.

The Playters used a friend's copper kettle until 1976, when they purchased their own. Some friends told them of the handmade kettles they had seen hanging in the window of a furniture store in New Harmony, Indiana. Upon inspecting them, the Playters chose a forty-gallon kettle. One thing that makes this kettle unique is the way the seams are joined. The bottom and side joints are formed by interlocked fingers soldered into place, creating a perfectly smooth seam. The kettle has a rounded bottom, with no corners where sauce can accumulate and burn.

Gently clean the kettle with vinegar, salt, and water solution to remove the tarnish. Then rinse thoroughly with water.

Someone should start the fire while the kettle is being cleaned. Although many old-timers preferred Osage orange hedge wood, which produced a more intense heat, the Playters prefer oak because it kindles much more quickly, and they do not care for such a hot fire. John seems to get best results from a moderately hot fire. A very hot fire may heat the kettle unevenly and cause the apples to scorch in some places. "We're not in any hurry," John said. "We've got all day." Use

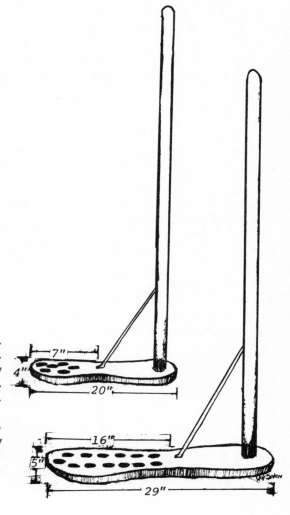

Even though some people use only one paddle throughout the process, the Playters have found that another, smaller, paddle is very useful in stirring the bulky apples as they cook down. The paddles have somewhat proportional dimensions, and their handles are the same size. Both paddles are made from one-inch birch boards.

two nonflammable, perhaps metal, wind shields to retain the flames and to prevent embers and ashes from being blown over the yard.

Pour one gallon of water per bushel of apples into the kettle and place it over the fire. Some people use apple cider instead of water, for a stronger flavor even though it is more expensive. Add approximately one half of the sliced apples and allow them to cook down. As they begin to lose their chunky appearance, the apples will take up less room in the kettle and will make stirring much easier. Then gradually add the remaining apples.

Stir the apples with the small homemade apple butter paddle. Paddles are often made of birch wood, for oak and pine do not withstand heat as well and may add an undesirable flavor to the apple butter. Never use a metal paddle, for metal will scratch the soft copper surface. Its smaller size makes the paddle easier to pull through the bulk of the quartered apples during the first cooking. Because of the right-angled design of the paddle, it needs a brace between the handle and the paddle itself.

Cook the apples two or three hours, or until they become very soft and mushy, and then remove the kettle from the fire. The apples are now ready to be strained through the colanders. Put a strong board or pole through the bail of the kettle, with one person supporting each end, and carry the kettle from the fire to a work table. Meanwhile, equip the table with two saucepans to dip out the apples, several colanders sitting in flat pans to catch the applesauce, stone crocks to hold all the resulting sauce and a long-handled spatula to scrape out every particle from the pans and utensils.

The Playters set up an assembly line using two people to dip the apples out of the kettle with saucepans into five or six colanders. Perhaps the hardest work of all is forcing the apple pulp through the tiny holes in the metal colanders with the wooden pestle. Persons working the colanders rotate the pestle around the sides of the colander until most of the pulp is pressed through the holes and only the dry peeling remains. They empty the peelings into a cardboard box or other garbage container. In past years, farmers fed this roughage to their hogs. As the pans fill with applesauce, other people empty them into the large stone crocks. When the kettle is empty, they rinse it thoroughly with water.

The apples are now ready for their second and final cooking. Put the kettle back onto the fire, empty the applesauce from the stone crocks back into it, and resume stirring.

This time the Playters use a larger, heavier wooden paddle with bigger holes and a longer handle. The larger paddle keeps the sauce

Cousin
Phyllis

Kent - Jane's
husband

Don-Phyllis
husband

Friend "Barb"

After the sliced apples have cooked until soft, they must be run through colanders to remove seeds and skins before continuing the cooking.

in a constant swirling motion, preventing the ingredients from settling. The larger holes help to mix the ingredients thoroughly, especially as the sugar and spices are added. The holes act much the same way as the slots in a slotted mixing spoon do, distributing the ingredients evenly throughout a mixture and creating a smooth blend of their flavors. The longer handle provides the increased leverage needed during the vigorous stirring.

Stirring is extremely important during this stage. John showed us a good pattern of stirring to keep the sauce constantly moving. "We go down the middle, around the side, back down the middle and around the other side. The bottom is smaller than the top, so if you do that, you pretty well cover the whole bottom. If you keep stirring in the middle, pretty soon you've let the sides stick. You constantly move everything on the bottom."

As the sauce thickens, especially after the sugar is added, it can easily scorch. "If you ever burn it and stick it," John warned, "you've had it. You've ruined the whole batch and the kettle, too. You've got to be careful."

Charlene gave two major precautions to take to avoid such a disaster. "Never stop stirring, and never let the firewood touch the bottom of the kettle, for that would make one little spot where it's too hot, and it would make it stick." Therefore, take care to keep the fire evenly spread beneath the kettle.

The curved edges of the paddle also help prevent sticking, because they somewhat fit the round shape of the kettle and can scrape more surface area. As the applesauce begins to boil, the bubbles break against the sides of the kettle, forming a thin film around the rim. A long-handled spatula is more convenient than the paddle for scraping it back into the mixture. The spatula is also helpful in removing leaves or other impurities that may blow into the kettle.

When the sauce is hot and boiling well, it is time to add the remaining ingredients to the five bushels of cooked apples.

1 box whole cloves
2 ounces stick cinnamon
4 pounds of red hots
75 pounds of sugar (or less depending on taste)

First enclose the cloves in a small bag made of cheesecloth. Then simply toss the loose pouch into the kettle. The porous cheesecloth serves as a strainer for the cloves, preventing the tiny, inedible nuggets from spreading throughout the sauce, while allowing the sauce to absorb the flavor.

Break the stick cinnamon into small pieces about one inch long, and add them to the bubbling contents of the kettle. Be careful not to crumble the sticks. They need to be visible so they can be removed when the apple butter is eaten.

Add the sugar slowly enough that the sauce never stops boiling. How well the sugar dissolves depends on the temperature of the applesauce. If the sauce is boiling, it will be hot enough to dissolve the sugar as it is added. Otherwise, the sugar crystals will quickly settle to the bottom of the kettle and may stick and burn. Therefore, vigorous stirring, especially on the bottom, is important during this stage. It is also advisable to wear long gloves to protect the hands and arms while adding the sugar, because the applesauce is very hot and may easily burn the skin. Gloves continue to protect as the apple butter thickens, for sometimes as the bubbles burst, they send splatters of hot apple butter in all directions.

Finally, add the bags of red hots all at once. The Playters use this cinnamon-flavored candy to add a rich, dark red color as well as the spicy flavor. Long ago before red hots were sold commercially, people used oil of cinnamon to obtain a similar flavor. They probably added a little less than a teaspoon of oil per gallon of apple butter. Some people continue to flavor their apple butter with the oil, but the finished product may not be as flavorful as apple butter flavored with red hots, and the rich red color is forfeited.

At this point the applesauce still has a thin consistency. Allow the sauce to thicken by maintaining a steady boil, still stirring constantly. This cooking time varies, depending on the fire and the weather, but usually takes another three or four hours. The sauce must be carefully watched as it begins to thicken so that it will be of the right consistency for apple butter.

The Playters perform thickness tests repeatedly until everyone agrees that the apple butter has just the right texture. "John and I always have to argue about that quite a little while," Charlene said. "Everyone's ready to eat it before John's ready to start canning. But he's always been the final judge, and he hasn't failed us yet."

The first test consists of simply observing the formation of the bubbles. When enough water has evaporated from the sauce, the bubbles become large and airy, taking a couple of seconds to reach their peak in height. As they burst, they make deep craters in the surface of the apple butter. After the apple butter has reached this stage, make a second test. Place a spoonful of the apple butter on a small saucer, and tilt the saucer to see whether the sample holds its shape. If a watery liquid separates from the sample, it needs to cook longer.

Test for doneness when large, airy bubbles form on the surface.

The finished product should be firm enough to hold its shape, yet moist enough that it can be spread. Of course, the degree of thickness depends on personal preference.

Since only John and Charlene are involved in the actual testing of the apple butter, there are plenty of others to prepare for the next process. Those in the kitchen sterilize the jars and boil the lids for proper seal and bring them out to the table, ready for canning.

"Now it is ready!" John and Charlene both agree. This pronouncement activates another assembly-line formation down both sides and ends of the work table. John and his son-in-law once again remove the blackened copper kettle from the fire and place it at the end of the table. As before, two people, equipped with gloves or hot pads to protect their hands, dip the apple butter from the kettle into a funnel in the top of the first jar. The next two people carefully wipe the top rim of the jar with soft white cloths to remove any spilled apple butter, assuring a good seal. The next down the line place the

Kent's Mother

Aunt Charlene

Don *Fay* *Barb* *Kent* *Old Friend* *Young Friend Phyllis* *Jane*

Uncle John

In late afternoon, when the apple butter is cooked just right, everyone helps fill the jars and seal them for future good eating.

cap on the rim of the jar and secure it with a metal ring. Next wipe the jar clean and put it in a box. One by one the jars are filled until the kettle is empty, and about 172 pints of rich, red apple butter is canned.

Though the apple butter is finished, the work is not, for there still remains the cleanup. The copper kettle needs immediate attention. Clean the inside of the kettle soon after the canning is finished, before the residue starts to dry. Use water to rinse the sticky inside and wipe it dry with a clean soft cloth. Cleaning the outside is a much harder job, usually not undertaken the same day. Apply a copper cleanser to the outside of the blackened kettle with a soft cloth and rub it clean. Copper is very easily dented and scratched, so take care in using the cooking utensils, and never use steel wool to clean the kettle. With diligent scrubbing the copper's warm, shiny glow will begin to appear from beneath the charred black coating of smoke and ashes.

After spending a long evening and the following day making homemade apple butter, its advantages may become camouflaged by the convenience of commercial brands. Does the taste of the homemade apple butter really compensate for the time and effort devoted? Some people who make it regularly believe that the taste is worth every bit of the effort. Others take a personal pride in making their own food products and in knowing exactly what they are eating. And still others simply enjoy making apple butter as a social event, uniting friends and family members in a worthwhile project.

Whatever the reason, the tradition of making apple butter each fall is not just a thing of the past. It is becoming a new tradition for a number of families, with others learning to make it each year. Perhaps you would like to start a tradition of making apple butter. If so, invite your neighbors in, polish up a copper kettle, fill it with tart, red apples, kindle a good smoky fire, and enjoy a taste of the past.

Cellars—A Store of Produce

"When we were growing up several years ago without deep freezers or refrigeration either one, a cellar was the only way we had to keep food," Bernice and Delmer Wade said as they showed their cellar, which is still well stocked with potatoes and home canned goods.

In years past, almost every home had some kind of cellar near the kitchen, to store foods in a safe, dark place free from extreme cold and summer heat. Some were fortunate enough to have a spring convenient enough to the house to store the perishable foods, but springhouses were of no value for storing root vegetables and other foods that needed to be dry. But any family could build a cellar almost anyplace they could dig in the ground.

Since electricity reached every farm in the 1940s, making refrigeration and home freezers possible, the importance and use of cellars has declined. Some people have abandoned them completely, others have torn their cellars down or filled them in, but still others, who continue to raise big gardens and do some canning, continue to make some use of them.

Though the use of and inside appearance of cellars did not vary a great deal, there were differences in how they were constructed. Some were built down into the ground, some built back into a hillside, and others were constructed under the house or other buildings such as a smokehouse.

The first cellars built were probably simply holes dug in the ground with a drain to carry off the water. They were crudely built with dirt walls or walls of split logs to help hold the shape and keep the dirt from eroding in. These types of cellars did not last long, though, because the logs would rot and fall in, making them dangerous.

Some people constructed double-boxed wooden structures. To insulate them, they put sawdust between the walls. The sawdust kept fruit from freezing in the coldest weather, especially if a bucket of ashes was set in overnight.

More permanent cellars were built under the house as the house was built. These proved to be safer, convenient, and usually freeze

A well-stocked cellar. Notice the potato bin on the left.

proof. The floor of the building would be the ceiling of the cellar. The houses would seldom have a full cellar, usually under one room or about sixteen by eighteen feet. However, if built under a smoke-house, the cellar was usually the same size as the building. The walls of the early cellars were usually sandstone or limestone, found nearby or even on the farm. The rocks were chipped by hand to fit together to form the walls. The mortar between the rocks, if any, was lime and sand, used only to seal the walls, not to strengthen them, for the rocks were laid to be their own support. The floor always had a drain and could be kept clean and dry even with a dirt floor, but some people hauled in river gravel to improve the footing. Later, when cement became available, builders made the walls of concrete.

In some houses there was a trap door in the floor of the kitchen as well as an outside entrance. If the house foundation was high enough, a few outside steps led down to the door which opened directly to the cellar. Others had an outside wooden door slanted like a roof that enclosed the steps leading down to the opening to the cellar proper. Sometimes there would be another door in the house foundation, but not always.

This cellar, built under a smokehouse, made good use of the steep hillside.

During the twenties and thirties many people built cellars of formed concrete. The majority of these were dug partially in the ground, with curved cement tops. Then the whole structure was covered with dirt for insulation.

It usually took about three weeks to build these cellars from the first digging until final tramping down the soil. The construction was generally done during dry weather, so the hole would not fill with water. Most of the people who had cellars built the structures themselves, with perhaps one or two neighbors to help. They chose a convenient spot near the house, but far enough from any tree to prevent the tree roots from cracking the concrete.

The first job was to dig the cellar and make a drain. The drain was dug from the lowest point of the cellar floor to let out the water that might accumulate. The drain would run slightly downhill to wherever it disposed of the water. The drain was made by digging a trench or deep ditch and then laying down pipe of some kind. Commonly used was red tile pipe. As Lorraine Davis put it, "It was no big job building the form and pouring the concrete, but digging the hole was something else."

A well-constructed concrete cellar still being used.

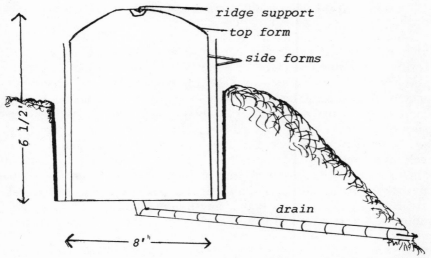

After digging a ditch and laying the drain and digging the hole for the cellar, build forms for the sides and one curved form for the top.

The digging was done by hand with a pick and shovel, digging downward to a depth of about five to six feet. Some cellars were dug deeper, or if the location was on a hillside, the depth and extent of the digging would depend on the location. The size would generally be eight by ten feet. The dirt dug out was saved for covering over the cellar later. The sides were dug straight, with square corners. The hole needed to be at least twenty-four inches larger than the inside dimensions of the cellars to allow for the walls, which were five to six inches thick, and to leave room to work with the forms. Almost as big a job as digging the hole might be digging the drain, depending on how far one had to dig.

After digging and laying the drain, the next job was making the forms. In some communities there were forms provided by the county Agricultural Extension Service that one could borrow. Most people, however, built their own, usually using green oak lumber, one-by-sixes or one-by-eights, for the sides and ends, which needed both inside and outside forms.

The form for the curved roof was made in a variety of ways. One way was to use green one-by-four boards, which were bent to the desired shape and fastened to the inside side forms. These boards were nailed flush together the entire length, strengthened and held in place with a ridge piece tacked underneath. A piece of tar paper over it all prevented cement from falling between the cracks.

Some people made flat roofs over their cellars. Though easier to build, the finished cellar was not as strong and could not support the dirt on top that was helpful for insulation.

When the forms were all in place, the builders began pouring the concrete. When these cellars were poured, there were no ready-mix concrete companies ready to come when called. The builders had to spend many hours hauling the fine gravel and sand mixture that they had shoveled by hand out of the gravel bars of the closest river or creek, often getting stuck several times. They hauled water in barrels from the creek or spring, or drew it by bucketfuls from the well. They shoveled one shovelful of cement and four of the sand and gravel mixture into a large open wooden tray-like box built for the purpose. Adding water, they mixed it well with a hoe. The job became easier and faster in later years, with cement mixers turned at first by hand and later powered by a belt from a tractor. Then hauling the cement by wheelbarrow loads, they dumped it into the forms.

To save cement, many people carefully placed in the wet cement inside the forms layers of rock, which they could pick up on almost any field. They strengthened the walls with iron wire, rods, old bedsprings, or any old scrap iron. The concrete was tamped in to fill all the spaces. It was especially important to make sure no rock or iron jutted against the form, but that the walls were all smooth concrete.

Pouring over the top was more difficult, for there was only one form. After laying the metal supports, workers shoveled on the cement and smoothed it out on top by hand tools. They usually worked from the back to the front, squatting on top of the form to smooth out the cement to the desired depth, finishing up above the entrance door.

After pouring the roof and sides, they would let the cement dry overnight or until well set before taking the forms down. The next step was to pour the cellar floor and make the stairs and door. Just like the cellars under the house, some had open outside steps leading down to the door, while others had covered steps, or, if built into a hillside, some had no steps at all, but a walk-in door.

The cellar had to have some type of ventilation to circulate the air and to aid in keeping foods from freezing. For that purpose a hole was left at the top of the cellar about four to six inches in diameter.

The next step was to cover the exposed parts of the cellar with dirt. The deeper the dirt layer the better the insulation—two feet

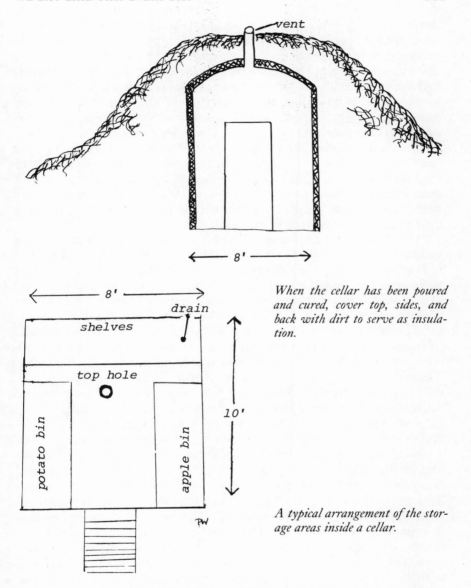

When the cellar has been poured and cured, cover top, sides, and back with dirt to serve as insulation.

A typical arrangement of the storage areas inside a cellar.

deep on top was adequate. Most people sowed grass or some plant on top to hold the dirt and help prevent erosion.

Correctly built and insulated with dirt, the cellar remained warm in winter and cool in the summer. During the summertime the average day temperature would stay about fifty to sixty degrees. At night during especially hot summers some people would leave the cellar door open to cool off, and then would close the door early the next morning to preserve the cool air during the day. Lorraine Davis said of his cellar, "You go down in that cellar in about zero degree weather and the thermometer will read about thirty-six degrees, while a spring house which is on top of the ground will run about thirty-four degrees. During the summer it will stay about fifty degrees. It just depends on how much dirt you have on your concrete."

For less well-insulated cellars, people would sometimes put hot coals in a big pan and place them in the cellar during winter to keep food from freezing. Although cellars usually wouldn't freeze in normal winter temperatures, most people would rather be safe than sorry. In more recent times, people left light bulbs burning or put in heat lamps during prolonged periods of extreme cold.

Good cellars won't freeze. Bernice Wade said of her cellar, which is in the ground at least five feet, "It doesn't freeze in this cellar. I've got potatoes in the potato bin next to the door. We don't cover the door with anything, and of course we don't have a solid door at the bottom of the stairs, and it didn't freeze last winter." [One of the coldest winters on record.]

The cellar was used for keeping a variety of foods. Lois Beard said, "Things we stored in a cellar were very precious to us, because it was our grocery store. We would prize the things we put in the cellar. There's nothing better tasting than an apple kept in an underground cellar. It gave them a flavor like the earth. Those of us who had cellars couldn't imagine kids coming to school without an apple."

And strange as it seems, Lorraine Davis assured us, "You store apples and potatoes together in your cellar, the potatoes won't sprout."

Besides apples and potatoes, cellars were storage places for stone jars filled with pickles, kraut, honey, molasses, apple butter, and pickled meats, all weighted down with a rock on a wooden lid that held the food under the preserving liquid. The early days also saw stone crocks with milk, cream, and butter set on tables near the door and baskets of eggs for market and for home use. After butchering, cellars held the stands of lard, which were kept cool enough during the hot summers that the lard did not become rancid. As sugar became cheap and available, jams, jellies, and preserves of all kinds covered the shelves, first in stone jars with a lid sealed with beeswax, then in glass jars. When cold-pack canning in glass jars in the early twenties and pressure cookers in the 1930s made home canning possible, shelves bulged with canned tomatoes, fruits, berries, green beans, peas, greens, corn, meat, relishes, and pickles.

Country schools, such as this one at Washington School District in Laclede County, used cellars for protection during tornadoes.

There were some foods that would not keep well in cellars. Pumpkins, onions, and sweet potatoes, because they needed lots of air, which cellars didn't have, spoiled quickly in a cellar. Some fresh foods were kept in cellars, but they wouldn't keep very long. Garden vegetables would keep three or four days—about as long as in a modern refrigerator—but milk would "get blinky in three days."

The way things were put into a cellar depended on the owner. Usually, on one side there would be an apple bin and a potato bin. There would always be plenty of shelves lining the back or sides to put canned foods on. In some cellars there was also a table used for butchering meat and straining the milk. Some kept stone crocks or jars by the door to store milk in the cellar, and others kept their egg cases there.

Besides being places of storage for food, cellars also served some other purposes—mainly that of a storm shelter. After the big tornado came through Webster and Laclede Counties in 1936, many people in its path built cellars. Being underground and close to the house, they were ideal protection. Many rural schools also built them for the children in case of a storm after that big storm blew one schoolhouse away and damaged another. Fortunately, the children were not hurt.

One of the many old, abandoned cellars one sees throughout the countryside.

When there was a storm, the people would often take an ax with them down into the cellar as a safety precaution, to prevent being trapped in case a tree or the house should blow over the cellar door. Some people today only use their cellars for storm protection. Some of them go to their cellars every time the wind gets strong or there is an alert on television. Others rarely go, but agree with Bernice Wade that, "It gives a good feeling knowing that the cellar is there."

Cellars offer refuge from the extreme heat as well as from storms. In the hot, dry summer months Lois and Cole Beard kept cots in their cellar in order to sleep there during the hot nights.

Animals in the cellars weren't very common occurrences, although most people have had at least one encounter with a varmint. Lorraine Davis had to build a fence around his cellar to keep his cattle from grazing on the grass on top and knocking off the dirt. Another nuisance was ground hogs. Lois Beard recalled, "I got a ground hog in the dirt by the cellar a few years ago and he dug him a hole. That ground hog would take a peep around the corner and look at me, and then I'd take a crack at him with an old .22. Never did kill him though."

An ever present worry was snakes. Although they weren't common occurrences either, a few would get in the cellars for shelter. Dorothy McMicken remembered a black snake that curled up in a gourd in her cellar. It was in so tight her husband had to break the gourd to get it out.

Along with other buildings used for food storage on the farm, such as springhouses, ice houses, and well houses, cellars have almost outlived their usefulness. But unlike the other structures, cellars are still valued by some people for storing their garden produce and for protection from storms.

EPILOGUE

Midway we close our story of the bittersweet earth, its rivers, its caves, and its people. Men, women, girls, and boys—taking, giving, struggling, working, playing, loving—all continually leave their marks on the land. This story has no end, but recurs like the seasons, as slow to develop as the caves and as temporary as turtles sunning on a log in the river.

And still it continues.

And still it continues.

LIST OF CONTRIBUTORS

Students

Following are the students on the staff of *Bittersweet* magazine who worked on articles that were chosen for this book.

Authors

Jim Baldwin
Rebecca Baldwin
Beverly Barber
Vicki Bench
Rick Bishop
Mike Doolin
Larry Doyle
Janet Florence
Kyra Gibson
Jimmie Harrelston
Jay Hillig
Nancy Honssinger
Daniel Hough
Ronnie Hough
Stephen Hough
Joe Jeffery
Gina Jennings
Terri Jones
Linda Lee
Kathy Long
Stephen Ludwig
Teresa Maddux
Vickie Massey

Robert McKenzie
Darrell Pollock
Carla Roberts
Emery Savage
Mary Schmalstig
Melinda Stewart
Lea Ann Sutherland
Todd Waterman
Tracy Waterman
Patsy Watts

Photographers

Jim Baldwin
Rebecca Baldwin
Rick Bishop
Lance Collins
Mark Elam
Mike Doolin
Daniel Hough
Stephen Hough
Joe Jeffery
Gina Jennings
Stephen Ludwig

Vickie Massey
Robert McKenzie
Karen Mulrenin
Larry Renken
Carla Roberts
Rita Saegar
Emery Savage
Mary Schmalstig
Doug Sharp

Artists

Kyle Burke
Alexa Hoke
Jimmie Harrelston
Nancy Honssinger
Jana Low
Teresa Maddux
Larry Renken
Emery Savage
Jill Splan
Melinda Stewart
Terry Tyre
Patsy Watts

Informants

Following are the men and women who helped with interviews and other information for the stories and material in this book, with place and date of interview and the subject.

Tom Aley, Underground Laboratories, Forsyth, Mo., July 17, 1974, geology and ecology of caves.

Ralph Amos, Lebanon, Mo., February 22, 1974, cave legends.

Lois Beard, Conway, Mo., March 1977, February 9, 1978, cellars; January 13, 1977, October 14, 1976, springhouses; February 3, 1978, wells.

Stanley and Helen Beard and Charlotte Davis, Lebanon, Mo., October 1975, cider.

Lee Berry and Geraldine Brewer, Buffalo, Mo., February 21, 1979, tie rafting.

Don Boyd, Lebanon, Mo., February 4, 1977, steamboating.

Sam Bradford, Lebanon, Mo., May 8, 1974, Indian legends.

David Bradshaw, Maude Bradshaw, Lebanon, Mo., July 6, 1978, Corkery.

Forrest and Ethel Bradshaw, Lebanon, Mo., April 27, 1978, Corkery.

Iva Bradshaw, Eldridge, Mo., December 18, 1977, reminiscences.

Gene Chambers, Conway, Mo., January 8, 1975, Bat Cave.

Warren Cook, Republic, Mo., April 17, 1978, June 13, 1978, old-time farming methods.

Lavern Cravens, Lebanon, Mo., 1978, river crossings.

H. L. Davis, Grovespring, Mo., April 5, 1978, cellars.

J. W. Davis, Lebanon, Mo., February 19, 1974, caves.

Ella Dunn, Walnut Shade, Mo., March 19, 1977, April 21, 1977, herbs.

Annie Fike, Lebanon, Mo., ice houses.

Adley Fulford, Lebanon, Mo., November 6, 1976, springs.

Russel Gerlach, Geography Department, Southwest Missouri State University, Springfield, Mo., geology of rivers and caves.

Ellen Gibson, Lebanon, Mo., November 19, 1975, greens.

Vernon Graven, Lebanon, Mo., April 4, 1979, tie rafting.

Ralph Gray, Gaithersburg, Md., 1978, wells.

Esther Griffin, Lebanon, Mo., September 12, 1973, cider.

Clay Gumm, Lebanon, Mo., February 21, 1979, cisterns.

Imo Honssinger, Richland, Mo., May 7, 1975, wild greens.

The Charles Hough Family and Myrtle and Elvie Hough, Lebanon, Mo., September 29, 30, October 3, 5, 6, 1973, October, 1975, sorghum molasses.

Elva Hough, Lebanon, Mo., April 12, 1977, November 10, 1977, bridges; October 1975, cider.

Ernie Hough, Lebanon, Mo., November 11, 1976, June 24, 1977, June 28, 1977; reminiscences; October 27, 1976, ice houses.

Myrtle Hough, Lebanon, Mo., March 6, 1975, cave legends; October, 1975, cider.

Lillian and Harold Humphreys, Lebanon, Mo., September 22, 1978, water witching.

Ed Johnson, Lebanon, Mo., April 20, 1978, Corkery.

Clayton H. Johnson, Department of Geology, University of Missouri, Columbia, Mo., rivers.

Esther Jones, Lebanon, Mo., October 1975, cider.

George Kastler, Lebanon, Mo., December 16, 1973, February 24, 1974, April 10, 1974, April 15, 1974, November 15, 1974, plus other cave trips, caves.

Rose Lowrance, Lebanon, Mo., December 10, 1976, reminiscences.

Katie Lowry, Lebanon, Mo., November 2, 23, 1976, reminiscences.

Dick Luthy, Lebanon, Mo., May 11, 1976, ice houses.

Dorothy and Lyn Marble, Falcon, Mo., February 14, 1978, water witching; February 22, 1978, cisterns.

David Massey, Lebanon, Mo., photography.
Emmitt Massey, Lebanon, Mo., February 11, 1974, cave legends.
Homer Massey, Lebanon, Mo., May 15, 1978, July 23, 1978, reminiscences.
Pearl Massey, Lebanon, Mo., 1979, springs.
Ruth Ellen Massey, Lebanon, Mo., photography.
Dorothy McMicken, Richland, Mo., 1978, cellars.
Mary Moore, Phillipsburg, Mo., April 18, 1975, reminiscences.
Walter Niewald, Owensville, Mo., September 23, 1977, reminiscences.
Loma L. Paulson, Kansas City, Mo., 1976, greens.
John and Charlene Playter, Bolivar, Mo., October 19, 20, 1979, apple butter.
Tom Price, Lebanon, Mo., September 15, 1977, tie making.
Jim Purcell, Salem, Mo., September 23, 1978, ferries.
Earl Rhoades, Lebanon, Mo., February 8, 1979, cisterns.
Earl Ripley, Eldridge, Mo., October 13, 1979, tie rafting.
Della Snyder, Lebanon, Mo., July 14, 1976, blackberrying.
Johnny Starnes, Richland, Mo., March 18, 1976, reminiscences.
Earl Stiles, Lebanon, Mo., May 5, 1977, March 31, 1977, herbs.
Clifford Summers, Creed Summers, Conway, Mo., May 3, 1976, springhouses.

Euel Sutton, Eminence, Mo., September 28, 1979, ferries.
Bernice and Delmer Wade, Lynchburg, Mo., April 27, 1979, cellars.
Clifford Wallace, Lebanon, Mo., February 16, 1978, wells.
Nora West, Lebanon, Mo., September 29, 1976, springhouses.
Homer Wright, Tuscumbia, Mo., March 30, 1977, steamboating.
Eula and Bill York, Stoutland, Mo., January 4, 1978, water witching;
    taffy candy.
Robert Zang, Aurora, Mo., April 13, 1977, steamboating.

Index

Horseradish (herb): 312-13
Hough, Charles and family: 334-51
Hough, Elva: 334, 355-61;
  photograph, 347
Hough, Ernie: 147, 152-55, 255,
  257-59; photograph, 153
Hough, Myrtle: 127-28, 258, 334,
  355-61; photograph, 347
Houses: 211
Housework: 149, 188-90
Howell Cave, Laclede County,
  Missouri: 127-28
Humphreys, Harold: 265
Humphreys, Lillian: 263-65;
  photographs, 264
Hunting: 73-74, 153-54, 159-60,
  170

I

Ice houses: 255-59
Illnesses: 68, 182, 194
Indian turnip (herb): 313
Indians:
  Bluff Dwellers, 121-22
  caves, 121-23, 127
  Corkery: 70-71
  See also Osage Indians
Industrial Revolution: 211

J

Jack's Fork River: 99
James River: 75, 99, 147;
  photographs, 91, 92
James, Jesse: 124
J. W. White (steamboat): 27
Johnboat: 80-81
Johnson, Fred: 66, 236
Johnson's Sink: photograph, 106
Jones, Esther: 355-61
Journegan Cave, Wright County,
  Missouri: 127

J. R. Wells (steamboat): 30

K

Kastler, George: 135, 138-39,
  142-44; photograph, 143
Keelboats: 27

L

Lady's slipper (herb): 313
Lake of the Ozarks: 237
Lamb's quarter (greens): 296
Lebanon, Missouri: 122-23, 125,
  158, 169
Lebanon High School, Lebanon,
  Missouri: xi-xiv
Legends:
  caves, 124-29
  Osage Indian, 4-5
Lettuce, wild (greens): 291
Lily of the valley (herb): 314-15
Lowrance, Rose: 147, 206
Lowry, Katie: 166-78; photograph,
  167, 168
Ludwig, Stephen: 184-96
Luthy, Dick: 255-59

M

Marble, Lyn: 262-63; photograph,
  262
Marriage customs: 173-74
Marvel Cave, Taney County,
  Missouri: 124
Massey, Emmitt: 128-29
Massey, Homer: 156-65, 205;
  photograph, 157
Massey, Vickie: 156-65
Mayapple (herb): 315
McKenzie, Robert: 140-42, 144-45
McMicken, Dorothy: 385

Bittersweet Earth

designed by Bill Cason, was set in various sizes of Caslon by the University of Oklahoma Press and printed offset on 55-pound Glatfelter Smooth Antique, a permanized sheet, with printing and case binding by Vail-Ballou Press, Inc.